Madame Letizia

A Portrait of Napoleon's Mother

BOOKS BY MONICA STIRLING

Novels

SIGH FOR A STRANGE LAND
SOME DARLING FOLLY
THE BOY IN BLUE
LADIES WITH A UNICORN
DRESS REHEARSAL
LOVERS AREN'T COMPANY

Biography

MADAME LETIZIA: *A Portrait of Napoleon's Mother*
THE FINE AND THE WICKED: *The Life and Times of Ouida*

MADAME LETIZIA

A Portrait of

Napoleon's Mother

BY MONICA STIRLING

Harper & Brothers: New York

Madame Letizia

FIRST EDITION

This book was published in England
under the title A PRIDE OF LIONS.

Library of Congress catalog card number: 62-7915

To Solita

JOSEPH (Giuseppe) 1768-1844	NAPOLEON (Napoleone) 1769-1821	LUCIEN (Lucciano) 1775-1840	ELISA (Maria-Anna) 1777-1820
married 1794 Julie Clary (1771-1844)	married (1) 1796 Joséphine de Beauharnais (1763-1814) Marriage dissolved 1809	married (1) 1794 Catherine Boyer (1773-1800)	married 1797 Felice Pasquale Bacciochi (1762-1841)
2 daughters		4 children	
	married (2) 1810 Marie-Louise, Archduchess of Austria (1791-1847)	married (2) 1803 Alexandrine Joubertbon (1778-1855)	5 children
	1 son	10 children	

Joseph's elder daughter, Zenaïde, married her first cousin, Lucien, a remarkable ornithologist.

In 1952 his great-great-great-grandson, Alessandro Giunta, married Mussolini's granddaughter, Raimonda Ciano di Cortellazzo. In 1954 Joseph's great-great-great-grandchildren numbered 41 Italian and 4 French.

Napoleon's son, Napoléon-François-Charles-Joseph (1811-32), was given the title King of Rome at birth. His mother took him to Vienna in 1814. In June 1815 he was legally proclaimed Napoleon II, but he never reigned, and died a prisoner in Vienna.

In 1954 his great-great-great-grandchildren numbered over 150: 103 Italian, the rest French, Spanish, Polish and British.

Lucien's great-grandson, the Comte Giuseppe Primoli (1852-1927), founded the Bonaparte Museum in Rome.

This branch now extinct.

The present Swedish royal family is descended from Joseph's sister-in-law, Désirée Clary, who married Marshal Bernadotte. He became Charles XIV of Sweden (1818-44).

CARLO BUONAPARTE (1746-85)

LOUIS (Luigi) 1778-1846	PAULINE (Maria-Paola) 1780-1825	CAROLINE (Maria-Annunziata) 1782-1839	JEROME (Girolamo) 1784-1860
married 1802 Hortense de Beauharnais (1783-1837)	married (1) 1797 Victor Emmanuel Leclerc (1772-1802)	married 1800 Joachim Murat (1771-1815)	married (1) 1803 Elizabeth Patterson (1785-1879) Marriage annulled 1804
3 sons	1 son (d. 1804)	4 children	1 child
	married (2) 1803 Prince Camillo Borghese (1775-1832)		married (2) 1807 Princess Catherine of Württemberg (1783-1835)
			3 children

Louis's youngest son, *Louis-Napoléon* (1808-73), reigned as *Napoleon III* (1852-70). After the Franco-Prussian War of 1870, he took refuge in England. His only son, the *Prince Imperial* (b. 1856), was killed in 1879 while serving with the British Army against the Zulus. This branch thus became extinct.

This branch now extinct.

In 1954 her great-great-great-grand-children numbered 38 Italian, 32 French, 3 Austrian, 3 Polish, 2 German and 1 English.

The 7th *Prince Murat* was killed in 1944 while serving in the French Army during the Liberation.

The American branch became extinct in 1945, but through Jérôme's American great-granddaughter there are now 6 Danish great-great-great-grandchildren.

Of the children of his second marriage, the youngest, *Prince Napoléon* (1822-91), married *Princess Clotilde of Savoy*, daughter of Victor Emmanuel II of Italy. Their son, *Prince Napoléon*, married *Princess Clémentine of Belgium*, daughter of Leopold II and great-granddaughter of Louis-Philippe of France. Their son, *Louis-Napoléon-Jérôme-Victor, Prince Napoleon* (b. 1914), is the present head of the family.

Contents

ILLUSTRATIONS APPEAR FOLLOWING PAGES 98 AND 194.

Acknowledgments

For generous help I want to thank His Excellency Monsieur Gaston Palewski, French Ambassador to the Quirinal; His Excellency Monsieur Roland de Margery, French Ambassador to the Holy See, and Madame de Margery; Monsieur le Vicomte Fleuriot de Langle, curator of the Marmottan Museum; the staff of the Bibliothèque Nationale in Paris and of the Museo Napoleonico in Rome. I am also very grateful to the Marchesa Misciattelli, Madame Odette Arnaud, Mrs. St. George Saunders, Signora Livia de Stefani, Madame la Comtesse de Caraman, Mr. and Mrs. T. C. V. Roe, Professor Carlo Pietrangeli, Inspector of Museums of the City of Rome, Monsieur Labauge and Monsieur Mardikian of the Librairie Galignani, and Monsieur Michel Richard of the cultural department of the French Foreign Office.

The publishers are grateful to Mrs. George Bambridge and Messrs. Macmillan and Co., Ltd., for permission to reproduce the four stanzas from " A St. Helena Lullaby " from *Rewards and Fairies* by Rudyard Kipling.

Author's Note

One of the problems I encountered in writing this book was that of selecting between contradictory pieces of evidence. There is an immense body of literature about Napoleon (the German bibliographer Kircheisen lists 200,000 titles), and many books have been devoted to his brothers and sisters. But of his mother I found only five biographies in French, one in English and one in German. The details concerning her are scattered through her children's biographies and letters and are often at variance. The Bonaparte story still arouses controversial passion because, as a man, Napoleon was the apotheosis of individualism, and by his genius dominated France at a period when France dominated Europe and Europe dominated the world.

Letizia Bonaparte's first biographer, Baron Larrey, son of the Baron Larrey who was surgeon-in-chief with Napoleon's armies, says it is difficult to establish the exact date of her birth as the Ajaccio archives were destroyed by fire in 1789. The date usually given in encyclopædias and books of reference is 1750, and I have accepted this because it is the date she herself gave in the brief *Souvenirs* she dictated in her old age; it is also the date listed in the *Almanach Impérial*, no copy of which went to press without having been checked by Napoleon.

In *Napoleon*, a widely admired book by the eminent Soviet historian Eugène Tarlé, the author states that after Napoleon left Elba in February 1815, to return to France, his mother never saw him again. This is not so. She joined him in Paris in April, was with him until he left for Waterloo, and, after this battle, took her last farewell of him at Malmaison. Several writers mention that Madame Letizia's faithful Corsican servant, Saveria, dined with her on board the ship that took them to Elba. I saw no reason to question this until I read the journal of Sir Neil Campbell, the English Commissioner who acted as Letizia's escort on this trip. He wrote : " Captain Battersby and two of his officers, M. Saveira, a passenger, and myself, all dined with Madame on deck." I mention these two points, one important the other trivial, because they are typical of the riddles that resulted from comparing the works of reputable authors.

Where sums of money are concerned I have quoted the original figures, thinking that attempts to give modern equivalents would lead to confusion unless accompanied by details of contemporary salaries, their purchasing power and relation to the cost of living, all of which varied wildly during the Revolution. Mr. Theodore Besterman, one of the greatest scholars of this period, wrote in 1953 that in mid-eighteenth century one French franc (livre) was equal to one modern American dollar. There seems no doubt that the franc was the stable currency in the world during the nineteenth century (as the pound sterling and the dollar were to become later), and from 1799-1914 the rate of exchange was approximately 100,000 francs (livres)= 20,000 dollars= £4,000.

I have used no fact for which there is not written evidence. Where the problem of contradictory statements seemed insoluble, I have given both versions ; otherwise I have given the one that seemed to me most in keeping with Madame Letizia's character.

For the text of her letters I was privileged to use the collection, mostly in the original Italian, in the Bonaparte Museum in Rome. There are several ways of spelling her name, but Letizia is how she always signed herself.

Morning : Corsica

1750-85

Elle était belle comme les amours.

NAPOLEON

. . . Letitia Ramolino, a young woman eminent for beauty and for strength of mind . . .

JOHN GIBSON LOCKHART: *Life of Napoleon Buonaparte*

Napoleon's mother was a woman comparable with Plutarch's heroines, with Portia, Cornelia and Madame Roland. Her impassive, firm and ardent nature recalls even more the Italian heroines of the Middle Ages. . . . It is by the perfectly Italian quality of Madame Letizia that her son's character must be explained.

STENDHAL: *Mémoires sur Napoléon*

How far is St. Helena from a little child at play?
What makes you want to wander there with all the world between?
Oh, Mother, call your son again or else he'll run away.
(*No one thinks of winter when the grass is green!*)

KIPLING: *A St. Helena Lullaby*

ON JUNE 3RD, 1764, a beautiful Corsican girl of nearly fourteen was married in Ajaccio Cathedral to Carlo-Maria Buonaparte, an eighteen-year-old law student whose family belonged to the island nobility. Born Letizia Ramolino, this girl was to enter history as Napoleon's mother, and while she owes her fame to her son, he owed her the powerful temperament that made his achievements possible.

Although Corsica was just then about to revolt once more against the domination of the Genoese Republic, political tension did not spoil the wedding celebrations. Political conflict was a commonplace in this often-invaded island, but the spectacle of a bride such as Letizia was rare. Ever since she was a small child, her black eyes, classic features, perfect teeth and chestnut-coloured hair had caused people to point her out to strangers as " Ajaccio's little marvel," and cathedral gossips said that her presence at mass was " more effective than an anchorite's virtue " in obtaining conversions. On her wedding-day the dramatic effect of Letizia's beauty was heightened by an escort of more than fifty handsome and energetic male cousins. In a country where the vendetta remained the popular form of justice, male relatives were as valuable a part of a girl's dowry as land, houses or money. (Later, when the English occupied Corsica, seventeen of these " terrible cousins " successfully ambushed fifty-four of the invaders.)

Of Italian origin, the Ramolinos were related to the Coll'Alto family that dominated Lombardy in the fourteenth century and settled in Corsica, the third largest island in the Mediterranean, about a hundred years later. In 1745, Letizia's father, Gian Girolamo Ramolino, captain of the garrison at Ajaccio, had married Angela-Maria di Pietra Santa, a young girl who came of an old Corsican family and grew up at Bocognano, a mountain village rich in bandits, vendettas and giant chestnut trees. Over half a century later, Napoleon said of Angela-Maria di Pietra Santa that when an " argument " arose, his maternal grand-mother could summon between two and three hundred militant mountaineers to support her side of it.

About the time of his marriage, Gian Girolamo Ramolino was made Inspector-General of Roads and Bridges, and fre-quently had occasion to offer hospitality to the French soldiers hired by Genoa to keep order in Corsica. Both Gian Girolamo's first child, which died in infancy, and his second, which sur-vived, were born during lulls in the conflict ; but for this second child, Maria-Letizia, born in Ajaccio on August 24th, 1750, peace soon acquired rarity value. She was only two when the French commander, the popular Marquis de Cursay, left the island, with the result that the patriots in the interior immedi-ately rose in arms. Three years later (the year Marie-Antoinette was born in Vienna) Gian Girolamo died, leaving his daughter to grow up surrounded by violence.

This same year the patriots chose Clemente Paoli to succeed their leader, Gaffori, who had just been killed. Aware that he lacked the requisite qualities for leadership, Clemente asked to be replaced by his thirty-year-old brother, Pasquale Paoli, who promptly returned from Naples, where he had been sharing his father's exile and serving as an officer in the Neapolitan army. Hostile to both Genoa and France, Paoli hoped for support from England, where, thanks to the publication in 1768 of Boswell's widely read *Journal of a Tour to Corsica; and Memoirs of Pascal Paoli*, he later became a popular hero.

When Letizia was seven her mother married again. Her second husband was Franz Fesch, an intelligent and industrious Swiss from Basle then serving in Corsica as a captain with the

Genoese marines. Angela-Maria refused to marry him unless he became a Catholic. He obeyed her wishes and was consequently disinherited by his family. Always disposed to love her relatives, Letizia became devoted to her stepfather, whose stories of " the mainland," as Corsicans called the Continent, together with those of the French soldiers befriended by her father, gave her her first impressions of the strange world beyond the Mediterranean that her son was one day to rule.

The next year Paoli drove the Genoese out of Corsica and established himself as a benevolent dictator. During the thirteen years he remained in power he built roads, abolished the rights of the brigand chiefs, founded schools, printing presses and a university at Corte, and with the church's help partially suppressed the *vendetta trasversa*, a system of collateral revenge permitting anyone whose enemy had escaped him to take revenge on that enemy's relatives. Paoli made collateral revenge punishable by death, also by a " pillar of infamy " intended to perpetuate the offender's shame. But despite Paoli's immense prestige (he modelled himself on Plutarch's heroes, and was widely believed to have prophetic powers), he could not alter the Corsicans overnight. A mixture of Greek, Roman, Phœnician and Etruscan, they were as ready to kill in a personal cause involving honour as they were loath to provide a hangman to kill on behalf of the state.

Corsica remained at that time very much what it had been when the Romans left it in the fifth century. For this its geographical conformation was largely responsible. Turkish, Tunisian and Barbary pirates constantly threatened the island's coasts, and interior communication was made difficult, in many regions impossible, by savage mountains and torrent-filled gorges. Villages were isolated and a primitive wooden plough was still the only kind available. Boswell reported that the Corsicans were extremely brave and would never attack a stranger unless he tried to seduce one of their women, in which case they would immediately kill him. He also observed that " the chief satisfaction of the islanders when not engaged in war or hunting seemed to be that of lying at their ease in the open air, recounting tales of the bravery of their countrymen, and singing in honour of the Corsicans, and against the Genoese." Letizia spent the first thirty-five years of her life in this small, incisive Mediterranean world, and she never subsequently lost the conviction, voiced by Napoleon in exile, that "everything there was better and more beautiful than anywhere else." The people she loved best throughout her long life all had roots in Corsica.

When Letizia was twelve, with a highly developed maternal instinct and a slender, upright figure that attracted as much attention as her lovely face, one of the most important figures in her life was born—her half-brother Giuseppe Fesch. From then on Letizia loved him as steadfastly as she was to love her own children. The cast of the greatest play in centuries was beginning to assemble. Five months later, across the Atlantic in the island of Martinique, one of Letizia's future daughters-in-law was born—Marie-Joséphine-Rose Tascher de la Pagerie.

The young man whom Letizia married came, as she did, of stock originally Italian ; but his ancestors, who belonged for the most part to what in France was called the " nobility of the robe " (administrators, men of law, or letters), had moved to Corsica about a hundred years later than the Ramolinos and settled farther inland, so that, although they belonged to the ruling class, contact with rebel territory had made them favour Corsican independence. Carlo was fourteen when his father died, leaving him to the care of an uncle, Lucciano Buonaparte, Archdeacon of Ajaccio and a friend of Letizia's uncle, who was a canon there. The first of his family to attend the new university at Corte, Carlo left Corsica at sixteen to go to the Continent and study law at Pisa. Handsome, graceful and animated, he neglected none of the opportunities Pisa offered for enjoying life and spending money. Always convinced that something would turn up, he had still not taken his degree when the time came for him to return home and marry Letizia, with whom he had been in love before going to Pisa.

The marriage caused some surprise locally as the Buonapartes and the Ramolinos held different political views. But Carlo and Letizia were wildly in love, and as Archdeacon Lucciano was inclined to be avaricious (prolonged contact with Carlo would probably have induced avarice in anyone, except the seven out of Carlo's eight children who inherited his devotion to pleasure), he thought less of politics than of Letizia's dowry, which consisted of 6,705 livres, partly in land and property. Despite temperamental differences, the marriage was to prove very successful. Letizia never loved another man, and although it is improbable that he was completely faithful to her, Carlo never ceased to love his wife. Later, when a friend remarked on her obvious joy in her husband, Letizia said, " How could I fail to be happy and proud to belong to him? He is good, handsome, celebrated, and he loves me." Her choice of attributes, and the order in which she placed them, are characteristic, as is the common-sense explanation for her uncommon radiance.

After their wedding the young couple lived at the Casa Buonaparte, then a three-storied house of chamois-coloured stone in a narrow street called Via Malerba at one end and Via Buonaparte at the other and overlooking a small rectangular piazza containing acacia trees. To-day this street is named the Rue Saint-Charles, and the piazza the Place Letizia. Only the second floor of the Casa Buonaparte belonged to Carlo and Letizia. The ground floor was occupied by the Archdeacon Lucciano and Carlo's mother, whom Letizia called Mamma Saveria, the third floor by a cousin, Maria, married to Antonio Pozzo di Borgo. It never occurred to Letizia to object to sharing a home with her new relatives. Corsican girls were taught to obey their husbands without question, and besides, she liked family life, indeed never seemed to have a surfeit of it. This was fortunate for her, since as she began so she would have to continue : one of a closely-knit clan.

Some years later Carlo was to bring a suit against Maria

Pozzo di Borgo for having deliberately emptied her slops over his head from an upper window. Lawsuits were almost as popular a diversion in Corsica as bull-fights are in Spain. This one sparked off a long family feud that was to have dramatic effects on Napoleon's career. For the moment, however, all was harmony in the crowded Casa Buonaparte.

HARMONY DID NOT, however, prevail outside their home. Two months after Carlo and Letizia were married, French soldiers arrived to garrison Ajaccio, Bastia, Calvi, St. Florent and Algajola. Louis XV lent these troops to the Genoese Republic as repayment of the 80,000 livres with which the Genoese had helped France finance her part in the Seven Years War. The new French commander, the Comte de Marbeuf, was a charming and competent man, later to show himself a good friend to the young Buonapartes. He introduced the culture of the potato into Corsica, and Boswell described him as a worthy, open-hearted Frenchman, gay without levity and judicious without severity, all of which was true, but did not console Corsican patriots for the French occupation of their island.

These patriots began moving inland to the *macchia*, uncultivated territory submerged by aromatic trees, shrubs and wild flowers : strawberries, myrtle, rosemary, ferns, broom, rock-roses, lavender, fennel, lilies, cyclamen, asphodel, thorn, arbutus, the whole mass six feet high in some parts and often so inextricably knitted together as to present an impassable barrier to strangers unfamiliar with the hidden trails that criss-crossed this great natural fortress. The wind carried the heady scent of the *macchia* out to sea, sometimes for as much as sixty miles. Outlaws who took refuge here were unlikely to be captured since no self-respecting citizen would betray them. It was from Corsica that the French Resistance in the Second World War adopted the expression " take to the maquis."

As sensitive to politics as a circus horse to music, Carlo began to feel a compulsion to perform and soon attracted public attention as an orator. Never loquacious, but fierier and more typically Corsican than her husband, Letizia shared his political views but was now occupied principally by child-bearing. Still very young for this, she lost her first child in 1765, the year he was born, and also a daughter born in 1767. The way she endured these bereavements (particularly cruel ones to a girl who longed for children in a country where the more children, and especially the more sons, a woman bore her husband, the more highly she was esteemed) revealed the extra-ordinary stoicism she possessed even in adolescence. She was also helped by a forceful, laconic piety that made her attend Mass every day throughout her long life, except when pre-vented by household crises, war or revolution. This piety sometimes expressed itself in puerile ways. All her life she retained the habit (which Napoleon inherited) of crossing herself and saying " Jesus ! " on hearing news that outraged or maddened her.

Reports of Carlo's powers as a political speaker reached Paoli at a time when the leader was drawing up a constitution and needed jurists, who were scarce in Corsica. He sent for Carlo, and was so impressed by his intelligence that he asked the young man to join him at Corte, legendary seat of the Moorish kings and at this time Corsica's political capital. This invitation from a childless leader on the lookout for young supporters fired not only Carlo's patriotism but his ambition. Thanks to Corsica's strategic position, Paoli was becoming an illustrious European figure. France could not attempt to regain the hold on India that she had recently lost to the English without send-ing troops out east and Corsica lay between the great French naval base of Toulon and the overland route east via Egypt. Carlo therefore accepted Paoli's offer without hesitation and sent for Letizia, who, prompt to join him, left Ajaccio for the first of many long and dangerous journeys.

She was seventeen when she made the three days' trip to Corte on horseback, guided by a shepherd ; away from the familiar vines, olives and fig trees, up through the *macchia* and the giant chestnut forests, past the fan-shaped waterfall known as the Bride's Veil and past her mother's birth-place, Bocognano, over the Vizzavona mountain pass to the village of Vivario, birth-place of a ninth-century pope, and on to Corte. This austere eagle's-nest town in the mountainous centre of Corsica was built defensively upon a rock, and its sombre grandeur was as different from sunlit Ajaccio on its beautiful seashore as Letizia's adult life was to be from her childhood.

Carlo and Letizia were welcomed into the eagle's nest by one of her uncles, Tommaso Arrighi di Casanova (father of the cousin Napoleon was later to make Duc de Padoue), and his wife Maria Biadelli. Their house had formerly belonged to the national hero, Gaffori, who had fought for Corsican independence thirty years earlier, and stories of his exploits and of his romantic wife Faustina exhilarated Letizia and strengthened her sense of partisanship. Equally exhilarating was her first personal contact with Paoli, described by Boswell as having " a steadfast, keen and penetrating eye that searched his interlocutor's very heart," and who, in the manner of Homer's Telemachus, kept a bodyguard of great dogs. Like many Corsicans, Paoli combined austere morality with a love of cutting a fine figure (his horse was caparisoned with crimson velvet and gold lace), and he admired Letizia, whom he compared with Cornelia, mother of the Gracchi, quite as much as he did Carlo, now his secretary and assistant. He missed no opportunity to bring her to the fore, and her beauty and dignity attracted particular attention at a luxurious reception he gave for the Tunisian ambassador. On this occasion, Paoli's way of treating the young Buonapartes as if they were his children aroused some jealousy among his followers, who feared that he was training Carlo to succeed him.

Paoli's childlessness was rumoured to be due to impotence. Years later, Napoleon, who remembered him as plump, fairskinned, more like an Englishman or a German than a Corsican, asked Letizia teasingly : " Come, Mother, now that it's all past history admit that Paoli tried to flirt with you "; to which she replied, " Oh no, had there been anything of that kind it would have been with my sister-in-law, but between ourselves we women knew *Paoli was incapable in that respect.*" In any case, Letizia's nature was not made for infidelity. Her sense of honour was inflexible and she loved Carlo as only a grave, tenacious nature can love a charming, frivolous one.

Presently Paoli sent Carlo on a mission to the Pope. The young man's courtesy and erudition made an admirable impression in Rome, but he spent so much money there that he had to borrow the fare home from the Pope's medical attendant Saliceti, who, luckily for Carlo, was a fellow Corsican. Although most of their money came from Letizia's dowry, she never criticised Carlo's passion for buying embroidered satin waistcoats and giving elaborate dinner-parties. There was more than wifely acceptance to this. She understood Carlo's meridional desire to cut a figure—*fare bella figura*—and, half a century later, Napoleon remembered his mother telling him when he was a small child that although he might always be poor, he must never forget that it was worth going short of food in order to be able to afford a handsome room, a fine jacket and a good horse. " The Buonapartes," added Napoleon, " took themselves for the Bourbons, and indeed they were the Bourbons of the island."

Letizia's third child, Giuseppe (her first to survive infancy), was named after Carlo's father and born in January, 1768, when Corte was in a ferment. Although Paoli's appeals to the rulers of Europe had produced no practical assistance beyond the gift of a sword from Frederick the Great inscribed *Patria Libertas* (" Foolish as we are," remarked Lord Holland, " we are not so foolish as to go to war because Mr. Boswell has been to Corsica "), Paoli began planning an assault on the neighbouring island of Capraia, then garrisoned entirely by Genoese troops. When news of this project reached the Continent, Genoa offered to sell Corsica to France. The offer was well-timed, as France had recently lost her possessions in Canada as well as in

India and was looking for new ones. French contingents reached Corsica in April, even before the deal was settled, and Letizia, who had been visiting the family in Ajaccio, rushed back to Corte accompanied by Carlo's uncle Napoleone, her devoted sister-in-law Geltruda, and her brother-in-law Niccolo Paraviccini. Meanwhile Louis XV's minister Choiseul had eagerly accepted Genoa's offer of a Mediterranean stepping-stone, and Corsica was signed over to France at Versailles on May 15th, 1768. Letizia's future children would be born French subjects.

Outraged by the spectacle of his countrymen being treated as chattels, Paoli rallied his partisans and asked them to choose between resistance and surrender. Carlo then made an impassioned speech, saying that if freedom could be obtained merely by wishing for it, everyone would be free, but that, on the contrary, it required unremitting effort, based not on the emotions but on an understanding of the true facts of the case— a statement that lost nothing from the emotional way in which it was made. The majority voted for resistance, and the meeting broke up amidst shouts of " *Libertà o Morte.*" Carlo's family was extremely proud of this speech, and Napoleon quoted from it at St. Helena. Perhaps still more remarkable was Paoli's caustic observation to Boswell : " If the event prove happy, we shall be considered great defenders of liberty. If the event prove unhappy, we shall be called unfortunate rebels."

TEN THOUSAND French troops landed at Bastia in August, bearers of Louis XV's declaration that the Corsicans were now his subjects and must act accordingly. The most spirited of the King's new subjects promptly took to the mountains, accompanied in many cases by their wives and children, since Corsican girls were taught that in times of danger their first duty was to load their husbands' rifles. Among the patriots were Carlo, now Paoli's aide-de-camp, and Letizia. This David and Goliath struggle appealed to European liberals much as the Greek fight for independence was to appeal to their descendants half a century later, and its genuinely epic quality kept this small campaign vivid in Letizia's mind long after she had seen crowns and coronets roll before her son's great armies in the first mighty cataclysms of the nineteenth century.

As the French had not anticipated resistance, they were taken by surprise and in several initial engagements defeated. Exasperated, and determined to conquer before winter set in, the French commander, Chauvelin, launched an attack at Borgo which proved unsuccessful. The Corsicans took five hundred prisoners and obtained a truce. Chauvelin then resigned, complaining that he had been given too few troops for his task. Although exultant, the Corsicans realised that the French were bound to make another attempt to master them, and would probably rely on superior numbers and equipment next time.

When French troopships were sighted off the Corsican coast in the spring of 1769, Letizia was again pregnant, but as determined as Carlo to fight to the death. It looked at first as if the partisans could do nothing else. The Comte de Vaux had engineers, artillery, three cavalry regiments and forty-five infantry battalions; the Corsicans had only courage and knowledge of the terrain. The French artillery opened fire near Borgo on May 3rd. Having no artillery, Paoli moved back out of firing range. Next day the Corsicans repelled the French at Rapale. At dawn on the third day the Comte de Vaux assembled all his troops on the St. Nicholas plateau and, threatened with encirclement, the Corsicans had to shift their headquarters back across the River Golo. In the confusion Letizia lost touch with Carlo and had to make for the rear on her own initiative. Although this part of the fighting was taking place in the north-east, far from Letizia's birth-place in the south-west, she had already acquired a minute knowledge of her untamed island, and when at last Carlo found her and proposed to take her to safety— she was six months pregnant with Napoleon—she unhesitatingly galloped beside him up the gorges of Restonico, through a forest of giant pines and up the slopes of Monte Rotondo, one of Corsica's least accessible mountains, to a wild place where granite caverns provided natural hide-outs. With the young Buonapartes went a little band of friends and survivors.

The cave in which they are supposed to have bivouacked is still known as " The Refugees' Grotto." At dawn, before the horizon was misted over, most of Corsica could be seen from there and even the coast of the mainland was visible as a distant blur. By a curious optical illusion, the islands of Elba, Pianosa, Formica and Monte Cristo appeared to be suspended in the sky. The refugees' only protection in this aerie was the wildness of the terrain between them and the French army. Meanwhile hardship was the rule. Their food consisted of flour provided by wandering shepherds and water from the nearby Triggione fountain. The nights were still icy at this altitude, and the caverns damp, but fire-smoke would have betrayed their whereabouts. At dusk the *voceratrice* (girls or women with a gift for improvising the tempestuous songs of mourning and prophecy so characteristic of Corsica) would celebrate their dead heroes, invoke heaven's wrath on their murderers and foretell the coming of an avenger. A typical lament was :

Povera, orfana, zittella,
Senza cugini carnali!
Ma per far la to vendetta
Sta siguru, vaste anche ella.

(A poor orphan maid without blood cousins—but be sure even she will suffice for the vendetta.)

There is a curiously Old Testament air about the scenes in which Letizia participated while carrying Napoleon, and he was later thought by some of his compatriots to be the promised avenger.

Napoleon is perhaps the only great soldier to have had pre-natal experience of the battlefield. When he was a French officer of twenty, in the last stages of his youthful obsession with Corsica, he told Paoli : " I was born when my country was perishing . . . I was cradled by the cries of the dying, the groans of the oppressed, the tears of despair." These words reveal an essential difference between his generation and that of his mother. Despite his feeling for Corsica, Napoleon was indelibly marked by his French education and by the romanti-cism of Jean-Jacques Rousseau, whose famous *Du Contrat Social* (1762), contained this remark about Corsica : " I have a presentiment that one day this little island will astonish Europe." Letizia's eyewitness view of Corsica's struggle was far nearer to ancient Rome than to the France of Rousseau or Voltaire. Sixty years later she still remembered this period of her life vividly and said that, sustained by the thought of Carlo and of Corsica, she had carried Napoleon " with the same joy, the same tranquil happiness, the same serenity, as I experienced later when holding him in my arms and feeding him. To obtain news of the army, I used to leave the steep rocky hide-outs assigned to the women, and make for the battlefields. Bullets whistled past my ears, but I trusted in the protection of the Virgin Mary, to whom I had consecrated my unborn son." Napoleon's knowledge of Letizia's courage made him very scornful at St. Helena of Lady

Lowe's refusal, on the grounds that she was pregnant, to pay a courtesy visit on Madame Bertrand : " A ridiculous excuse. My mother crossed the Corsican mountains on horseback when she was carrying me." Four days after Letizia's narrow escape, the Corsicans were forced back to the Tenda Pass and next morning a disaster brought the struggle to an abrupt and ugly end. The French Lieutenant-Colonel Geoffre made a feigned attack on Calenzana, a village famous for its oil and honey, followed by a feigned retreat. Convinced of imminent victory, Paoli recrossed the River Golo, only to find the entire French army massed here for a counter-attack. Heavily outnumbered, the Corsicans were driven back across the bridge to a barrier of stones erected by their own men. This barrier was manned by German deserters from the French army, who had been in-structed by the Corsicans to fire on anyone (anyone meaning any enemy) trying to pass them. In the confusion of the unexpected retreat some of the Germans, and some of the Corsicans who had remained on the farther bank, fired on their own side. A massacre resulted. Carlo's uncle, Napoleone, was among the day's dead. A French officer who questioned wounded Corsicans received answers worthy of Corneille's *Le Cid* :

" Where are your hospitals ? "

" We have none."

" Then what becomes of you ? "

" We die."

Meanwhile, the refugees of Monte Rotondo were unaware that, far from wishing to pursue them, the Comte de Vaux was eager to come to terms and stop the murderous guerrilla fighting still continuing in isolated pockets of Corsica. They were astonished when a French officer arrived on May 23rd with a white flag and the news that they might return to their homes unmolested. Paoli had agreed to go aboard an English warship into honourable exile, and the Comte de Vaux re-quested the partisans to appoint a delegation to meet him and discuss his plans, which were " to their advantage."

Carlo's first impulse was to take Letizia home, then accompany Paoli to England. But his irrepressible sense of opportunity told him that Paoli's cause was finally lost, and those who wanted him to form part of the delegation to the French pointed out that Corsica's situation would become desperate if all patriots emigrated. So he and Letizia went to Corte, where the Comte de Vaux received him in a most flattering manner. This was not so surprising as it may seem now. In addition to being a charming, well-bred, influential citizen who had proved himself a brave adversary, Carlo was one of the tiny minority of educated Corsicans who spoke French well, which made him a valuable potential ally.

When Carlo and Letizia left Corte for Ajaccio, they decided to take the less direct route in order to avoid the French army, who might well prove less amenable in the field than at headquarters. They broke their journey at Vico, where they had friends with whom Letizia was able to rest. Soon after leaving there they reached the River Liamone, swollen at this season by melted snow. As they rode alongside it, Letizia's horse slipped down the bank and into the thundering water. Dominating herself and her horse, she swung the terrified animal back on to the bank without losing her head or her baby. It was incidents of this kind that made Stendhal compare her with the heroines of medieval Italy whom he admired for their combination of beauty, courage and initiative.

When the young couple reached Ajaccio on June 1st, Archdeacon Lucciano assured Carlo he had done right not to emigrate, that his place was at home with his own people. Uncles are still powerful members of Corsican families (a current Corsican anecdote mentions an uncle saying reprovingly to a father, " Ah, it's easy to see you have no nephews "), and since the archdeacon was both father and uncle to him, Carlo was confirmed in his decision to come to terms with the French authorities. That he did so with a good conscience is shown by Letizia's having urged him to make the arduous journey to Bastia—at least a week's ride each way—to bid Paoli farewell. The French commander at Ajaccio thought none the less of Carlo for this, but, on the contrary, made a point of welcoming him warmly on his return. There was much savagery about, but also a great deal of chivalry.

Nine days before Letizia's nineteenth birthday she attended a mass in Ajaccio Cathedral celebrated by Archdeacon Lucciano. By her stood her six-year-old half-brother and her sister-in-law Geltruda. It was the Feast of the Assumption, celebrated in Corsica as a national holiday. Bells had been pealing since dawn, and through the surrounding countryside rode brown-clad horsemen who looked like bandits, thanks to their rifles and stilettos, but were merely prosperous peasants eager to honour the Virgin and enjoy the city's music, flowers, banners and processions. As Letizia knelt before the altar, her labour began. Although the Casa Buonaparte was a minute's walk away, she reached home only just in time to give birth to a son on the sitting-room couch. Small and fragile, with a large head and a loud voice, the baby was named Napoleone for the uncle killed in the struggle for Corsican independence. According to Doctor Héreau, who attended both Letizia and, later, Napoleon's second wife, the only abnormal feature of Napoleon's birth was that it cost his mother no physical suffering.

Years later, when Napoleon's sparsely documented childhood had become the quarry from which innumerable legends were created, his admirers swore that Letizia had given birth to him on a carpet embroidered with a portrait of Julius Cæsar. The first time Letizia heard this she said scornfully : " *Farlo nascere sulla testa di Cesare! Aveva bisogna di questo? D'altronde' noi non avevamo tappeti nella casa corsu, d'estate ancora meno d'inverno.*" (Pretending he was born on Cæsar's head ! Did he need that ? Besides, we did not have carpets in Corsican homes—not even in winter, much less in summer.) Detractors, equally inventive, suggested that Napoleon was fathered by the fifty-six-year-old Comte de Marbeuf, but this is chronologically impossible. Letizia and Carlo were at Corte with the patriots at the time of Napoleon's conception. Apart from this, and the family likeness that stamped all Letizia's and Carlo's children as definitely as a hallmark stamps silver, the most convincing refutation of the libel is provided by Letizia's uncompromising character.

At this stage in his life the most interesting fact about Napoleone was that, after being carried in his mother's womb through a battle against France, he was the first of her children to be born a French subject.

SOON AFTER Napoleone's birth, Carlo returned to Pisa to take the law degree he had neglected to obtain during his first stay there. He left Corsica full of excellent resolutions, but, as foreign students were not obliged to attend lectures assiduously, he was soon caught up in his habitual round of pleasure. Letizia's life, meanwhile, was reduced to domestic interests. Her fighting years seemed over, and she did not regret them. Like many of history's most genuinely romantic figures, she had not a romantic temperament, and far from considering domesticity dull, found in it a unique source of joy.

In organising her household young Letizia showed not only a soldierly precision but strong nerves, since she who had so marked a gift for silence was often surrounded by noise. For example, although her mother-in-law and Napoleone's first nurse, Mammucia Caterina, were fond of each other, they nevertheless revelled in a feud to which each contributed voluble backchat as to how certain household tasks should or should not be performed—mostly not. The children, too, had the lungs of Italian tenors, and Letizia showed herself in advance of her time in making no attempt to curb the noisiness healthy at that age. In her *Souvenirs* she mentions that she cleared a large room where they played and fought without interference on wet days and were allowed to draw on the walls. Most inestimable of free benefits were sun and sea. She put them on horseback as soon as they could walk and often sent them off for long rides with their Aunt Geltruda, who taught them all she knew of local methods of farming. It may have been during these rides that Napoleone learnt to deplore the way goats damaged the young trees, a subject that was to lead him into many an argument with Archdeacon Lucciano, who considered his great-nephew's hostility to goats to be the result of the " new philosophy." But just as Letizia encouraged her sons to be adventurous, so she insisted on their taking knocks stoically. Her highly developed sense of the inevitability of tragedy in everyday life made her consider bravery an indispensable weapon rather than a pleasing attribute.

Although strictly domestic, her life was not a lonely one. Her mother, mother-in-law and sister-in-law paid her daily visits, and a host of aunts, uncles and cousins shared her adoration of her two little boys. Many of these visitors required hospitality, the duties of which were traditionally considered almost as sacred as those of religion. Corsica possessed few inns, so travellers relied on relatives, and no matter how plain the daily fare, it was a matter of pride that entertainment be elaborate. (Boswell relates that when he dined with Paoli's nephew-in-law he was offered twelve " well-drest dishes " served on Dresden china and a variety of local wines and liqueur.)

Nevertheless, life at the Casa Buonaparte was frugal for everyone but Carlo, who had the charm of a spoilt child and was treated accordingly. Clothes and furniture had to be paid for with ready money, so were made to last as long as possible, but food (except for imported coffee, sugar and rice) was home grown. Wheat came from family fields, wine from family vineyards, oil from family olive groves. There were only two groves of olive trees in Ajaccio, one belonging to the Jesuits, the other to the Buonapartes. Napoleone often heard his great-uncle Lucciano say proudly : " The Buonapartes have never paid for bread, wine or oil." Great-uncle Lucciano also said: " One must never sell one's land, rather debts than that." The family (a portmanteau word that included grandparents, parents, aunts, uncles and cousins to the furthest degrees) was given wine and oil free of charge. Peasant customers paid with goats, cheese or milk. Butchers' meat was exchanged for its equivalent in sheep, cattle or goats. Blankets were woven at home from goat hair. Letizia's dowry included a flour mill and a public oven where all the local people baked their bread, paying in flour or fish.

The Buonapartes' food was traditional—figs, goats' milk, cakes of maize, and a cream cheese called *bruccio* were the basis of their diet, with small octopi, local game, chestnut bread and the luscious island cherries as their gastronomic treats—but their standard of personal cleanliness was far in advance of their time. In an epoch that was by modern standards very dirty, Letizia trained her children to clean their teeth and take daily baths. They all had, and kept, beautiful teeth and a love of water. Years later, when Napoleon was planning cities, he showed an unusual interest in the creation of fountains and of clean water supplies.

Letizia's tasks did not lack variety. Carlo and the archdeacon were constantly occupied with lawsuits, and it was she who organised the delivery of food supplies from the family lands, she who doctored and nursed the children, and she who did most of the household spinning. In addition, she attended church punctiliously—after Napoleone's birth she went sooner than was obligatory to the churching ceremony at which Corsican mothers made an offering to the Virgin of bread and a coin in thanks for a safe delivery—and yet found time to tell her children episodes of Corsican history that fostered their love for the island. Stendhal commented on Napoleone's childhood : " By good fortune such as seldom befalls kings' sons, there was nothing mean or small about the people who surrounded Napoleon's cradle. Suppose he had been born in 1769, the son of a marquis in Picardy . . . what would he have heard first ? Anecdotes of gallantry, lies about the antiquity of his family, gossip concerning some petty quarrel between his father and a neighbour belonging to the minor nobility, etc. Instead of this . . . Napoleon heard how the National Guard of a little island of a hundred and eighty thousand inhabitants, headed by an elected leader, dared stand up to the Kingdom of France . . .

and these stories were related to the child by a mother personally acquainted with the battlefield. . . . Few existences have been as free of hypocrisy and, in my opinion, as noble as that of Madame Letizia Bonaparte."

Meanwhile Carlo was turning his stay at Pisa to some good use. By November 30th, he had presented his thesis and received his degree. He was inscribed in the university's *Libro di Dottorati* as " *il Sig. Carlo del Qm Signor Giuseppe Buonaparte, Nob. Patrizio Fiorentino, Samminiatese & di Ajaccio.*" He was the fourteenth Buonaparte to take a degree at Pisa since Antonio Francesco Buonaparte had done so in 1633, and he celebrated his doctorate by giving a banquet that, according to Napoleon, cost the family two years' income. The occasion did warrant a celebration, however, for with this doctorate Carlo had, without knowing it, added an item to the collection of official documents without which his older children could not have had the excellent French education he was to secure for them. He had a genuine if over-optimistic sense of the value of any opportunity, and in his volatile but loving way was as good a father as Letizia was a mother.

IN THE SPRING OF 1770, a month before the fifteen-year-old dauphin married the fourteen-year-old Austrian Archduchess Marie-Antoinette, Louis XV offered privileges similar to those of the French nobility to Corsicans whose families had lived on the island for two hundred years and who could provide documentary proof of having ranked as nobles during that period. There were three kinds of nobility in Corsica, the *anciens seigneurs*, descendants of the old feudal lords, such as the Colonna and d'Istria families ; the *Caporals*, like the Casabiancas and the Arrighis, whose ancestors had revolted against feudalism in the tenth century ; and the *étrangers*, such as the Buonapartes, who had come from Tuscany or Genoa. In each case the requisite documents, or " parchments " had to be ratified by the local Courts of Justice.

The originals of Carlo's parchments are now in the French National Archives. They include his baptism certificate ; an acknowledgment of kinship from the Tuscan Buonapartes to Carlo's father (*un acte de reconnaissance de la famille Buonaparte de Toscane du juin 28, 1759 qui jouit du patriciat, et par conséquence de la plus grande noblesse, comme il est constaté par un extrait des lettres de noblesse du 28 mai 1757 délivré par le Grand Duc de Toscane*) ; letters patent of nobility from the Archbishop of Pisa (*lettres patentes de l'Archevêque de Pise en Toscane qui accordent au dit Charles l'exercice du titre de noble et de Patrice du 30 novembre 1769*) ; an act of ratification from the local Court of Justice (*certificat des principaux nobles de la ville d'Ajaccio du 19 août 1771 qui prouve que la famille Buonaparte a été toujours au nombre des plus anciennes et nobles, tant pour son côté, que par rapport aux alliances qu'elle a contractées avec la noblesse du Royaume la plus distinguée*); and a testimony to his nobility by the Corsican Upper Chamber (*arrêt du Conseil Supérieur de Corse du 13 septembre 1771 qui déclare la famille Buonaparte noble de noblesse prouvée au dela des deux cents ans*).

The Comte de Marbeuf had persuaded Louis XV to grant Corsica a measure of self-government through a locally re-cruited States-General. When the Corsican States-General assembled for the first time on May 1st, 1772, Carlo was elected member of the Council of Twelve Nobles. He was already Assessor of Ajaccio's Court of Justice, and was later to be chosen as one of the deputies to represent Corsican interests at Versailles. In order to provide an appropriate setting for his new undertakings, Carlo began enlarging his house. First he built a banqueting gallery, then a terrace for after-dinner relaxation. (It was from Carlo that the Buonaparte children inherited their immoderate passion for building.) He also added to his library, already an impressive one for the time and place, over a thousand volumes. A born spendthrift, he had some reason to feel that he had money to play with, since between them he and Letizia owned three houses, apart from their share of the one they lived in, three stories of a fourth house, three vineyards, and the Milelli, a little country villa in an olive grove on the coast out-side Ajaccio, where the family spent the summers. Although Letizia was only twenty-four, she had already borne six children (four of whom died in infancy) by the time her husband paid his first visit to the capital their second son was one day to rule. Carlo had been given the honour of offering Louis XVI and Marie-Antoinette the Corsican nobility's congratulations on their accession to the throne. For once he seems not to have spent more than the money allotted him for expenses. He was enchanted by Versailles, at last a building as grand as his dreams, and by the little King and Queen, who, still shy and eager to please, listened respectfully to his fluent account of how agri-culture might be developed in Corsica. Like Balzac, the imagin-ative Carlo was prompt to see the financial possibilities of undertakings for which the time had not yet come, and on this occasion he spoke so plausibly of what mulberry groves might mean to Corsica that he was awarded a government subsidy to carry out his plans.

Prompted by the Comte de Marbeuf, the young King decided to give the children of poor Corsican nobles the same opportunities for free education as were available to the indigent French nobility. When Carlo told Letizia he wanted to take advantage of this offer, she immediately agreed, and asked that her half-brother Fesch be included in Carlo's plan. She bore her seventh child, Lucciano (the third to survive infancy), in 1775, and Carlo had no difficulty in obtaining the " certificate of indigence " required by the French government as proof of his inability to pay for the education of all his sons.

Both Letizia and Carlo were determined their children should be well educated. Education, like bravery, came under the heading of useful weapons. All the handsome little Buonapartes showed promise of great energy, but Napoleone was the most intrepid of them all. Even as a child he had a passion for military life, and would exchange the white bread given to him to take to school for lunch for a piece of the coarse dark bread issued to the local troops. When Letizia discovered this and questioned him, he insisted he preferred the dark bread, and " as I am going to be a soldier, I ought to get used to it." The only way in which his love of the army differed from that of millions of other small boys was in its enduring nature. He inherited tenacity from Letizia, and perhaps from the maternal grandmother who could summon two or three hundred Corsican mountaineers to support her side of an argument. He also inherited Letizia's capacity for concentration, her sense of order and responsibility, and the classical profile, piercing gaze and grave expression that were to make Stendhal describe her face as sublime in its tranquillity : " only the eyes moved."

As a small child, Napoleone was not an outstanding pupil, except at mathematics, but he was always avid for information, and his abnormally energetic temperament made one of his teachers describe him as " granite heated in a volcano." Letizia was quite capable, however, of dealing with granite. The violence of her love for her children made her strict with them. She sometimes sent them supperless to bed, not as a punishment but to train them " to bear discomfort without showing it," and they soon learnt that when they had been disobedient, untruthful, or deficient in respect for their elders, not even their easygoing papa could save them from a whipping. Carlo disliked unpleasantness in every form, so he would often ask for the offender to be let off just this once, but Letizia invariably replied " This is my business," which was in accordance with tradition. A Corsican wife obeyed her husband, but was obeyed by her children. Later, during the Empire, Letizia said laughingly that no one had ever slapped so many future kings and princesses as she had. Without her lioness's paw, the little Buonapartes would have had no discipline, for, as she said, " My mother-in-law and husband were so indulgent with the children that at the slightest cry, the slightest complaint, they ran to caress them. For my part, I was severe or indulgent as the occasion warranted."

One of these occasions occurred when Napoleon was home on leave as a seventeen-year-old officer. He and his baby sister Maria-Paola were caught by Letizia in the act of imitating their grandmother's rheumatic gait. Maria-Paola was promptly put across Letizia's knee and spanked, while Napoleon, thinking that despite his mother's expression (which " boded no good ") he was safe from such undignified retribution, slipped out of the house. Letizia made no further comment on the incident, but next morning she refused his kiss. Later in the day she told him he had better hurry and change as he had been invited to dine with the governor. Delighted, he hurried upstairs—and into the trap she had prepared for him. While he was changing, she entered the room and, having taken him by surprise, locked the door behind her ; then, with Carlo's whip, she gave him the beating she considered warranted. Many years later, at St.

Helena, he spoke with mixed admiration and indignation of the way she had ambushed him that day.

None of Letizia's children resented her severity nor, which is perhaps more remarkable, did they despise Carlo's indulgence. Even Napoleone, who soon realised that " my father would have eaten up all his money if Madame had not checked him," found Carlo so endearing that once, when Letizia sent him to a local café to see if Papa were gambling again, the child's only fear was " lest Papa's feelings be hurt."

Maria-Anna, Letizia's eighth child and first daughter to survive infancy, was born in 1777, a year after the American Declaration of Independence. The family seemed likely to prove a large one, and when Carlo was re-elected deputy for the Corsican nobility the following year he decided to take his two eldest sons and young Fesch to France with him. Fesch had been granted a scholarship to the seminary of Aix-en-Provence, Carlo was paying for Giuseppe to go to the college at Autun that would prepare him for the seminary, and Napoleone was to accompany his brother and study French until the result of Carlo's request for a military school scholarship for him came through. The Abbé Varese, a cousin of Letizia's who had been appointed subdeacon of Autun Cathedral, accompanied them. Three months before they left, Letizia's ninth child, Luigi, was born.

Leaving Corsica was a turning point in the children's lives. Giuseppe was ten, Napoleone nine, and neither could speak French. Next time Napoleon saw his home he would be a man, a young French artillery officer who had shed the final " e " from his Christian name, though not yet the " u " from his surname, and had almost forgotten his native tongue.

On the evening of December 11th, 1778, Letizia took the two children to the Lazarists to be blessed by the father superior. Next day they set out on horseback and by mules as far as Corte, where they took a carriage, lent them by the Comte de Marbeuf, to Bastia, the ancient capital that originated as a fourteenth-century citadel and is to-day a small edition of Genoa. There they spent the night in an uncomfortable inn. Years later Napoleon retained vivid memories of an old man who had dragged a few mattresses, too few to go round, into the room assigned to the party. Carlo's mother and the servants had wept bitterly when the boys left, and at the final parting only Letizia and Napoleone remained outwardly calm. Her last word to him was " *Coraggio* " (Courage). This was the first of many partings, each of which was to increase Letizia's fears for her second son's safety. A world of victories lay between him and St. Helena, and he was about to take the first step towards defeat.

CARLO WAS STILL at Versailles in March, 1779, when the French Minister of War notified him that Napoleon had been granted a scholarship to the military school at Brienne. He immediately wrote to Marbeuf's nephew, the Bishop of Autun, who arranged for Napoleon's transfer. The parting between the two little boys at Autun was very painful. Giuseppe (now known as Joseph) sobbed piteously, and although Napoleon shed only a single tear, the master who witnessed the scene said that his grief seemed even greater than Joseph's. As a child and a young man Napoleon adored his elder brother, and even later, when Joseph often, if unwittingly, served him ill he continued to care for him. He could never entirely forget that Joseph was the eldest son, and that in Corsica the head of the family's word is law.

By the time Napoleon entered Brienne he could speak French fluently, but his schoolfellows jeered at his strong Corsican accent. He suffered ferociously from homesickness, which transformed him from an exuberant child into a taciturn one. Like his father, and later, his brothers and sisters, he felt a compulsion to express himself on paper, and traces of his homesickness still exist in a composition he wrote at this time about a Tahitian's overwhelming joy on seeing a tree from his native land. Lack of pocket money made him cut a poor figure beside the sons of French noblemen, and, smarting with humiliation, he wrote imploring his father to send him an allowance or else remove him from the school and let him learn a manual trade.

Unfortunately for Napoleon, it was Letizia who read this appeal. Neither her youth nor her circumstances made for indulgence, and her determination that her children should respect their father was strengthened by her knowledge of Carlo's extravagance. He had bought himself twelve embroidered waistcoats on his last trip to Versailles, and these, together with his elegant knee-breeches, silk stockings, silver-buckled shoes and habit of wearing a sword, caused him to be known locally, half admiringly, half ironically, as " Buonaparte the Magnificent." She knew too that as a result of this magnificence, the bedridden Uncle Lucciano had taken to hiding his savings in his mattress. But none of this was, in her opinion, the business of Carlo's nine-year-old son. Letizia and Napoleon were alike in so many respects that from the first she expected more of him than of his brothers and sisters. So now she wrote :

Figlio mio [throughout her life Letizia wrote her correspondence in Italian, and when French was required, had her letters translated by her children or, later, by her secretaries], I have received your letter ; at least, the handwriting and signature indicate that it comes from you. You are my favourite son, but if ever I get another such letter from you, I shall wash my hands of Napoleone. Where did you acquire the notion that a son might address his father in such terms ? You may thank heaven your father is not at home, otherwise an affront of this kind would have sent him straight to Brienne to punish you for your insolence. I shall hide your letter, in the hope that you regret having written it.

You have the right to tell us your needs, but you must realise we cannot do more than we are doing for you, hence our silence. It is not on account of your admonitions or threats that I am sending you a letter of change for 300 francs. This should convince you of our love . . . Napoleone, I hope you will be more discreet in future, and more respectful, and will not force me to write to you again in this way. If so, I shall sign myself, as always,

Your loving Mother

The prospect of kindly, spendthrift Carlo setting out for

Brienne in the spirit of an Old Testament prophet is strikingly unconvincing, but Corsican fathers had the power of life and death over their children, and had often been known to exercise it, so Napoleon understood Letizia's attitude. He also knew that she had every reason to worry about the family revenues.

Letizia's life was in many respects a hard one at this time. She was only thirty when she bore her tenth child, Maria-Paola, and her eleventh, Maria-Annunziata, arrived fifteen months later. Her health was so good that it had become second nature to her to put too great a strain on it, but after a prolonged attack of puerperal fever her doctor urged her to go to France and take the waters at Bourbonne-les-Bains. So she accompanied Carlo the next time his political duties took him to Versailles. The authenticity of this trip has been contested, but expenses for it are entered in Carlo's account book under June, 1782.

Ironically, the splendour of Versailles appealed far more to Carlo, who would have loved to live in such a place, than to Letizia, who was to return there as a royal personage twenty years after Carlo's death. At the time of her first visit there were between seventeen and eighteen thousand people at Versailles (sixteen thousand at the King's service, the rest courtiers without definite functions), and Letizia distrusted the superficiality of this glittering, alien world. She has often been laughed at for saying "*Pourvu que ça dure*" (Provided it lasts) of Napoleon's glory, as if this remark indicated a dourly suspicious peasant mentality ; but it really sprang from the prophetic instinct that caused her to be intensely troubled at Versailles by the sense of doom she discerned in the face of the gay and frivolous young Queen.

On their return journey the Buonapartes went to Autun, the old Burgundian city full of Roman remains, to see their eldest son. One of Joseph's schoolfellows described Carlo on this occasion as tall and slender, wearing a powdered wig, silk coat and a sword ; and Letizia as still young, carrying herself superbly, in a white silk frock with panniers, and with a lace veil over thick, chestnut-coloured hair arranged in a chignon. As the most popular portraits of Napoleon are those showing him as a thin, burning-eyed young general, the epitome of the Revolution in arms, there is a lifelike incongruity about this distinctly *ancien régime* picture of his handsome and youthful parents returning home from Versailles. Next they went to Brienne, where, to Napoleon's proud delight, all his schoolfellows pronounced Letizia as " *belle comme les amours* " (as beautiful as the loves). On her side, joy at seeing her favourite son was mixed with consternation at what school discipline had done to him. Years later, in St. Helena, Napoleon told General Montholon : " She was so alarmed by my thinness and altered expression that she alleged they had changed me beyond immediate recognition. I was indeed changed, since I used to work right through our recreation time, and often spent my nights thinking over what I had learnt during the day." She was equally alarmed by the prospect that he might be assigned to the Navy and, twenty-two years later, she told the British officer who escorted her to Elba that she had done all she could to dissuade Napoleon from a naval career. (" My child, in the Navy you have to contend with fire and water.") But no matter what Letizia said at Brienne, no matter how steadfastly they were to continue to love each other, Napoleon was already soaring beyond the sphere of her protection, and what alarmed her most was the chilling shadow of her son's future greatness.

WHEN LUCCIANO WAS eight years old, he went to join his eldest brother Joseph at the College of Autun. Letizia hated parting with him. Very like his father, Lucciano was a particularly loving child, with a feminine gift for small attentions of the heart, and because she missed Joseph, Napoleon and young Fesch, Letizia had spoilt him as she had never spoilt the others. He had also, since Carlo was now a public figure in Corsica, more self-confidence than his elder brothers had had at his age. As a result he was, for the time being, utterly charming. Letizia was impressed by Napoleon, whose smouldering force matched her own, but Lucciano disarmed her.

After Lucciano's departure for the Continent came that of seven-year-old Maria-Anna, for whom Carlo had obtained a scholarship to the famous school for girls founded by Louis XIV's morganatic wife, Madame de Maintenon, at St. Cyr. Letizia did not accompany her husband and daughter to France in the summer of 1784 as she was expecting another child. During this trip Carlo went to fetch Lucciano (now Lucien) from Autun, where Joseph took the opportunity to tell his father that he no longer wanted to go into the Church but would prefer an army career. This was a blow to Carlo, who had already spent a good deal on his eldest son's education, but he promised to discuss the matter with Napoleon when he took Lucien to Brienne. Carlo's attitude at this juncture suggests that, although he may not have been aware of it, he already considered Napoleon rather than Joseph as the future head of the family.

His children's prospects were much in Carlo's mind just

then. He was only thirty-eight, but his health had lately become alarmingly bad. Always slender, he had suddenly lost weight, and was subject to attacks of pain and sickness that, with characteristic optimism, he at first attributed to indigestion. This optimism had not prevented him from recently writing to the French Minister of Finance : " As ill-health precludes my paying court to you, I am taking the liberty of sending you four memoranda . . . I have seven children, Monseigneur, and am expecting an eighth, and I am almost without means, for reasons explained in the said memoranda. I have the honour, therefore, to ask for your protection, and for justice for my poor family."

When Carlo and Napoleon met at Brienne, they found themselves in complete agreement on every point. Separation from home and family had made Napoleon mature early, and far from rebelling against paternal authority, he appreciated all Carlo had done to give his children the best education available to them, and all he was still doing to help Corsica make the best of its connexion with France. He deplored his elder brother's change of heart, and said that Joseph's good looks and faculty for turning a pretty compliment would make him an admirable garrison officer, but nothing more. Like his father, Napoleon counted on young Fesch, now twenty and about to be ordained, to persuade Joseph to continue his education at the seminary. The loving and respectful letter Napoleon wrote Carlo after this meeting, which was to be their last, must have pleased Letizia far more than his desperate demand for pocket money had vexed her. Napoleon said later : " My father was an extremely handsome man of lively imagination and ardent passions. He had a fanatical love of liberty, but dreamed of a liberty that cannot exist at the beginning of a revolution that overturns everything. My father would have died with the Girondins."

Carlo took Joseph back to Corsica with him, hoping that the boy would either think better of his rash decision or agree to follow in his father's footsteps and study law. Napoleon,

meanwhile, was making a great fuss of Lucien, whom he had
not seen since the latter was a baby. His precocious paternal
instinct was strongly aroused and he wrote home : " Lucien
shows great ability and willingness. He will write you a note on
the back of this. I won't help him, as I want you to see how well
he writes." Unfortunately for both their futures, Lucien did not
appreciate his elder brother's affection. Accustomed to being
king of the nursery castle at home and to getting his own way
through charm, he found Napoleon's love too pedagogic. Nor
did the two brothers have much time to get to know each other.
Four months after Lucien's arrival at Brienne, Napoleon was
admitted to the École Militaire in Paris. His brevet of admission
as a gentleman cadet was signed by the Comte de Ségur, then
Minister of War. Sixteen years later, when Napoleon was First
Consul, he gave the old count a pension and ordered the
Consular Guards at the Tuileries to present arms when he
appeared.

By the time Napoleon left Brienne for Paris, Carlo was so ill
that Letizia, then in her last month of pregnancy, borrowed
fifty livres in gold from the governor of the island and insisted
that her husband return to France and consult the famous court
doctor, Lassonne, whose earlier treatment had seemed to do him
good. Joseph and young Fesch, now an abbé, accompanied him.
None of them guessed that Carlo's illness might be cancer, and
it is unlikely that Letizia had a premonition that this was their
final parting.

The crossing to the Continent was stormy. Carlo put up a
brave show, but by the time they reached Aix, where Fesch left
for the seminary, Carlo was too ill to travel on to Paris. A well-
known Provençal doctor advised them to try Montpellier,
famous as a medical centre. Father and son went to a cheap inn
while awaiting the Montpellier doctor's verdict, then moved to
more comfortable lodgings just outside the town. While in
Montpellier they were shown great kindness by Madame
Permon, a compatriot of theirs who had married a Frenchman,
and whose new-born baby daughter, Laure, was to marry one of

Napoleon's generals, become Duchesse d'Abrantès, and eventually contribute a great deal of Napoleonic lore to the novels of her young lover, Honoré de Balzac. The Bonaparte story is full of first and last meetings, strange coincidences and collisions, and many a writer of memoirs was to exploit these opportunities for drama. When Letizia was asked as an old woman what she thought of the Duchesse d'Abrantès's Memoirs, she said dryly that they amounted to fiction " and very bad fiction."

Carlo's courage survived his realisation that he was doomed. He talked constantly of Letizia and longed for her presence, but forbade Joseph to summon her, saying again and again that she would need every franc they possessed for the future. Furthermore she had given birth to her twelfth child, Girolamo, only ten days after Carlo left Corsica.

Christmas passed without Carlo's being able to leave Montpellier and by the New Year he was weakening rapidly. Joseph sent for the Abbé Fesch, who administered the last rites on February 24th. That afternoon Carlo's pain-clouded mind began to wander. In his delirium he called repeatedly for Napoleon, crying in hazy anguish, "Why doesn't he come with his great sword and protect his father? " Still ready to gamble on the unlikeliest chance, Carlo struggled against death until evening, when his heart at last yielded.

Since the doctors suspected cancer, an autopsy was performed. This was most unusual at that period. Even in Paris there were no more than a hundred autopsies a year, and medical students had to depend on stolen bodies for dissecting. Carlo was buried in Montpellier, in a crypt belonging to a Franciscan order. He would have been thirty-nine the following month.

There is no record of how Letizia received the news of Carlo's death, nor of how she survived the first shock of a bereavement unsoftened by those funeral ceremonies which, by dramatically acknowledging grief, make it slightly more bearable. But nearly half a century later she wrote to a widowed granddaughter: " I know by my own experience that it is very difficult to control grief caused by the loss of those we love, yet I beg you to do as I do and harden yourself against irremediable misfortune." As a widow of thirty-four, Letizia had no choice but to harden herself against irremediable misfortunes if she was to protect her eight children, five of them still less than ten years old.

II

Transformation

1785-93

Je trouvai appui dans le grand caractère de ma mère, et elle parlait de l'appui consolateur qu'elle trouvait en moi.

NAPOLEON

Lorsque la guerre de la Révolution éclata, les rois ne la comprirent point ; ils virent une révolte ou ils auraient dû voir le changement des nations, la fin et le commencement d'un monde . . .

CHATEAUBRIAND : *Mémoires d'Outre-Tombe*

How far is St. Helena from a fight in Paris street ?
I haven't time to answer now—the men are falling fast.
The guns begin to thunder, and the drums begin to beat.
(*If you take the first step you will take the last!*)

KIPLING : *A St. Helena Lullaby*

THE DETERMINATIVE figure in Letizia's life was now fifteen-year-old Napoleon, the only one of her children trained for a profession. Far away from her in Paris, he did not hear of his father's death until a month after it had taken place, and his immediate reaction was characteristic. In cases of bereavement a cadet was allowed the privacy of the school infirmary, but Napoleon refused this favour, saying, " Women must weep but a man should know how to suffer. I have not reached my age without thinking of death." His letter to Letizia was curiously formal, probably because he knew it would be read by his instructors before being mailed.

" Now that the first shock is over," he wrote, " I hasten to tell you of the profound gratitude I feel for all your goodness to us. Try to be comforted, dear Mother; the circumstances demand this. We all feel redoubled tenderness for you, and shall work to the utmost, happy if our obedience can compensate you a little for the inestimable loss of a cherished husband." Fortunately for Letizia, she did not realise at this point that Napoleon was the only one of her children who understood the verb " to work " as she herself understood it.

As the eldest son and nominal head of the family, Joseph had hurried home to manage what remained of the family property. There was no question now of his being able to enter the Army, so he decided to go to Pisa and study for a law degree in order to obtain a post in Corsica similar to his father's. From Paris, Napoleon helped his elder brother by soliciting grants and writing again and again to various ministers about the long-overdue subsidies for Carlo's mulberry groves. In struggling to turn his father's fancies into facts, Napoleon displayed a literal-minded tenacity very like his mother's, and since he was a born conqueror and had none of his father's talent for begging charmingly, he rapidly acquired a coldly authoritative manner.

By September of that same year Napoleon was ready to present himself for the École Militaire's final examinations. Most of the other candidates had already been graduated from the famous Metz artillery school. Napoleon had had only one year's preparation, but, thanks to systematically intelligent overwork, he passed forty-second in a class of fifty-eight. This enabled him to skip the stage of serving as a pupil-officer and become a lieutenant at sixteen. He was the first Corsican officer to be graduated from the Ecole Militaire into the artillery. Being sent to the La Fère regiment at Valence was particularly lucky from his point of view, since Valence lay on the direct route to Corsica, and owing to the disorderliness of the times (this was the year of the famous Queen's necklace scandal, which Goethe called " the preface to the French Revolution "), he soon managed to secure an inordinate amount of leave.

Napoleon was as proud of his uniform as any of Stendhal's young heroes, and became passionately vexed when one of the Permon girls (daughter of the Madame Permon who befriended Carlo at Montpellier) noticed how thin his legs were, and nicknamed him " Puss-in-Boots." He proudly described his regiment as the best in Europe, his officers as the " most paternal, the best and worthiest people in the world." He enjoyed even his off-duty pursuits, and had his first flirtation with a young girl named Caroline du Columbier—a very innocent matter of holding hands and picking cherries in the nearby countryside.

Yet for all Napoleon's absorption in his profession, his family was seldom out of his mind. He applied for leave as soon as regulations permitted and was allowed to go home on September 1st, 1786. With him went a trunk of books : Plato, Montaigne, Tacitus, Livy, Voltaire, Montesquieu, Racine and Corneille, whose superb plays, through which the alexandrines march like an army with banners to support honour and glory, were among his favourite reading.

Napoleon landed in Ajaccio seven years and nine months after leaving it. All the family was on the quay to meet him, except Lucien, at school in Brienne, and Maria-Anna, still at St. Cyr. At first both he and his family were disconcerted. Letizia had said goodbye to a Corsican child. She welcomed back a French officer in a blue-and-scarlet uniform, barely able to speak to her in their native tongue. Napoleon was at that time small and thin, with brilliant blue-grey eyes that darkened in moments of passion, hollow cheeks, and delicately shaped lips already compressed from the concentrated attention he paid to whatever came his way. His brown hair hung straight to his shoulders and he had a lean and hungry look. Almost at once, though, Letizia found in this emaciated young stranger her greatest comfort since Carlo's death. Years later he himself wrote : " I drew support from my mother's strength of character and she spoke of the comfort she found in me." Eager to help them both was young Fesch, who had succeeded the now bedridden Archdeacon Lucciano at the cathedral, and was thus, at twenty-four, the most important ecclesiastic in Ajaccio.

Introductions as well as reunions marked Napoleon's arrival home. He could not recognise his eight-year-old brother, Luigi, whom he had last seen in the cradle, and two sisters and a brother were entirely new to him : six-year-old Maria-Paola, four-year-old Maria-Annunziata, and the baby Girolamo. The one who impressed him most was Maria-Paola, a dazzlingly beautiful child, who could already twist everyone, even her mother, round her little finger. With this child (the future Princess Borghese), Napoleon regained the capacity for youthful laughter that he had lost when he left home. She became his favourite sister, and never lost her power to reduce him to laughter, even when he was genuinely angered by her latest folly.

It was with his mother, though, that Napoleon was first concerned. He found her more exhausted than he had ever seen her. Carlo had spent most of her dowry and she was doing all the housework herself. She was so driven that she asked her confessor for a dispensation from churchgoing, saying : " I believe it is a Christian obligation to attend church daily, and indispensable on feast days, but I do not believe the Church demands this of people who have work to do or who are mothers of families." Yet neither grief nor drudgery had crushed her spirit. She mourned Carlo, but she delighted in his children. Nothing would ever mean as much to her as *la Famiglia*, and she is known to have refused two offers to marry again. Unlike her extremely amorous children, she was able to forgo sexual love while still young. The explanation appears to lie in her single-mindedness. Having given her heart and body in childhood entirely to one man, she was incapable of making herself over to anyone else. Yet she was as free from prudery as any great lady of the eighteenth century, and her letters to her grandchildren were to show a vigorous and matter-of-fact desire that they should avail themselves of the pleasures appropriate to youth.

No matter how busy she was, she found time to listen to Napoleon when, stimulated by new ideas, he wanted to expound Rousseau or Plutarch to her and to Joseph. She would listen by the hour to the pair of them declaiming Corneille :

La tendresse n'est point de l'amour d'un héros :
Il est honteux pour lui d'écouter des sanglots ;
Et parmi la douceur des plus illustres flammes,
Un peu de dureté sied bien aux grandes âmes.

(Tenderness is out of place in a hero's life, it is shameful for him to heed sobs and even in the midst of the tenderest and most illustrious passion a little harshness becomes a great spirit.)

Before long she found the French poet's inflexible sense of grandeur, rectitude and duty striking a response from her own heart. It was not surprising that she should share the enthusiasms of this grown-up son who had seemed a stranger for a minute on the quayside. Though they laughed easily in the family circle, and both had a mordant sense of sarcasm, Letizia and Napoleon were fundamentally grave, even melancholy, and at this stage in their lives he repulsed mediocrity with youthful ferocity while she had never encountered it. Still lithe and ardent, she had already given birth and endured bereavement, shown skill in the home and courage on the battlefield, and become familiar with joy and grief; yet what made her so precious to Napoleon were the splendid negatives in her experience. At thirty-six she had never lived in an ugly landscape or drab climate, had never been intimately acquainted with people lacking energy or fortitude, and had never come across synthetic food, fatuous entertainment or meretricious writing. Paoli's famous words to Napoleon, "There is nothing modern about you, you are a character out of Plutarch," were even more applicable to Letizia than to her favourite son. All this, which appealed so strongly to Napoleon, was to prove a source of strength to Letizia throughout her long life, but would not render her easily comprehensible to courtiers.

Stimulated by his mother and his homecoming, Napoleon spent the beginning of his leave in working on his long-cherished plan to write a history of Corsica and in trying to organise a Corsican National Guard and see what could be done towards replacing the French personnel of the municipal authorities by Corsicans. His fervour reminded her of that shown by his father in the same cause twenty years earlier. She took it seriously and, always prompt to give practical expression to her sympathies, built a little summer-house at the end of Carlo's terrace where Napoleon could work undisturbed by the children's noise.

By the time the family moved to the Villa Milelli for the hottest months of the summer, Napoleon was once more on terms of close friendship with Joseph and had established loving relations with the children. Because he had left home and shouldered responsibility so early, Napoleon developed a tendency to treat his brothers and sisters as if they were his children, which, when they were all adults, made him alternately over-authoritative or over-indulgent with them. By postulating

" family reasons " he prolonged his leave until he had been home for nearly a year, but he was certainly not idle, for in addition to studying and writing on his own account, he helped Joseph superintend the family properties and their various harvests, escorted Letizia to take the waters at Cuagno, and bombarded the French authorities with requests for payment of the long-overdue subsidy on Carlo's mulberry groves. When Archdeacon Lucciano's gout became much worse and local doctors proved powerless to help him, it was Napoleon who thought of writing to the famous Doctor Tissot of Lausanne for advice. But Doctor Tissot merely noted in the margin of this letter : " of slight interest, not answered." When all his letters about the mulberry groves proved equally fruitless, Napoleon decided to go to Paris and see what could be achieved on the spot.

He reached Paris in October, 1787, and the following month obtained an audience with Monseigneur de Brienne, the recently appointed Controller-General of Finances. Nothing came of this but promises, which confirmed Napoleon in his contempt for the dilatoriness of bureaucrats. More instructive was an experience he came by as the result of a walk in the gardens of the Palais-Royal (described by the historian Michelet as a place for " *le plaisir rapide, grossier, violent, le plaisir exterminateur* "). Here Napoleon met a young woman with whom he fell into conversation. With an earnestness worthy of Rousseau, he asked her what had driven her to choose her profession. Her replies were equally earnest. (The first six books of Rousseau's famous *Confessions* had been published six years earlier and his theory that man is naturally good influenced even people who had not read him.) At the end of this literary exchange Napoleon accompanied the young woman to her room, and thus had his first sexual experience with a prostitute. No sooner was he back in his hotel than he hastened to write an account of the meeting in his private notebook. Few of the male Buonapartes considered any experience complete unless described in writing.

In December, Napoleon obtained a further six months' leave and returned to Corsica. During his absence Letizia's financial worries had increased. Joseph needed money for his law studies, and Lucien had suddenly decided, after two years at the military school at Brienne, that he wanted to be a priest, which involved giving up his military scholarship with no guarantee that he would get one to a seminary. Such chopping and changing exasperated Napoleon, himself phenomenally single-minded. The equally single-minded Letizia was determined, however, to give each of her fatherless sons an opportunity to follow the profession to which he was best suited. In this case Napoleon's intolerance was speedily justified. No scholarship could be obtained at a seminary, and before long Lucien realised he had no vocation either. Few Buonapartes had vocations involving celibacy. Eventually Lucien returned to Ajaccio and spent a happy, undisciplined adolescence developing his natural taste for politics. Letizia did not discourage him, since she felt that he had inherited this proclivity from his father—and Lucien was indeed as brilliant a speaker as his father had been.

During Napoleon's absence Letizia had injured a finger while doing housework and was in urgent need of domestic help. On his return Napoleon made her write to Joseph, urging him to spend as little as possible in Pisa (advice as wasted on Joseph as it would have been on Carlo), and asking him to engage a servant. " I would prefer an experienced woman," she told Joseph, " not too young, about forty, for indoor work. I would like her to do the washing, though that is not essential, but she must be able to do the simple cooking we require, also to sew and iron, and she must be trustworthy."

Having done the little he could to ease Letizia's situation, Napoleon rejoined his regiment, now at Auxonne, a small Burgundian town with an artillery school presided over by the regiment's commander, the Baron du Teil. This excellent officer, who loved his profession, soon noticed Napoleon's intelligence and took special pains to teach him artillery tactics. (Napoleon never missed an opportunity to learn something. Once, when confined to barracks in a room containing nothing to read but a volume of Justinian's *Juris Civilis Corpus*, he studied this so thoroughly that, fifteen years later, when drawing up his famous Code Civil, he amazed the Council of State by his knowledge of Roman Law.)

Absorbed by Corsican affairs, Letizia had no detailed knowledge of the violence brewing in France until this was provided by Napoleon, the first of the family to come into physical contact with the revolution that was to uproot the Buonapartes and help turn them first into beggars, then into kings. Four months before his twentieth birthday, rioting broke out in Seurre and Napoleon's company was sent to stop it. As his instinctive respect for army discipline was far stronger than his ephemeral sympathy with Rousseau's belief in human goodness, Napoleon did not question the justice of the orders he had been given. Even at nineteen he possessed great authority, and was able to disperse a threatening crowd merely by ordering his men to prepare to fire and then proclaiming, " Let honest folk go home, I fire only on riff-raff."

Back in Auxonne more violence came his way. In July, rioters began wrecking the Customs House. Napoleon wrote home that the news from Paris was astonishing and " singularly alarming." Thousands of labourers were drifting to the capital, where approximately 120,000 out of 650,000 inhabitants were already out of work. The King summoned the States-General (which had not been convened since 1614), and troops were called out to stop rioting in the Faubourg Saint-Antoine.

On July 14th, the populace of Paris stormed the Bastille prison. Excitement spread over Europe. A Norwegian called Steffens wrote in his Memoirs : " I was sixteen at the time. My father came home beside himself, called his sons and said, ' How fortunate you are, what a splendid future is opening before you ! If you do not each achieve an independent position now, it will be your own fault. Birth and poverty will no longer be obstacles . . .' He stopped, overcome by emotion . . . Then he told us how the Bastille had been taken and the victims of despotism freed." There were in fact only seven prisoners in the Bastille at the time, four of them forgers, two lunatics, and one confined there at the request of his family. This did not prevent people from sharing Steffens's feeling that "Those first moments of enthusiasm, to be followed by terrible ruins, had about them a purity that will never be forgotten." It was the beginning of the revolutionary mood that made the youthful Wordsworth write, "Bliss was it in that dawn to be alive."

A desire to remain alive produced the first emigration of aristocrats, headed by Louis XVI's youngest brother, the Comte d'Artois (the future Charles X), and by particularly unpopular aristocratic families, such as the Polignacs. Having seen little as yet of the mob violence that was soon to revolt him, Napoleon thought it "intoxicating" to see people "fired by the idea of liberty after centuries of oppression." But despite the sensations natural to his age and position, his point of view was still that of an onlooker. For the past three years he had spent half his time with his family, and his first concern now was with the effect all this was likely to have on Corsica. Not Letizia herself was more closely bound to their island home than Napoleon on the eve of the Revolution of which he was soon to be described as the armed embodiment.

W HEN NAPOLEON arrived home on leave two months after the fall of the Bastille, Corsica had already sent four deputies to the French States-General and was expecting to be freed at any moment from the Royal Commissioners' overlordship. Letizia was elated, and both Joseph and Napoleon were obsessed by the hope that Corsica would at last achieve self-government. Joseph's immediate personal aim was to be elected deputy, Napoleon's to command the local militia. Both confided their plans to Letizia, who not only helped but understood them. As soon as she understood what was happening in France she had urged Napoleon not to emigrate. Excess was a part of her nature, and just as she could be avaricious when family interests were at stake, so she could be extravagant, even reckless, in the same cause. On this occasion she gave her sons both backing and money she could ill afford. Carlo's banqueting gallery became once more the scene of political dramas, and the local ultra-royalists complained that Napoleon was fomenting trouble in his home town and should be ordered back to his regiment. In December, 1789, after the newly formed Constituent Assembly had declared Corsica no longer a French possession but an integral part of France, Napoleon was so carried away by enthusiasm that he asked Letizia to decorate the Casa Buonaparte with a flag bearing the words " *Vive la Nation! Vive Paoli! Vive Mirabeau!* " This she did. She was capable, too, of taking an active part in events on her own initiative, and on one occasion she put a stop to a violent clash between pro- and anti-revolutionaries—deploying in the process a typical mixture of physical fearlessness and shrewd exploitation of the would-be adversaries' family relationships.

It was Mirabeau who had urged the new French Government to invite Paoli back from exile to be military governor of Corsica. Joseph was one of the three Corsican delegates chosen to welcome the returning hero. Paoli's hopes for his country's future had been encouraged by the reception given him in Paris by Louis XVI and Marie-Antoinette, and he greeted Joseph like a long-lost son and presented him with a drawing of himself made by Carlo twenty years earlier on the back of a playing card, a gift treasured by Letizia. At first disposed to take the entire family under his wing, Paoli was soon forced to realise how profoundly uncomfortable they would all find that attitude. He went out of his way, on visiting Ajaccio, to show particular deference to Letizia, and they were both moved by their common memories of Carlo as a brilliant impetuous boy ; nevertheless, he disappointed Carlo's sons by his lukewarm attitude towards the local revolutionary club. Time and circumstances had moderated Paoli's views. Exile in London had made him fond of the English—and small wonder, since much of his time had been spent in the stimulating company of Boswell and Doctor Johnson (who declared that General Paoli had " the loftiest port of any man he had ever seen ")—and at sixty-four the former rebel was easily exasperated by whipper-snappers who, no matter how courteous their attitude, clearly felt that the desire to fight for liberty was their personal discovery. But Paoli got no support from Letizia, who was still near enough to her own youth, and above all to Carlo's, to feel with, as well as for, her dynamic and dogmatic sons. Small misunderstandings produced larger ones, and six months after Paoli's return Napoleon wrote a manifesto in which he called the old leader a political charlatan. The municipal authorities of Ajaccio retorted by ordering an effigy of Napoleon to be publicly burnt. Fortunately for Letizia's peace of mind, he was due to rejoin his regiment.

In order to lighten her domestic responsibilities, Napoleon

took his twelve-year-old brother, Luigi, to France with him. No scholarship had been forthcoming for Luigi, so Napoleon planned to support the little boy out of his pay and devote his spare time to teaching him. Although this imposed a great strain on Napoleon, who was already working at a pace that would have prostrated an ordinary man, he was enchanted to have the responsibility of " Monsieur Louis," as he nicknamed his small brother. In return, Louis worshipped the brother he thought of as a father, and did all he could to make himself useful to him. Before long Napoleon wrote home : " Louis is working hard and learning to write French. I am teaching him mathematics and geography. He reads history by himself. He will certainly do well . . . all the women here are in love with him. He has acquired a thoroughly French manner, knows how to enter a room full of people, and asks the right questions as solemnly as if he were thirty. He is obviously going to be the best of the four of us . . . he works hard as much from inclination as from pride, and is full of sensibility."

The revolution was soon to interrupt Louis's peaceful reading of history. Six days after Napoleon had been transferred back to Valence, Louis XVI escaped from the Tuileries with Marie-Antoinette, his two children and his sister, Madame Elizabeth. The royal family's flight from France had been carefully planned, but the King's unwieldy carriage proved too slow for the plan to succeed. Troop movements aroused suspicion among the already exasperated populace and the royal family was arrested at Varennes. Dread of foreign invasion spread through France, and with reason, since Leopold II of Germany and Frederick William II of Prussia declared that they would use force to restore the King's power to rule " according to the rights of sovereigns." This threat of foreign interference naturally outraged the majoriy of Frenchmen and worsened the unfortunate King's situation.

Three months after the flight to Varennes, Napoleon again obtained leave and took Louis home with him. It was becoming obvious that Corsica would not be able to maintain an independent position but must choose between the domination of France or England. Letizia and her three elder sons believed it would be best for Corsica to support France. This made Paoli distrust the entire Buonaparte family. When reminded that Carlo and Letizia had risked their lives for Corsica, he retorted that they had nevertheless accepted French rule and that Joseph, Napoleon and Lucien were now virtually Frenchmen. Political tension in Ajaccio was still on the increase in October, 1791, when the Archdeacon Lucciano died, leaving Letizia with no older man to whom to turn for advice.

She who seldom wept did so at the bedside of the shrewd old priest, who had been like a father to her as well as to his nephew Carlo. His ideas and conception of life had had a strong influence on her and she was disturbed too by his prophetic last words. Joseph, although never one to belittle himself, admitted in his Memoirs that the archdeacon had told him at the last, " You are the firstborn, but he "—pointing at Napoleon— " will be the head of the family." Napoleon, too, never forgot " *Tu poi, Napoleone, sarai un omone* "—nor that the old man had urged them to keep an eye on Lucien lest his hotheadedness cause them trouble. The archdeacon may have been merely an intelligent psychologist, but in a country so rich in superstitious beliefs his words lingered, helping to create what they foretold.

All the gold the archdeacon had hoarded in his mattress was left to Letizia, and although thrift had become instinctive to her, she gave Joseph and Napoleon unrestricted use of this windfall to further their political plans. Three months later Napoleon was appointed Adjutant-Major with the Corsican Volunteers. As this was a post reserved for professional soldiers, permission for him to accept it had to be obtained from the Minister of War in Paris. It was granted, but not before Napoleon had been so affected by the politically heady atmosphere of Ajaccio that he considered resigning from the French Army and making his career in Corsica. Yet he wanted Corsica to remain French, and himself sided wholeheartedly with the new Government. Unfortunately for Napoleon's immediate plans, the Minister of War gave permission for his new appointment without taking into account a law passed three weeks earlier forbidding regular French Army officers to join volunteer corps, and ordering those who had already done so to rejoin their original regiments by April 1st. Exception was made, however, for volunteer officers with the rank of lieutenant-colonel, so Napoleon ignored the fact that he was absent without leave, and set about getting himself elected lieutenant-colonel. Competition was keen, but after the Buonapartist faction had gone so far as to kidnap one of the most influential electors, Napoleon got his way and was appointed lieutenant-colonel.

A week later, on Easter Sunday, after the Volunteers had been attacked in the street by Paolists and a lieutenant killed, Napoleon and Quenza decided to enter the citadel, then in the hands of a French regiment commanded by Colonel Maillard. The colonel refused to admit them, and in order to avoid further trouble ordered them to evacuate their men from Ajaccio. Napoleon defied him without hesitation and obtained a counter-order from the public prosecutor. Three days of sporadic skirmishing followed, during which Napoleon vainly tried to seize the highest and most impregnable house in the town. By now the Paolists were so enraged that they sent denunciations to Paris, charging that " *Napoleone è causa di tutto.* (Napoleon is the cause of everything.)" The French Government at once sent two commissioners to Ajaccio to get the facts. Napoleon rode to Bocognano to meet them and make sure they heard his version first.

Both Paolists and royalists were determined to get rid of Napoleon. Since he was still, technically, absent from his regiment without leave, and therefore liable to court martial, they had plenty of scope for their denunciations of this brash, iron-willed young officer. Letizia and Joseph urged him to go to Paris to defend himself at the highest level and obtain his reinstatement in the French Army. According to Baron Larrey,

Letizia went so far as to say : " Corsica is merely a barren rock, an imperceptible corner of the earth. France, on the contrary, is large, rich and densely populated. Now France is ablaze—it is a noble bonfire, my son, and worth taking the risk of being burnt!"

BEFORE LEAVING home for Paris Napoleon assured Letizia that she need not worry about him, since he had done his duty as a French officer and would certainly be exonerated of blame. His naïve confidence proved justified. France had been at war with Austria since April and the Government could not afford to waste trained men. Nevertheless, he was two months in Paris waiting for his commission as a captain in the artillery to come through.

As soon as Letizia heard that Napoleon had been reinstated, she wrote Louis XVI a letter of thanks, one of the last of its kind the poor man received. Unfortunately this letter has not survived. She also wrote to Napoleon, advising him to remain in Paris on the supposition that he would be safer there than at home. She had no idea how dangerous the political atmosphere had already become in the capital. All religious orders had been suppressed, *émigré* property was being confiscated, and revolutionaries advertised their convictions by wearing green-and-yellow striped trousers instead of breeches (hence the term " *sans-culottes* "). In July the famous cry " *La Patrie est en danger !* " echoed across Europe. A fortnight later the Duke of Brunswick, who was preparing to invade France, issued a manifesto declaring that Prussia and Austria meant to rescue Louis XVI and Marie-Antoinette, and that if any violence were inflicted on the royal family Paris would be sacked and mass executions would follow. This naturally increased revolutionary fervour throughout France, as well as revolutionary fury.

The Tuileries was attacked in August. The sound of the tocsin filled the air with threats of the bloodshed. Three days later the royal family was imprisoned in the Temple. By this time Napoleon's genuine but theoretical enthusiasm for the Revolution had lessened. He wrote home : " The men at the top are poor creatures. When one sees events at close quarters, one is forced to admit that the masses are not worth the trouble individuals take to win their support. What is happening here in Paris is Ajaccio all over again, except that people here seem even more small minded than at home, even more addicted to calumny and bickering. . . ." All he saw now contributed to his opinion that there can be no revolution without terrorism and that a revolution is the greatest misfortune of the generation that carries it through.

The next private problem thrust upon Letizia by the pressure of public events was the removal of fifteen-year-old Maria-Anna from her conspicuously aristocratic school at St. Cyr. By the time Napoleon hurried to his sister's rescue, travelling had become more dangerous than usual. Even the humblest vehicle was liable to be held up by self-appointed " deputations " who would order travellers to shout " *Vive la Nation !* " and become violent unless obeyed with enthusiasm. While Napoleon and Maria-Anna (henceforth to be called Elisa) were on the road, news that the invading Prussian army was at Verdun reached Paris, where fanatics immediately broke into the prisons and began murdering the inmates. Between 1,100 and 1,400 prisoners were butchered during five days of these famous September Massacres.

On their way back to Paris, brother and sister were several times stopped by " chamber-pots," the nickname for the vehicles used by the Versailles revolutionaries ; and even at their modest hotel, the recently renamed *Hôtel des Patriotes Hollandais*, they were again and again asked to show their papers. All this was very alarming to Elisa. Physically the most like Napoleon of his three sisters, she was now a clever French bluestocking, indelibly marked by the educational system Madame de Maintenon had devised for noblemen's daughters. Familiar with Fénelon, Racine and Madame de Sévigné, she knew more about Louis

XIV and the gallantries of Versailles than about the revolutionary world in which she now found herself. Napoleon's uniform and passport still served as a protection for them, but he found it difficult to explain Elisa's presence.

" Where is she from ? "

" Her convent."

" Which convent? "

No sooner was St. Cyr named than they asked aggressively if she was a *ci-devant* aristocrat. Fortunately, Elisa's looks were not of the kind then fashionable. Napoleon said later that had beautiful Maria-Paolina been in Elisa's place " things would have gone badly " with them. As it was, he and Elisa managed to catch a post-chaise to Toulon. Whenever they were stopped *en route*, his assertion that Elisa was his sister aroused catcalls, but at least not envy, that most dangerous emotion. Asked if they were aristocrats, Napoleon replied, " We don't have *ci-devants* in Corsica. We have always fought for liberty." As most of the hecklers did not even know where Corsica was, they could not contest this.

Napoleon and Elisa reached Ajaccio in October, nearly a month after the ragged revolutionary army won its first great victory at Valmy, defeating the Prussians in a battle that, as Goethe said, marked a new epoch in world history. Royalty was abolished in France the next day and its place taken by the first French republic, called the Convention in honour of the American assembly that had met five years earlier, under the leadership of George Washington, to draw up the constitution of the United States of America. Soon after Napoleon and Elisa reached Corsica, a French naval squadron appeared there. On board was Charles-Louis Huguet Sémonville, the new French Ambassador to Constantinople, with secret instructions from the Convention to undermine Paoli's influence in Corsica. A minor Talleyrand, this forty-two-year-old revolutionary marquis captivated the Buonapartes while compromising them in the eyes of anti-French Corsicans. With Sémonville was his nine-year-old stepson, the Marquis de Montholon, who, twenty-three years later, would accompany Napoleon into exile.

Both ambassador and admiral stayed with the Buonapartes, the former making a great impression on seventeen-year-old Lucien—who acted as his interpreter at the revolutionary club and later went as his secretary to Toulon with dramatic results—and the latter bewitching Elisa, who found his manners as polished as those to which she had become accustomed at St. Cyr. The admiral seemed equally charmed by Elisa. Far the most intelligent of the Buonaparte girls, she was amorous in the extreme, as they all were, and possessed some of the volcanic quality that distinguished Napoleon. Letizia was wholeheartedly in favour of the match. At Elisa's age she herself had already been married for two years, and, like the Buonapartist Stendhal, she found it hard to resist a well-washed revolutionary with the manners of an aristocrat. But public events moved too fast for this private matter. The admiral returned to sea, and distance put an end to what proximity had scarcely had time to begin.

The Convention aimed to take Sardinia early in 1793. The two Corsican volunteer battalions, still nominally under Paoli's command, were to begin their offensive by landing on the islets of the Madeleine, opposite the Corsican port of Bonifacio. This small campaign, Napoleon's first and Paoli's last, started badly. Paoli's heart was not in it. He regarded the Sardinians as brothers and was disgusted by the republican sailors sent to transport the Corsican troops. They were the scum of the French ports, and as soon as they heard enemy shots, behaved so badly that a retreat had to be sounded and the cannon left behind.

The execution of Louis XVI completed Paoli's disillusionment with the Revolution. He told Lucien, " The wretches have guillotined their King, the best of men, a saint ! No, Corsica wants nothing to do with them ! It would be better to become Genoese subjects once more . . . Shame on anyone who sides with the brigands ! " Paoli then got in communication with

Admiral Hood, commander of the British fleet in the Mediterranean. Informed of this, the Convention sent three commissioners to investigate the matter. They were still at work when word came that Paoli was to be arrested as an English agent. When this startling move proved to be the direct result of a speech Lucien had made against Paoli at the Toulon revolutionary club, Corsicans divided into Paolists and Buonapartists. Napoleon said later that Lucien's speech had been prompted by Sémonville, which is indeed probable; but whatever its cause, it fulfilled the archdeacon's prophecy and endangered the Buonapartes' lives.

While the mass of Paoli's followers assembled at Corte, pro-French partisans made for Bastia, Joseph among them. Paolists in Ajaccio were ordered to capture Napoleon alive or dead, but Letizia was informed that no harm would befall her provided she gave a written statement disapproving of her sons' conduct. Her only recorded comment—" I thought Paoli knew me better than that "—showed that she was as ready to fight at forty-two as she had been at eighteen.

Having escaped an attempt to assassinate him, Napoleon slipped out of Ajaccio only to be trapped at Corsacci. Local partisans helped him escape and return to Ajaccio. So as not to endanger Letizia, he kept away from the Casa Buonaparte and hid in the house of a kinsman, Levié. Other kinsmen rallied to him, and when a Paolist search-party invaded the house at midnight there was no trace of Napoleon, who escaped by boat to Macinaggio and from there rode to Bastia. This was Letizia's first experience of the dread lest Napoleon be killed in war or assassinated in peace that were to dominate the next twenty-nine years of her life. A Corsican vendetta may seem an insignificant matter compared with the struggles that lay ahead of Napoleon, but it cannot have appeared insignificant to Letizia when she had her first encounter with the Revolution in that beloved landscape and among the familiar figures of the island that was never again to be her home for long.

While Napoleon sailed to Bastia, the frustrated Paolists

decided to take the forbidden collateral revenge on his family. Letizia prepared to barricade her house and fight as Faustina Gaffori had done half a century earlier, but she was dissuaded from this useless gallantry by Costa of Bastelica, a devoted partisan who arrived on May 23rd with a group of young mountaineers armed with carbines and stilettos and very similar to those who had been at her mother's beck and call. (Napoleon never forgot what Costa had done for Letizia, and he left him 100,000 francs in his will.) They wanted to escort her to the *macchia* in accordance with Napoleon's laconic message: " Prepare yourselves. This country is not for us."

Letizia immediately entrusted her two youngest children, Maria-Nunziata and Girolamo, to her mother, and dressed the others for flight. She gave her keys to a cousin, Tommaso Braccini, who removed her private papers, including recent letters from Joseph and Lucien, to a safe place. Then she set out. The young men of Bastelica led the way and those from Bocognano brought up the rear. Letizia walked between them, holding Maria-Paola by the hand, and Elisa and Louis kept close to their uncle, the Abbé Fesch. As they hurried through the darkness, Costa told Letizia that the pro-French party meant to seize all the ports but that Napoleon was sailing back from Bastia with a French naval squadron headed for Ajaccio. If the French attempt to land should fail, Napoleon planned to make for the tower of Capitello, east of the Gulf of Ajaccio, so that Letizia would have a chance of joining him there. Every now and again the fugitives fancied they heard movements in the thick undergrowth around them. Scratched by the bushes, the terrified children began to whimper. Letizia managed to quieten them by pointing out that since she was not crying there was no need for them to cry. It was typical of her that at this intensely dramatic moment she appealed to their problematic reason rather than to their prolific emotions—and with success.

Their friend the Abbé Coti met them at Milelli with the news that the Paolists had sacked the Casa Buonaparte in Ajaccio and were now close on their heels. Without a pause they hastened on for Capitello, avoiding all villages. It was a dark night and they had to pass ravines, struggle through brushwood, and cross the Campo dell'Oro bogs. Near the end of their trek they came upon a torrent too deep and rough for the children to wade through. Their only horse was loaded with provisions and exhausted. Suddenly Costa remembered that he knew a man who lived nearby and owned a horse accustomed to fording this stream. The man was providentially at home and willing to lend his horse. Letizia rode across the torrent with her two daughters as successfully as, twenty-four years earlier, she had ridden out of another torrent with Napoleon in her womb. After she dismounted, the horse was taken back for Louis. Then the grateful fugitives parted from all their supporters except Costa, who continued with them, guiding the borrowed horse. They did not know that Paoli was about to pass a decree banishing the Buonapartes from Corsica.

On the other side of the river they almost ran into a group of Paolists who were on their way to Ajaccio and talking fiercely of what they had in store for the Buonapartes once they laid hands on them. Letizia managed to keep the trembling children silent, and long afterwards her most vivid memory of the incident was of how their horse stood motionless, as if it too understood the situation. At last they reached the ruined tower of Capitello, built long ago by the Genoese. All Letizia could do now was wait for Napoleon to keep the rendezvous.

Shepherds brought them food, and on the morning of May 30th, Letizia heard the sound of gunfire. The French naval squadron was bombarding the citadel of Ajaccio. Answering shots rang back. The citadel showed no signs of surrendering, and since the French commander had not enough men for a landing-party he decided to give up the attempt. From across the gulf Letizia saw the ships move out to sea. Now, it seemed, she and her younger children were lost. As always in moments of danger, she took refuge in silence and stoicism. No wonder she felt at home in the world of Corneille :

Sa probité sévère est digne qu'on l'estime;
Elle a tout ce qui fait un grand homme de bien.

Finally the little group watching from the tower saw a three-master sailing in their direction. From it a long-boat came rapidly towards the beach. A thin figure in a blue French uniform jumped out. It was Napoleon. He ran through the water, took his mother in his arms and burst into tears. Then he rowed them all out to the three-master and accompanied them to Giraglia. From there he sent them overland to pro-French Calvi, where, although faced by the usual refugee problems, they at least had plenty of relatives and friends. Letizia and Maria-Paola were welcomed by the Giubegas (Napoleon's godfather's family); Fesch found lodgings for Elisa, Louis and himself; and when the younger children arrived, Maria-Nunziata went to the Paraviccinis, and Girolamo, who was ill, was cared for by the Casabiancas. Once again the clan provided a haven for its members. Their family solidarity is illustrated by the fact that during this time not one of the Buonapartes is recorded as blaming Lucien for the perils to which he had exposed them.

Joseph hurried from Bastia to plan their future with Letizia and Napoleon. Immediate action was essential, as they knew Calvi was about to be besieged by the Paolists. There seemed no solution but flight. The Buonapartes sailed from Corsica on June 11th, 1793, aboard a coaster belonging to a cousin who was an old hand at slipping through the British fleet. Letizia's passport and those of the younger children (except Luigi's which seems to have disappeared) read :

BUONAPARTE, LETIZIA, dressmaker, age 56 [she was 42], passport number 576.

BUONAPARTE, MARIANNE [Elisa], dressmaker, age 18 [she was 16], passport number 577.

BUONAPARTE, PAULETTE, dressmaker, age 15 [she was 12], passport number 578.

BUONAPARTE, ANONTIATA [*sic*], dressmaker, age 13 [she was 11], passport number 579.

BUONAPARTE, JÉRÔME [Girolamo], schoolboy, age 11 [he
was 9], passport number 580.
This covey of dressmakers reached Toulon in two days.
There they found the family orator, Lucien, delighted to see
them and disarmingly pleased with himself for having taken so
vigorous a political stand.

III

Afternoon : France

1793-1814

La vie intime et particulière appartenant à chaque homme continuait son cours sous la vie générale, l'ensanglantement des batailles et la transformation des empires.

CHATEAUBRIAND : Mémoires d'Outre-Tombe

What a chequered life was here! In her girlish days she had been the beauty of Corsica : when she became a wife, she had to follow her husband through great trials and dangers, but not great enough to quell her dauntless spirit ; she was, while still young, left a widow with eight children, to support whom she struggled hard ; she lived to see these children raised to the highest ranks of earthly greatness and grandeur, and she lived also to see them fall more suddenly than they rose ; but throughout her long career no prosperity could raise, no adversity could depress, her calm, indomitable spirit.

WILLIAM HAZLITT : Life of Napoleon Buonaparte

How far is St. Helena from an Emperor of France ?
I cannot see—I cannot tell—the crowns they dazzle so.
The Kings sit down to dinner, and the Queens stand up to dance.
(*After open weather you may look for snow!*)

KIPLING : A St. Helena Lullaby

At TOULON LETIZIA found herself in a world of anarchy and bloodshed far more horrible than any battlefield. The port was controlled by the St. Jean revolutionary club, extremists who flouted government orders, held up arms destined for Corsica and refused to allow the fleet out of harbour. At every front door hung a list of the house's occupants and their means of livelihood. As usual in times of social upheaval, envy, prying and denunciation masqueraded as civic virtues. A hundred leading citizens had just been arrested and a scarlet guillotine was already in action in the centre of the town. (It is one of history's ironies that the guillotine, which came to symbolise the Terror, should have been invented by the humane Doctor Guillotin in order to lessen the sufferings of men condemned to death.) For the first time Letizia saw heads paraded on pikes. Inured to hardship, she had never before experienced bestiality.

Determined to remove his mother from a mob violence equally distasteful to himself, Napoleon found lodgings for her with a Widow Cordeil at La Valette, a small village on the outskirts of Toulon. Then he gave her all the money he could spare and left to join his regiment at Nice, promising to send her part of his pay regularly. Fortunately, he found on arrival that he had 3,000 livres of back pay awaiting him. From June until September, Letizia and her five younger children depended entirely on this. Joseph wrote from Paris, where he had gone to try his luck, that the Convention had voted a relief fund of 600,000 livres for Corsican patriots, but as there were the usual bureaucratic delays in distributing the money, this was no immediate help.

The situation was confusing for native-born citizens, let alone refugees. The Convention had sent representatives to the province with full powers to hasten the levying of 300,000 men, arrest suspects and dismiss moderate administrators. Widespread resentment resulted, and soon after Letizia's arrival in Toulon an army of southern insurgents marched against Paris. In August the local revolutionaries were defeated, and Toulon fell into the hands of the English Admiral Hood, who took possession of it with 7,000 Spaniards, 2,000 Piedmontese, 6,000 Neapolitans and 2,000 Englishmen " in the name of the King of France." (As Louis XVI had already been executed, this meant his little son, whose death in prison has still not been proved.) Letizia and her children fled north from Toulon, first to Beausset, then to Reonnes, a village on the road to Brignoles, where kindly neighbours gave them food. Accustomed to independence, Letizia never forgot this humiliating period. Later, when reproached for showing avarice at the height of the family fortunes, she would say dryly, " I may one day have to find bread for all these kings I have borne."

Matters improved for her slightly in September, when Joseph, for whom Napoleon had obtained the job of secretary to their compatriot Saliceti, became a war commissioner. He immediately arranged for Letizia and the children to go to Marseille, where they were granted two rooms in a requisitioned house that had belonged to an *émigré* and contained " voluptuous wall decorations but no furniture." Whenever possible Letizia took Maria-Paola (now known as Pauline or Paulette), Maria-Nunziata (now Caroline) and Jérôme to school, sometimes remaining to study with them so as to improve her own French. But apart from this she could teach her daughters only the most primitive household management. Years later, when the girls had all acquired coronets, an old servant said she could remember the modesty with which at this time they took it in turns to prepare a *plat sucré* for dessert ; but as food was far too scarce to allow for girlish efforts at dainty recipes, this is probably one of those pious tales designed to convince the obscure that the famous are " just like you and me." Modest the Buonapartes' lives certainly were, and when, long afterwards, Napoleon came across a libellous account of Letizia's stay in Marseille, he cried indignantly, " Ah, Madame ! . . . Poor Madame, with her pride ! If she were to read this ! "

But while Letizia was struggling to maintain the standards of Corsican family life in revolutionary Marseille, Napoleon's position was about to undergo a sensational change. Hitherto he had waited impatiently in the wings of history ; now he appeared on the stage he was soon to dominate. While serving with his regiment at Nice, he attracted the attention of Jean du Teil, artillery commander of the Army of Italy and brother of the general who had noticed Napoleon's intelligence at Auxonne. As a result he was sent to Avignon to organise convoys to the Army of Italy. On discovering that he could not carry out his orders until Avignon was liberated from the insurgent federalists, he spent his enforced wait outside the city in writing a political brochure entitled *Le Souper de Beaucaire*. Well written in dialogue form, it demonstrated the futility of the federalists' attempts to defy the Convention. Napoleon paid for this to be printed in the hope that it might attract attention and procure him advancement. This proved an astute decision. The brochure was read by Joseph's benefactor, Saliceti, now one of the commissioners sent by the Convention to accompany General Carteaux's army on its mission to quell revolt in southern France. After proving successful in Avignon, Nice and Marseille, Carteaux was checked by prolonged resistance in Toulon.

In September, Saliceti, who was at army headquarters, received a visit from Napoleon returning to Nice with a convoy. Carteaux's artillery commander had just been badly wounded, so Saliceti quickly suggested that Captain Buonaparte be requisitioned to replace him. The siege of Toulon was proceeding so unsuccessfully that it was felt matters could scarcely be made worse. Saliceti therefore got his way—and the obscure young

Corsican took command of the artillery. There, wrote Las Cases in the *Mémorial de Sainte-Hélène*, " history took possession of him and his immortality began." In the past, while waiting in Toulon for a boat to Corsica, Napoleon had often spent his time walking about the town and examining its fortifications. (Eleven years later, when the young Prince de Bade complained there was nothing to see in Mainz, Napoleon told him that whenever one was at a loss in an unfamiliar town one should investigate the fortifications, " in case one ever had to besiege the city.") He had thus discovered that whichever side controlled a point called L'Eguillette controlled the roadstead. Once the English ships were within range of the French cannon, Toulon would be forced to surrender to the government troops. Napoleon's ceaseless energy, spirit of enterprise and habit of sleeping only briefly and always on the ground beside his battery, irritated the middle-aged Carteaux ; but the latter was relieved of his command in October and in the following month a Council of War gave Napoleon a free hand to carry out his plans. As a result, the English evacuated Toulon on December 18th and Jean du Teil wrote to the Minister of War : " I lack words to describe Buonaparte's merits. He has tremendous skill, equal intelligence and too much bravery. It is up to you, Minister to consecrate him to the service of the Republic."

Promoted Brigadier-General at twenty-four, Napoleon thought immediately of the effect on his family. Thanks to tours of inspection which took him to Marseille, he was able to see Letizia early in the New Year. Her pride in him was mixed with anxiety, for he had not fought unscathed. He had had his horse killed under him, the first of many, he had received a bayonet thrust in the thigh that nearly cost him his leg, and— what was to prove more troublesome than his wound—he had caught a virulent attack of scabies from a dead gunner whose place he had taken. Yet, thin and exhausted, he was prouder than ever of his profession, and for the rest of his life would always help a soldier of whom he was told " he was at Toulon." In February he was given command of the artillery of the Army of Italy, and soon afterwards arranged for Letizia and the children to live with him at Château-Sallé, a comfortable country house just outside Antibes, with gaily painted shutters and a garden full of orange trees, palms, mimosas and eucalyptus.

Here neighbours devoted to equality, if not to liberty and fraternity, were edified by the spectacle of young General Buonaparte's beautiful mother doing the family washing in the river that ran through her garden. (Napoleon had given her an allowance of 150,000 livres a year, but recent experiences had developed her sense of fortune's fickleness. A year ago it had never occurred to her that she could live cut off from Corsica, yet now her home was occupied by English soldiers invited there by Paoli, beside whom, not so long ago, Carlo had fought for Corsican independence.) Neighbours were less edified when young General Buonaparte's beautiful sister, thirteen-year-old Pauline, demonstrated her belief in the pursuit of happiness by climbing their walls and enjoying their figs.

Before Letizia had had two months of this idyllic life, nineteen-year-old Lucien gave her a distressing shock, the first of many he was to cause her. Although he now had a lucrative job as supervisor of army supplies at Saint-Maximin, only sixty miles from his family, he could not keep away from politics and had managed to get himself elected president of the local revolutionary club. Then, in May, he defied Corsican tradition by marrying without asking the consent of the head of the family—in this case Letizia. As he was still a minor, he faked his birth certificate. His bride, Catherine Boyer, was the illiterate twenty-one-year-old sister of the innkeeper with whom Lucien lodged at Saint-Maximin. " I have met a girl who is poor and virtuous and I have married her," he told his family. (Jean-Jacques Rousseau again.)

Once she had met and talked with Catherine, Letizia appreciated the girl's gentle, loving nature, perfectly adapted to conjugal life. But Napoleon, who was struggling with all his might to build up the family fortunes, thought Lucien had made an idiotic marriage and refused to be placated. This was the first of those quarrels between Napoleon and Lucien that were to be the source of some of Letizia's bitterest griefs. It was a great relief to her when, three months later, Joseph made a marriage of which she entirely approved. His bride, Julie, was the twenty-three-year-old daughter of François Clary, a prosperous bourgeois of Marseille, who had left his children a fortune earned in textiles. He had also left them dangerously situated politically, since they had ties with the provincial nobility. One member of the family committed suicide for fear of arrest, three more members emigrated. As a result, the Clarys were the first French family to consider the Buonapartes, with their impeccably revolutionary background, as politically useful friends. They had every reason to do so, since Joseph helped save Etienne Clary from the guillotine, thus becoming the hero of the family before he entered it as a brother-in-law. Although small and plain, Julie was also sweet-natured, loving, devout and rich—and could display a dry wit when with people she trusted, as she did her mother-in-law. Letizia liked Julie so much that she was delighted when Napoleon fell in love with her pretty younger sister, Désirée (later to become the Queen of Sweden).

But within a week of Joseph's marriage Napoleon was in no position to think of following his example. Robespierre had been overthrown and guillotined a month earlier, and in consequence anyone connected with him, however remotely, was suspect in government circles. Napoleon had been on friendly terms with Robespierre's younger brother since the siege of Toulon, and had only recently been sent to Genoa by him on a secret mission to examine the terrain over which the Army of Italy would have to fight. Napoleon was therefore arrested and, on August 9th, imprisoned in the Fort Carré, within sight of Letizia's house. While he was in prison, his friend and aide-de-camp, Junot (Junot had been a sergeant when his courage attracted Napoleon's attention and friendship at Toulon, and was to end as a general and Duc d'Abrantès), called on Letizia and offered to organise Napoleon's escape. Letizia often said that she would never forget Junot kissing her hands and sobbing

as he swore he would liberate Napoleon or die with him:
"From that moment I considered him the sixth of my sons."
Napoleon refused, however, to attempt to escape, sure that,
being innocent, he would be exonerated. This was an extremely
irrational belief, but once again he was proved right, although
the influence of his friend and commander Dumerbion, who
considered him an irreplaceable officer, had far more to do with
his narrow escape than had his innocence.

The accusations against Napoleon were so ridiculous that
his career seemed unlikely to suffer from them until nine months
later, when he was ordered to leave the Army of Italy for the
Army of the West, then fighting the royalist rebels in the
Vendée. As this meant transferring from the artillery to the
infantry, Napoleon objected violently and set out for Paris to
try to get his orders changed. With him went Junot, Marmont
(another of Napoleon's future marshals) and his brother Louis.
Letizia and her four younger children moved back to Marseille.

No sooner was Napoleon gone that Letizia heard that Lucien
had been arrested for "Robespierrisme," and was in the very
prison in Aix where only recently a group of royalists had
murdered the inmates. (There was little to choose between
revolutionary and royalist terrorism.) Joseph, who had lost his
job as a war commissioner, was away in Genoa on business for
his wife's family, so Letizia had to act on her own initiative. She
wrote to Chiappe, the Convention's representative to the Army
of Italy:

Citizen Representative,

I have just learnt from this morning's courier of the
arrest of my son Lucien. As none of his brothers is here and
I do not know to whom to turn, I am addressing you in the
hope that you will interest yourself in his case. He was
denounced at Saint-Maximin to one of your colleagues
whose name I do not know. I cannot imagine what he is
accused of, since there were no *émigrés* there, and no one
perished at the hands of the law. Only a few people were
denounced, but I do not know why. I beg you, Citizen

Representative, to write to your colleague Isoard, who is here. I await this proof of your friendship, and hope you will not disdain my supplications. If your sister-in-law is still at Nice, please remember me to her.

I am, Citizen Representative, with respect,

Your fellow citizen,

LETIZIA BUONAPARTE

When the news of Lucien's imprisonment reached Napoleon he was hanging around Paris on half-pay, waiting for the result of his demand for sick leave. His health was bad at this period, and his sombre, brooding air earned him the reputation of " the kind of youth one would not care to encounter at a dark street corner." He was also the kind of youth Stendhal was to immortalise thirty-five years later in the character of Julien Sorel, hero of *Le Rouge et le Noir*. Immediately he heard of Lucien's plight, he used his influence to obtain his brother's release and sent him the money to come to Paris. Letizia was becoming accustomed to treating Napoleon as her most responsible child.

In August he was employed in the topographical department of the Ministry of War, and by the end of the month had become the Government's unofficial adviser on military operations. His plan for the invasion of Italy won him promotion. He was head of his department when the question of his joining the Army of the West came up again. He still objected to this transfer, and had decided to leave the country rather than submit, when he heard that the Sultan of Turkey wanted French artillery officers to train his army. As Napoleon had been fascinated since boyhood by both the Orient in general and the exploits of Alexander the Great in particular, he immediately offered his services and started making plans to get Joseph appointed French Consul in Constantinople. He told Joseph that one must live in the present : " A brave man must despise the future."

Then, in September, he received two astonishingly contradictory pieces of news. The first was that he had been struck off the army list for having failed to take up his command with the Army of the West ; the second that he had been appointed head of a military mission to Turkey. He did not have to leave immediately, and a month later history suddenly played into Napoleon's hands, transforming him overnight from a suspect officer on half-pay into a national hero.

ALTHOUGH NAPOLEON had always been generous to his mother, she was astonished when, in October, 1795, she received a present of 2,000 livres from him. With this came a letter saying, " It is all over now and my first idea is to send you the news." What was over was Napoleon's apprenticeship. He had just saved the Government from being overthrown by the insurgent National Guard.

For months the Convention had been in a precarious position, attacked from within and without. After the death of Louis XVI's son was announced, the boy's *émigré* uncle, the Comte de Provence, assumed the title of Louis XVIII and royalist bands such as the *Compagnons de Jésus* and *Compagnons du Soleil* attacked revolutionaries in Lyons, Aix, Tarascon and Marseille. Other royalists rose in the Vendée, and in June the English landed 12,000 *émigrés* in Brittany. With food scarce, business at a standstill, the army unpaid, and corruption rampant, even people without political views were grumbling, and the bourgeoisie was becoming almost as hostile to the Government as were the royalists. By the beginning of October, 20,000 insurgents, *sections* of the National Guard, already controlled part of Paris, and had found a leader who drew up a plan for them to assault the Tuileries in two converging groups. The Convention determined to fight back, but by October 4th it was rumoured all over Paris that the Government had capitulated. In a last-minute attempt to save the situation, the Convention made Barras head of the Army of the Interior.

That evening, Napoleon was at the Théâtre Feydeau with his friend Junot. He remarked that had he been leading the insurgents, he would soon have made short work of the Convention. A few hours later he was in command of the Convention's troops, having been called in by Barras, an intelligent, corrupt and ambitious viscount from Provence, who was then a member of the Convention. Barras had met Napoleon about the time of the siege of Toulon and been unforgettably struck by his shabbiness, intransigence and precocious military skill.

Among the men now under Napoleon's orders was his future brother-in-law Major Joachim Murat, the histrionically handsome and courageous son of a Lot innkeeper. Realising that swords and bullets would not suffice to defend the Tuileries, Napoleon sent a squadron under Murat galloping to fetch the cannon in the Parc de Sablons before the insurgents could capture them. Rain delayed the insurgents, and when they reached the church of St. Roch in the Rue Saint-Honoré they were confronted by forty cannon. Two or three hundred of the insurgents were killed on the spot and Napoleon's troops routed the rest. He had made short work of the insurrection. Three weeks later " Général Vendémiaire," as he was now nicknamed (because October 5th was 13th Vendémiaire in the Revolutionary calendar), was promoted commander of the Army of the Interior, and the Convention was replaced by the Directory, a government headed by five directors who were all former members of the Convention, including Barras, the former lover of the woman Napoleon was soon to marry.

Napoleon's first reaction to success was typically Corsican. " Now our family shall lack nothing," he wrote home. He arranged for his mother and sisters to move from their two rooms in Marseille to a handsome apartment in the same street, and he even thought to send clothes for his sisters, who had started going to balls where they attracted the kind of attention nowadays given to film stars. It was the period of the eccentric fashions of the *Merveilleuses* and *Incroyables*, which showed as much as possible of the female figure without complete nudity, fashions entirely pleasing to the nymph-like adolescent Pauline. He gave Joseph a consular appointment, letters of introduction to the Spanish Ambassador, expert advice on Julie's financial problems and special facilities for cashing money orders. Indeed, he seemed unable to do enough for his elder brother. When Joseph wanted to buy shares in two privateers, Napoleon arranged it; when Joseph grew bored in Genoa, Napoleon invited him to be his guest in Paris. He secured a post for Lucien as Commissioner with the Army of the North, and also a special assignment to accompany Fréron, Commissioner-Extraordinary to Southern France, on an official tour of inspection that would make it possible for him to visit Letizia. Louis became a lieutenant in Napoleon's old regiment and a month later was appointed his brother's aide-de-camp. Jérôme was sent to a good school. Letizia's half-brother, Fesch, was given the profitable job of purveyor to the Army of Italy. Joseph's brother-in-law gained command of a battalion of engineers. Nor, in his desire to please his mother, did Napoleon forget distant cousins, Ramolinos, Buonapartes, Arrighis. No matter how often individual members of the family might disagree with one another, the Buonapartes were united by bonds like those of a secret society. Years later, when he was ending his life in exile, Napoleon told Las Cases : " Joseph would have adorned society anywhere, and Lucien any political assembly. Jérôme would have governed well in maturity. Louis would have charmed and attracted attention anywhere. My sister Elisa had a masculine intellect, a vigorous spirit : she must have shown great philosophy in adversity. Caroline is very skilful and capable. Pauline, perhaps the most beautiful woman of her time, was and will be to the end of her life the best creature in the world. As for my mother, she deserves every type of veneration. What large family could present a more handsome ensemble ! On top of that, apart from political dissensions, we loved one another. As for me, I have never lost my brotherly feelings. I loved them all, and I think that fundamentally they all loved me."

Letizia's joy at this flowering of the family fortunes was abruptly checked by an affront she had never anticipated.

Away in Paris, Napoleon suddenly married a stranger without even telling his mother, let alone asking her consent. This deviation from Corsican tradition was all the more painful to Letizia because Lucien had already committed the same offence.

According to what most modern historians now dismiss as a " pious legend," a small incident led to Napoleon's marriage. Immediately after his victory at St. Roch, civilians were ordered to turn in their arms. A boy of fourteen, Eugène de Beauharnais, called at Napoleon's headquarters to ask permission to keep a sword that had belonged to his father, the Vicomte de Beauharnais, a revolutionary noble who had served as a general with the Army of the Rhine, then been guillotined during the Terror. Touched by the boy's courage and filial loyalty, Napoleon not only gave permission, but gave it charmingly. He was just beginning to discover that he could control people otherwise than by force, and even those who disliked him, as did Chateaubriand, admitted that his charm and his smile could be irresistible. A few days later the boy's mother, Joséphine de Beauharnais, came to thank the young general for his kindness to her son. She was a seductive creole from Martinique, where her aristocratic father had been a sugar planter. Born Joséphine-Rose Tascher de la Pagerie and married at fourteen, she was now thirty-three, seven years older than Napoleon, and as great a conqueror in the alcove as he was on the battlefield. Whether or not there is any truth in this story, Napoleon certainly met Joséphine at this time and took to attending her receptions, where he met not only many of the most powerful figures of the day, but older men who would sometimes forget his presence and assuage their nostalgia for the *ancien régime* by saying, " Let's take a turn at Versailles," and then settling down to talk of the past.

As a fashionable member of what would now be called the Barras set, Joséphine knew Napoleon was highly esteemed in Government circles, so, instinctively, she set out to charm him. This was not difficult, for like many brilliant young men who have devoted most of their time to work, Napoleon was naïve sexually. He had never before seen a woman like Joséphine and was soon at her beck and call. All thoughts of ingenuous Désirée Clary vanished from his mind as he rapidly became obsessed by his passion for Joséphine. Years later Joséphine's daughter, Hortense, wrote in her Memoirs that at this period, when she was thirteen, she had found herself seated at dinner beside a young general who in order to talk to her mother " pushed himself forward with such energy and perseverance that he wore me out and forced me to lean back. In spite of myself, I examined his face, which was beautiful, very expressive, but remarkably pale. He spoke passionately and seemed aware of nothing but my mother."

Flattered and indolent, Joséphine did nothing to discourage her " funny little Corsican," and four months after his first visit to her house they were married, and settled in a charming little house between courtyard and garden in the Rue Chantereine (later renamed Rue de la Victoire in Napoleon's honour) that Joséphine had rented for the past six months from Julie Careau, wife of Napoleon's friend Talma, the famous actor. Joséphine had maintained the house's dramatic traditions by furnishing the bedroom with stools shaped like drums, chairs with backs that imitated cross-bows supported by sheaves of arrows, and a bed draped to resemble a tent. Napoleon was not to enjoy this boudoir battlefield long. He had recently been appointed General-in-Chief of the Army of Italy (malicious gossip said that this was a wedding present from Barras), and he was obliged to leave his bride two days after their wedding.

On his way to join the Army of Italy Napoleon stopped at Marseille to see Letizia. As this was his first visit there since Vendémiaire the city gave him an official welcome, and for the first time Letizia was publicly honoured as Napoleon's mother and was presented with the palms of victory. Nevertheless, the moment was not, from Napoleon's viewpoint, well chosen for a family reunion. Letizia was having trouble with Pauline, the most amorous of her incandescent daughters. (Balzac later made an *ancien régime* character in *Une Double Famille* say to his

[Photo Maurice Petit]

Letizia Bonaparte

Above left: Carlo Bonaparte, father of Napoleon; *right:* Letizia Bonaparte, mother of Napoleon. *Left:* General Pasquale Paoli, Corsican patriot.

Corte, as it was in Letizia's time

The Bonapartes' house in Ajaccio

The Bonaparte family escaping from Corsica as refugees, 1793

Joseph Bonaparte

Jérôme Bonaparte

Lucien Bonaparte

Pauline Bonaparte

Joachim Murat

Caroline Murat,
née Bonaparte

Louis Bonaparte

Hortense Bonaparte,
née de Beauharnais

Joseph Bonaparte,
with his wife Julie,
née Clary

Elizabeth Patterson of Baltimore,
first wife of Jérôme Bonaparte

prudish son, "Without the Emperor's sisters, what would become of us ? ") Pauline had fallen in love with Lucien's superior, the forty-year-old commissioner, Louis-Stanislas Fréron. The son of a Catholic and royalist journalist and the godson of King Stanislas of Poland, Fréron had backed the revolutionary party and founded a successfully violent left-wing newspaper, *L'Orateur du Peuple*, to which Marat contributed. Fréron had no more genuine talent as a journalist than he had courage as a soldier, but he was in advance of his time in his sense of the value of publicity. Completely heartless, he had a genius for turning against old friends at crucial moments. But although he had been involved in some very bloody deeds, there was superficially nothing of the *sans-culotte* about him. Like Robespierre, with whom he had been at school, he dressed as a dandy and powdered his hair. His personality was as outwardly brilliant as it was inwardly crapulous, and he easily dazzled the ingenuous and ignorant Pauline. The only one of Letizia's children who had escaped any formal education, she was at fifteen more than ready to embark on her lifelong pursuit of love. Jaded Fréron was overwhelmed by her beauty and freshness and welcomed her childish and passionate letters : " *Ti amo sempre e passionatissimamente, per sempre ti amo, ti amo, ti amo, sbell'idol mio, sei cuore mio, tenero amico, ti amo, amo, amo, si amatissimo amante.*" (I love you always, most passionately, I love you for ever, I love you, my beloved idol, my heart, my tender friend, I love you, love you, love you, my most beloved lover.) This was a typical fragment. Pauline's world was still that of the old Corsican serenade :

> *S'entrassi 'ndru Paradisu santu, santu,*
> *E nun truvassi a tia, mi n'esciria.*

(If I entered Paradise and found you were not there I would flee from it.)

Letizia had hoped Napoleon would control Pauline, who adored him, but now that he had married " an old woman with grown-up children " (the family view of Joséphine), Letizia felt he was in no position to advise anyone about matrimony. To her dismay, he seemed as totally bewitched by love as Pauline. Indeed, he had scarcely left Joséphine's arms before he was writing to her: " Every instant takes me farther from you, adorable one, and every instant I miss you more unbearably." Love and genius were devouring him. It was the most feverishly imaginative period of his life, the only one in which he could write : " What is the future ? What is the past ? What are we ? What is the magic fluid that surrounds us and conceals the things we most need to know ? We live and die in the midst of marvels."

As Letizia could no longer beat him nor send him to bed without supper, she made the best of his marriage outwardly and wrote a socially acceptable reply to the letter he had brought her from Joséphine :

I have received your letter, Madame. It could not, of course, add to the charming impression I had already formed of you. My son has told me of his happiness, which is enough to ensure not only my consent, but my approval. My own happiness lacks nothing but the pleasure of meeting you. I already consider you one of my children.

My son has encouraged me to hope that, as your letter suggests, you may come through Marseille on your way to join him, I look forward to the pleasure of having you stay with me.

My daughters join me in the hope that you will soon be here. Until then, my children, like myself, offer you the same friendship and affection as they feel for their brother.

You may be assured, Madame, of the loving attachment of

LETIZIA BUONAPARTE, Mère

It was during this visit that Napoleon begged Letizia, with particular emphasis to take care of herself. " If you were to die I should have only inferiors in the world," were his words. Napoleon was to love both his wives, in very different ways, and at least two of his mistresses, but although he treated all the women in his life generously, he never respected any woman as he respected Letizia. The natural bond between mother and child was strengthened instead of weakened by time, and by the course of history which gave each of them new reasons to admire the other's fortitude.

That he was himself passionately in love did not make Napoleon sympathise with Pauline's infatuation. He knew too much about Fréron's unsavoury private life (his actress mistress was currently expecting her third child by him) not to urge Letizia to withhold her consent. This was enough to cause Lucien, still angry with Napoleon for disapproving of Catherine, to support Pauline. Elisa, as usual at this stage in their lives, stood by Lucien, and the cross and clever pair complicated matters for Letizia by asking insinuatingly in what way Fréron was inferior to Joséphine. So far as all the Buonapartes except Napoleon were concerned, they were already committed in thought, if not in deed, to a vendetta against the Beauharnais family. None of this affected Napoleon's attitude, and by the time he left to take up command of the army in Italy Pauline was so distraught at his opposition that Letizia could not bring herself to forbid all communication between the lovers, as is shown by Pauline's letter to Fréron :

Everyone is against us. I see by your letters that all your friends have failed you, including Napoleon's wife, on whose support you counted. In fact, she told her husband that I would demean myself by marrying you, and that she hoped to prevent our marriage ! What harm have we done to her ? Everyone is against us, we are in a miserable situation.

Do write to Napoleon. I would like to write myself. What do you think ? Address your letter to me care of Mamma. I shall love you all my life. Love me always. My soul, my blessing, my tender friend, I breathe only to love you.

Indefatigable in matters of the heart, Pauline did write to Napoleon several times. But he was too busy to attend to her. At twenty-six he had reached one of the most fabulous moments of his career, the moment evoked by Stendhal in the opening paragraph of *La Chartreuse de Parme* :

On May 15th, 1796, General Bonaparte entered Milan at the head of the young army that had just crossed the bridge of Lodi and shown the world that, after all these centuries, Cæsar and Alexander had a successor.

W HEN NAPOLEON reached Nice, he found the Army of Italy openly rebellious. Thirty-eight thousand unpaid and ill-equipped French soldiers faced the prospect of fighting seventy thousand crack Austrian troops, and were prepared to despise any general sent them by " those incompetent civilians in Paris." Within a few days, however, they were won over by the precision of Napoleon's orders, his unaffected interest in the smallest detail of their lives, and above all by his challenging words : " You lack boots, clothes and bread. The enemy has plenty of everything. It is up to you to conquer. You want to— you can—forward ! " Even so toughly recalcitrant a character as General Augereau, twelve years Napoleon's senior, was subjugated. " The little bugger positively frightened me," he said later. " I can't understand what came over me at his first glance."

With his army finally in hand, Napoleon began to execute his long-meditated plan for driving the Austrians out of Italy. A year later, when the Austrians had to beg him to come to terms with them, he was within sixty miles of Vienna, and had fought fourteen battles, seventy lesser combats and taken 100,000 prisoners. Stendhal said that no general had previously won so many great battles in so short a time or against such heavy odds. While accumulating these victories in Italy, Napoleon received his first and very flattering letter from Talleyrand, exnoble, bishop and *émigré*, recently returned to France and government office. Now forty-three, the brilliant and wily Talleyrand was adept at reading the writing on the wall, and he immediately divined something of the young general's genius.

When the two men met each was favourably impressed by the other. Talleyrand wrote of Napoleon : " At first sight his face appeared to me charming. A score of victories go so well with youth, with fine eyes, with pallor and an air of exhaustion." Nevertheless, their association, which seemed likely at first to benefit both France and themselves, finally proved fatal to Napoleon's empire.

From the start, this first Campaign of Italy provided splendid material for the Napoleonic legend, and stirred not only the popular imagination but that of the greatest French writers of the period. No historians have done more to immortalise Napoleon than Balzac, Stendhal, Victor Hugo and even Napoleon's enemy, Chateaubriand. In *Le Médecin de Campagne* Balzac makes a veteran say of the beginning of this campaign : " So then Napoleon, who was still merely Bonaparte, put the heart into us, God knows how, and we marched by day and we marched by night, and we thrashed them at Montenotte, and we went on to make short work of them at Rivoli, Lodi, Arcola, Millesime : we gave them no quarter. Soldiers soon acquire a taste for victory ! " Those first French victories were rapturously welcomed by the Italians, to whom they meant liberation from the Austrians.

Napoleon soon became so popular that after each battle the old soldiers held a meeting and conferred promotion on him, as if raising him from the ranks. It was at Lodi that they gave him the famous nickname " the Little Corporal." It was at Lodi, too, that Napoleon first realised that he might play a decisive part in history : " *Je sentais le monde fuir sous moi.*" (I felt the world flee beneath me.) When, at Arcola, Napoleon seized the flag and led his troops across the bridge, a slender, heroic figure with flying hair who narrowly escaped death, he entered not only history but legend.

While the peace terms were being arranged, Napoleon set up headquarters at Milan and invited Letizia and his family to join him. Joséphine had been reluctant to leave Paris, and as he suspected her of infidelity, he had already sent for Pauline in the hope that his sister's presence would have a restraining effect on his wife. (This is the only occasion on record when anyone who knew Pauline well expected restraint from her.) His brothers, Joseph and Louis, were already in Italy fulfilling their obligations. Louis had shown extreme bravery during the campaign and had been the first French soldier to cross the Po. But the troublesome Lucien, who ought to have been at his post with the Army of the North, was lingering in Paris without leave and inciting Fréron to feel ill-used. When Napoleon ordered him to resume his duties, Lucien complained to Letizia that his wife's miscarriage had been due to their having been forced to travel just then, and that Joséphine was always balefully influencing Napoleon against him. It is difficult to see what advantages the happy-go-lucky Joséphine could have obtained from urging Napoleon (who needed no urging) to order Lucien back to work for which he was drawing payment, but Letizia was so suspicious of Joséphine that she was inclined to believe Lucien's tale.

Just as Letizia had found it natural to treat Napoleon as a man while he was still an overworked boy, so she sometimes found it difficult not to continue to indulge Lucien as she had done when he was the only child left in her nursery. He had a quicksilver quality that reminded her of Carlo, and also, being a person of projects rather than achievements, a disarming availability. It was because he alone of her sons was available just then that she turned to him when his favourite sister, Elisa, received an offer of marriage from Felice Pasquale Bacciochi, a thirty-five-year-old army officer from Ajaccio, who had lodged in the same house as the Buonapartes in Marseille. As Bacciochi was Corsican, a soldier, and related to the Buonapartes through his mother, Letizia favoured the match despite the Bacciochis' having been pro-Paolist. Lucien realised that Napoleon was sure to object to the introduction of pro-Paolist elements into the family, but since he was still angry with his brother for objecting to his own marriage with Catherine Boyer, he urged Letizia to give Elisa and Bacciochi their way. His advice encouraged Letizia's own inclinations, since she thought Elisa too old—

nearly twenty—for celibacy, and it was extremely evident that Elisa shared this view. Both Letizia and Elisa had already asked Napoleon for his consent, but by the time his answer arrived and proved to be a refusal, Lucien had overcome his mother's doubts. Elisa and Bacciochi were married on May 1st, 1797.

Letizia therefore sailed for Italy accompanied not only by Elisa, Bacciochi, Caroline and Jérôme, but also by an uneasy conscience. Napoleon was to be told that his veto had arrived only after his sister was already married, and Letizia hoped that Napoleon would make the best of this, just as she herself had made the best of his marriage.

This was Letizia's first trip to Italy, where so much of her life, including her most tragic years, was to be spent. She landed at Genoa just as Napoleon's aide-de-camp, Lavalette, was concluding arrangements for the Genoese Republic to surrender to France. The city was in an uproar and its fairy-tale marble palaces and hanging gardens were surrounded by anti-French demonstrators. Lavalette had not expected Letizia so soon and insisted she have the protection of a military escort as far as Milan. Letizia refused with a typical mixture of courage and common sense, pointing out that as Napoleon was holding several important Genoese citizens as hostages, no one was likely to attack his mother.

To Lavalette's amazement, this proved correct. Moreover, whenever Letizia appeared in public she was hailed as the mother of the Liberator of Italy with all the enthusiasm of a country where mothers are revered as a matter of course and closely associated in the popular mind with the Madonna. As she approached Milan, Napoleon rode out to meet her, accompanied by Joséphine, Fesch, Joseph, Louis and Pauline. When he dismounted and ran to embrace her, she said, " To-day I am the happiest mother in the world," words Napoleon quoted at St. Helena as having been among his life's greatest rewards.

Here for the first time Letizia saw her extraordinary son the centre of an extraordinary setting. Mombello, where Napoleon had established his headquarters, was a square castle on a hill outside Milan, overlooking the plain of Lombardy. Its grounds abounded in shady alleys, grottoes and fountains, and an immense avenue led up to a double flight of steps and a terrace that surrounded the castle. Even more astonishing to Letizia than the décor, were the actors. Three hundred Polish lancers in blue-and-amaranth uniforms and shapskas were on guard. The poet Arnault has left an eyewitness account : " High-ranking officers, administrators, heads of government and magistrates stood around Napoleon at a respectful distance. Nothing impressed me so much as the attitude of this little man in the midst of the giants whom he dominated by his character . . . Berthier, Kilmane, Clarke, even Augereau, waited in silence for him to address them, a favour he did not grant to everyone . . . Never has a military headquarters more closely resembled a court. The atmosphere was exactly like that of the Tuileries a few years later . . . ' That man,' I told Regnand on our way home, ' is a man apart. Everything yields to his genius . . . he is born to rule as others are born to be ruled. If he is not fortunate enough to be carried off by a bullet, he will in four years' time be either in exile or on the throne.' " It was at this point in his career that Napoleon dropped the " u " from his surname and henceforward signed official papers Bonaparte, until the day when the signature Napoleon sufficed.

To Letizia's relief, Napoleon accepted Elisa's marriage calmly. He was not pleased by it, but nevertheless he gave his sister a dowry of 40,000 francs and secured a military command at Ajaccio for Bacciochi. The only condition he imposed was that the civil ceremony by which Elisa and Bacciochi had been married in France should be followed by a religious one at Mombello. As this was in accordance with Letizia's own wishes, Napoleon seized the opportunity to get her to consent to the marriage he had planned for Pauline. The prospective husband, Victor-Emmanuel Leclerc, was a brave and handsome officer of twenty-five, recently promoted general. The son of a wealthy flour merchant of Pontoise, Leclerc had received a good education before volunteering at nineteen for the Seine-et-Oise battalion. He and Napoleon had been friends since the siege of Toulon, and Leclerc had fallen in love with Pauline at a time when she was too infatuated with Fréron to notice the younger man. Letizia had no difficulty in convincing her that she would be happy with Leclerc. The inflammable little girl promptly fell in love with him. Pauline's affections were extremely catholic, and she was in love from now on until the day she died, though seldom for long with the same man. She married Leclerc there and then, and the priest who had performed the ceremony also married Elisa and Bacciochi. Like Elisa, Pauline received 40,000 francs as dowry from her brother.

Now that Letizia was able to relax she began to long for Corsica. Napoleon had foreseen this. He himself once said, long after he had grown accustomed to palaces, that to lose the house one was born in, the garden where one played as a child, was to lose one's country. So when Corsica was liberated the previous October he had ordered that the Casa Buonaparte be repaired against his mother's return. This proof of her favourite son's imaginative care for her was for Letizia the climax of a glowing summer, during which Carlo's grandiose ambitions for her children had begun to appear extremely modest and rational.

Before parting from Napoleon, Letizia asked herself whether she ought to tell him that Joséphine was the mistress of Hippolyte Charles, an entertaining nonentity who amused her idle days. Letizia had been informed of the affair by Pauline, who still bore Joséphine a grudge for the part she fancied her sister-in-law had played in preventing her marriage to Fréron. Revolted by Joséphine's infidelity and unable to pardon her for not having given Napoleon a child, Letizia nevertheless hesitated. Finally she said nothing. Napoleon was still helplessly in love and Letizia was not a trouble-maker. Silence came naturally to her.

THE NEWS THAT Letizia was on her way home stirred up noisy enthusiasm in Corsica. When she landed the quay-side was packed with cheering crowds. Ajaccio was illuminated and guns roared a salute in honour of the mother of the Victor of Italy, the Liberator of Corsica. Letizia accepted this calmly. It was the sight and scent of the island itself that moved her, not the shouting inhabitants. She did not forget that many of those now cheering her return had only four years earlier driven her into exile.

Despite Napoleon's orders, the Casa Buonaparte still had the bedraggled look of a building recently vacated by an army of occupation. (It is another of history's small ironies that Napoleon's future gaoler, Hudson Lowe, was among the English officers billeted here.) Most of the furniture had been destroyed or stolen, but the French Government had voted compensation for " victims of the Paolist counter-revolution," so Letizia eventually received 97,500 francs from Paris. Helped by Elisa, Bacciochi and Lucien, who always fell on his feet and was now a French commissioner in Corsica, she arranged her surviving possessions and sent to Madame Clary on the mainland for what could not be bought in Ajaccio—such as white cord for curtains, chairs upholstered in yellow damask and rolls of red, yellow and red-and-white wall-paper. She did not grudge expense since she expected to remain in Ajaccio henceforward and to make her house the permanent family headquarters. Joseph favoured this plan and bought the part of the house that did not belong to her. Her half-brother Fesch also joined her there and invested some of his recently acquired money in land around Ajaccio.

Her homecoming was not, however, as opportune as it seemed. Despite the apparent fervour with which she had been, welcomed, Corsica was still politically divided. Unpopular government measures such as conscription, forced loans, the law of hostages and the persecution of priests who refused to take the Civil Oath, roused a violent hostility, exacerbated by former Paolists who attributed every move they disliked to " Buona-parte-influence " and chose this moment to pay off old grudges. By the spring of 1798 a clash seemed imminent.

Letizia did not immediately realise what was going on, for at this point she had a severe attack of malaria and, in addition, she was preoccupied by anxiety about Napoleon, who had sailed from Toulon in May in an attempt to conquer Egypt and open the route to India. With him had gone an army of 38,000 men, two of the Republic's best generals (Kléber and Desaix), a group of scholars, writers and archæologists, and his brother Louis. News travelled slowly by to-day's standards and mail from Egypt was often seized by the British fleet in the Mediterranean, so Letizia was constantly in suspense. Anti-French Corsicans added to her torments by spreading rumours of disaster, and she was once goaded into declaring, " My son will not perish miserably in Egypt as his enemies hope. I know a higher destiny awaits him."

Relief finally arrived in the form of a surprise visit from Louis, who, while carrying Napoleon's trophies to Paris, had been driven on to the coast of Corsica by unfavourable winds. He was still suffering from prolonged sea-sickness, and it says much for his resilience that he managed to give Letizia a spirited account of Napoleon's initial victories. After leaving Toulon, the French had occupied Malta, landed at Aboukir and taken Alexandria. Although Egypt was nominally ruled by the Sultan of Turkey, it was in fact controlled by the feudal Mamelukes, fearless horsemen who had attempted to halt the French Army when it reached Giza, opposite Cairo, after its exhausting march across the desert. In vain the Mamelukes had flung themselves against the French infantry, which lost only thirty men as against two thousand of the enemy. This was the famous Battle of the Pyramids (" Soldiers, from the heights of these pyramids, forty centuries look down on you ") that made Napoleon master of Cairo.

Besides this public news Louis brought private information. Napoleon had at last been told of Joséphine's infidelity and was wild with grief. Four months after he sailed for Egypt Joséphine had acquired Malmaison, a charming country house with forty-five acres of parks and gardens beside the Seine between Paris and Saint-Germain-en-Laye, where she indulged her passion for gardening and, equally openly, for her lover, Hippolyte Charles. (Recently discovered letters show that Joséphine was completely infatuated by this futile young man and, while the infatuation lasted, spoke to him of the Bonapartes as " those monsters.") Louis's report that Napoleon was considering divorce aroused in Letizia an emotion as fiercely implacable as that which prompted the Corsican *vociferatrice* to call down heaven's vengeance on the enemies of their husbands and sons.

After their family news had been exchanged, mother and son discussed the situation in Corsica. Determined that his mother should not be driven from her home a second time, Louis tried to persuade her to return to France with him. Her doctor, who wanted her to take the waters at a French spa, added his arguments. Letizia finally yielded, though unwillingly. Unaware that her life in Corsica was over, she promised herself as the ship sailed that she would return. She was unable to keep this promise until fifteen years later, when, for the last time, she spent a few hours in the island that represented to her youth and love.

AFTER TAKING THE WATERS at Vichy with Louis, Letizia went to Paris to stay with Joseph and Julie. She found the capital so dilapidated that she scarcely recognised it as the city she had visited with Carlo seventeen years earlier. The aristocrats' houses, for the most part abandoned by their owners, were mouldering and in need of fresh paint, secularised churches were serving as government offices and looked correspondingly drab, the streets were dirty and without pavements, and neither light nor water supplies could be relied upon. But in spite of all this Joseph had found and bought a splendid house, built by the great architect Gabriel for Mademoiselle Grandi of the Opéra, in the fashionable Rue du Rocher. All the Bonapartes except Letizia and Napoleon took an immoderate delight in luxury, especially in houses, objects of art and clothes. Only over food and drink were they all naturally abstemious. Whatever their tastes, they could henceforth indulge them, since the positions to which Napoleon raised his brothers and sisters enabled them to acquire fortunes without in any way running counter to the financial ethics of the period. One has only to read Balzac, in whose novels money plays so dramatic a part, to see the startling ease with which fortunes were made and lost in this era.

By bringing Letizia to France Louis had thought to rescue her from troubled air. But Paris proved no calmer than Ajaccio. While Napoleon was in Egypt the political situation in France had taken a turn for the worse. Anarchy was on the increase and with it talk of reforming the constitution and electing a " perpetual president." Fouché, the sinister, ambiguous Minister of Police who had been trained for the priesthood and was described by Talleyrand as a man " whose countenance, manner and conversation exhibited profligacy and ferocity, energy and restlessness," thought that the country needed a figurehead. So did his associate, the former Abbé Sieyès, that enigmatic statesman who, when asked what he had done during the Revolution, said " I survived." Together this formidable pair of intriguers started looking about for a picturesque public figure, preferably a soldier, since, as Sieyès told Fouché, " Two things are necessary, a head and a sword." While pursuing their investigations, they often attended the lively receptions given by the amiable and hospitable Joseph. Madame de Staël, Benjamin Constant, Talleyrand and Madame Récamier were among the guests who circulated before the observant gaze of the self-contained Letizia, and Napoleon was often mentioned by them as a brilliant soldier. Sieyès began to think that General Bonaparte might prove more useful than the previously suggested General Bernadotte, " who looks like an eagle but is really a goose," and both Sieyès and Fouché made the mistake of considering Napoleon as a sword they could handle. Just so, on a smaller scale, had social gaiety and political plotting been combined in Carlo's banqueting gallery.

After this taste of Parisian life, Letizia accompanied Julie and Joseph to their country house at Mortefontaine, near Chantilly. This house, now vanished, was built beside the fish-ponds installed by the monks of Chaalis and possessed a park laid out in the romantic style made fashionable by Rousseau, with a profusion of temples, grottoes, columns and ruins. Watteau set his " Embarquement pour Cythère " in this typical Île-de-France landscape, Corot painted a " Souvenir de Mortefontaine," and it was here that Chateaubriand read his novel *Atala* to Louis Bonaparte. Here too that gentle genius Gérard de Nerval lived as a child, after his mother had died in Germany while accompanying his father, an army surgeon, on one of Napoleon's vast campaigns. The child's first visits to his uncle's little house in the woods occurred at the same period as Letizia's last visit to her son's large one and the descriptions de Nerval was to write of this delicate countryside with its ancient legends and lingering traditions help us understand why Mortefontaine was the first place in France where Letizia felt at home.

It was not, however, much quieter than Paris. Guests filled the place with gaiety. Letizia enjoyed watching her handsome, good-natured eldest son playing host, but she obstinately refused to contribute to the social pageantry by ordering new dresses for herself. When Pauline, who adored clothes and was already spending a fortune on them, teased her for her avarice, Letizia said, " Quiet, spendthrift. I have to save for your brothers. They are not all in settled positions yet. It is natural at your age to think of pleasure, but I have more serious matters to consider. I do not want Bonaparte [Napoleon was the only one of her sons she called Bonaparte] to have cause for complaint. You take advantage of his good nature." Letizia usually meant precisely what she said (which is probably why many people found her enigmatic) and, since she did indeed think it natural the children should seek pleasure, she made no attempt to check their high spirits and, so far as everyday matters were concerned, fell in with all their plans. She never objected to meals at irregular hours, and when they returned from an outing she was always eager to hear about it. Experienced courtiers already realised that her children were the key to her heart. Whenever anyone praised them, " her deliberately serene expression made way for animation."

While his brothers and sisters were amusing themselves, Napoleon was still fighting. In April, 1799, he defeated the Turks at Mont-Thabor ; then lack of artillery drove him back to Egypt, where, in July, he repulsed the Turkish Army landed by the English at Aboukir. A month later he learnt of a new alliance against France through newspapers sent him with ironical intent by the English Admiral, Sir Sidney Smith, and immediately decided to find out for himself what was happening in Paris. Without asking permission, he left General Kléber in charge of the army, slipped through the English fleet by what seemed a miracle, and made a stop in Ajaccio, where he gave a dinner for forty guests in his father's banqueting gallery. This was the last time it was used by one of Carlo's sons for the purpose for which it had been intended. Napoleon's officers were delighted with Corsica and pronounced Ajaccio a splendid town, the women seductive and the food and drink excellent. It was harvest time and Napoleon gave them plenty of wine, grapes, pears and wild boar brought him by the peasants. This was a valedictory as well as a festive visit, for although Napoleon was still young, thirty, he was more than half-way through his life and would never see Corsica again.

When he reached Fréjus in October, he found France in a chaotic state. Royalists were up in arms in southern and western France, and also in Belgium, annexed to France for the second time in 1794. Dread of extreme measures prevailed, yet only extreme measures could reform the constitution. The Jacobin clubs had been closed, the extreme left-wing newspapers suppressed and the Directory was massing troops in Paris. It had also, in desperation, sent to Egypt for Napoleon, although not until after he had already left for home on his own initiative. His arrival had therefore been expected by the Government, but not his arrival as early as this and certainly not its startling effect on the masses. From the moment he landed in France popular sympathy, excitement and fervour crystallised round the victorious young general, who appeared an image of courage and probity in the greatest contrast to the noxious manipulators in power.

Stendhal noted that when news of Napoleon's arrival in France reached Paris, Fouché was ordered to arrest him but objected, " He is not the man to let himself be arrested and I am not the man to arrest him." It would certainly have been difficult to stop Napoleon then. All along the route crowds shouted " Long live Bonaparte ! Long live the Little Corporal ! He has returned to save us ! " From Pontarlier the municipal authorities reported : " The news of Napoleon's arrival in France so electrified our commune that many people were taken ill, others cried for joy and everyone felt this must be a dream."

Napoleon's stepdaughter Hortense, who accompanied Joséphine in a vain attempt to reach him before he saw his brothers and sisters (there were two main roads south and, not knowing which Napoleon had chosen, Joséphine took the wrong one and missed him), reported : " Whenever we stopped to change horses, crowds pressed round the carriage and asked if it were true that their ' saviour ' had arrived, for that was what all France was calling him now. With Italy lost, the treasury bankrupt, the Government devoid of both strength and reputation, Napoleon's return seemed a blessing from heaven. The journey from Fréjus to Paris was a series of triumphs that showed both him and his enemies what France wanted of him . . ."

He reached his house in Paris at six in the morning of October 16th, 1799. There he found Letizia, too eager to embrace him after more than two years' separation to have waited at Joseph's house. To his amusement she showed no surprise at the excitement aroused by his homecoming. Contemporary onlookers were again and again to wonder at her equanimity—which, because of the grandiose settings in which it was displayed, seemed to them both mysterious and disconcerting, and presently became legendary. It did not, apparently, occur to them that she was in many respects as literal-minded as she was forceful. In this case, the widespread belief that Napoleon had only to return to undo the blunders of lesser men and substitute order for chaos, prosperity for indigence, seemed to her well-founded. At thirty Napoleon had already quelled a mob, rescued his family first from death then from destitution, conquered a port supposed impregnable, prevented a tottering government from falling, and transformed a horde of discontented tatterdemalions into one of the finest armies ever destined to enter history with banners flying. Now he had arrived home, on his own initiative, at the very moment when he was most needed. Small wonder that Letizia thought it natural her belief in him should be shared by others.

Louis's report from Egypt had led Letizia to believe that

Napoleon was at last aware that both honour and dignity required him to divorce Joséphine. No religious obstacle existed, as they had not been married in church. When Letizia told him this, Napoleon agreed with her. He was full of bitterness against his wife, and later, when the clan gathered, his brothers and sisters did not hesitate to pour forth all the scandalous gossip about Joséphine that Letizia had preferred to omit. They had two days in which to harden his heart, and they made the best of them. Then Joséphine returned to Paris.

No sooner was she in front of him, distraught, tender, imploring forgiveness, than Napoleon's determination wavered. He always found it difficult to resist any woman's tears, and he still loved Joséphine. Her explanations were persuasive, her presence even more so. They had been married only three and a half years and for more than half that period had been separated. When Napoleon's brothers hastened to his house to find out the result of the interview between husband and wife, they learnt that Napoleon and Joséphine were in bed. In the street named after Napoleon's victories, Joséphine was still the conqueror.

Incensed by what she called such weakness, Letizia forgot that she herself had been equally weak with Carlo and was still equally weak where her daughters rather than her daughters-in-law were concerned. Again and again, throughout her long life, Letizia displayed equity, common sense, magnanimity and a formal but unaffected benevolence in keeping with her appearance ; but woe betide anyone within her reach who betrayed a child of hers ! When this happened her emotions divided swiftly and unconsciously into two working-parties, preparing mercy for her children but only justice for their enemies.

N APOLEON WAS NOT long kept idle in Paris this time. On the 18th Brumaire (November 9th), the Directory was overthrown and he received his first taste of purely political power. The *coup d'état* had been planned by a group of conspirators, including Fouché, Sieyès and Talleyrand, who planned to force all five Directors to resign and leave the executive posts vacant. The Council of Elders and the Council of Five Hundred were then to be induced to nominate three provisional Consuls to replace the Directors and draw up a new constitution. As one of these Consuls, Napoleon would be the indispensable figurehead. The Minister of Justice was a party to the conspiracy and the great majority of generals then in Paris could be relied on to support it. Lucien, who had been elected President of the Council of Five Hundred in spite of his being under the statutory age for this post, had been active in preparing the terrain. Attracted though he was by political intrigue, Lucien undoubtedly believed he was acting in the best interests of France, and for once he and Napoleon were in agreement.

The curtain went up when the President of the Council of Elders, who was in the plot, announced that a conspiracy to overthrow the Government had just been discovered. This immediately created a dramatic atmosphere, in which those councillors not in the conspiracy readily supported a proposal to transfer both Councils outside Paris to Saint-Cloud : a move designed to prevent popular interference with what was to follow. The Council appointed General Bonaparte commander of all the armed forces in Paris and entrusted him with the safety of both Councils. Napoleon promptly led a brilliant group of officers and men to the Council of Elders and said : " You have passed a law promising public safety. Our arms will ensure this. We desire a republic based on liberty, equality and the sacred principles of national representation, and I swear we will have it ! "

By next day those members of the Council of Elders who were not in the plot had had time to realise they were being duped and to plan concerted action with the Council of Five Hundred. As a result, the Council of Five Hundred opened the afternoon session by voting to maintain the constitution as it stood. After a clumsy intervention by the Council of Elders, Napoleon appeared before them, only to be greeted with yells of " Down with the dictator ! " This shook him. Fearless on the battlefield, he was nonplussed by civilian violence. The Council of Five Hundred displayed even greater hostility, crying " *Hors la loi!* (Outlaw !) "—words which, taken literally, amounted to a death sentence. Some of his grenadiers rushed to protect him, and Lucien, retaining his sense of political procedure with remarkable sang-froid, divested himself of his parliamentary insignia, toga and toque very slowly so as to retard the moment of voting.

Once outside and on horseback, Napoleon was acclaimed by his own troops, but the Corps Législatif's guards, for the most part hardened revolutionaries, were hesitant. Lucien joined his brother and, on horseback beside him, made an impassioned speech to the troops : " The President of the Five Hundred declares that the immense majority of the Council is momentarily at the mercy of an armed minority . . . these reckless brigands, no doubt in the pay of the English, are setting themselves up against the Council of Elders, and have dared to speak of outlawing the general charged with carrying out its decrees. I tell you that it is this ferocious minority that is outlawed—outlawed by itself ! I trust the Army to protect the majority of their representatives. Generals, soldiers, and all of you, citizens, you will acknowledge as your legislators only those who join me now ! "

Led by Murat and Leclerc and with drums beating, the grenadiers entered the hall and expelled the recalcitrant deputies. At nine o'clock that evening the Elders, and those who had rallied to them, voted the liquidation of the Directory and its replacement by three Consuls : Sieyès, Ducos and Napoleon. After which the Councils adjourned and two Commissions of twenty-five members each were asked to prepare a reformed constitution under the supervision of the Consuls. From the first there was no doubt as to which of the three Consuls was the most important.

On the evening of the 19th Brumaire, Letizia was in Paris, attending a performance at the Théâtre Feydeau (now the Opéra-Comique) with Pauline, Madame Permon, and her daughter Laure and Junot. In her Memoirs, Laure wrote of this evening :

Ever since we arrived, Madame Bonaparte had seemed agitated and uneasy. She said nothing, but kept glancing at the door of the box, and my mother and I saw that she was expecting someone. The curtain went up, the little play began peacefully, when the manager came on to the stage, bowed and announced in a loud voice :

" Citizens, General Bonaparte has narrowly escaped being assassinated at Saint-Cloud by traitors to our country ! "

At these words Madame Leclerc [Pauline] gave a piercing scream and began to agitate herself violently, while her mother, although just as painfully affected, was occupied only in calming her.

Madame Letizia Bonaparte was as pale as a marble statue, but no matter how wounded her heart, the only sign of this on her still beautiful face was a slight contraction of the lips.

Leaning over her daughter, she took her hands, held them tightly in hers, and said in a trenchant voice, " Pauline! Why make such a scene? Be quiet. Didn't you hear that no harm has befallen your brother ? . . . Be quiet then . . . and come away. We must go and find out the news."

Her mother's tone had more effect on Madame Leclerc than all our attempts to comfort her . . . At last we were able to leave . . . crowds were streaming from the theatre, eager for news . . . several people called out " There's the General's mother and sister." . . . " Where do you want to go ? " my mother asked Madame Letizia. " To the Rue du Rocher [Joseph's house] or to the Rue Chantereine [Napoleon's house] ? " " To the Rue Chantereine," said Madame Letizia after a moment's thought. " Joseph won't be at home, and Julie will know nothing."

So it was with Joséphine that Letizia learnt that the son who at nine years old had feared lest lack of pocket money shame him in an aristocratic French school, was at thirty virtually the ruler of France.

WHEN NAPOLEON arrived on the political scene the public's desire for a stable government and material prosperity outweighed any fear of dictatorship. The Paris factories were employing only one eighth of the number of workers employed on the eve of the Revolution, the number of *canuts* (the famous Lyons silk workers) had fallen from 8,000 to 1,500 and Marseille was doing less trade in a year than it had formerly done in six weeks. In the west, 40,000 Chouans (devout royalists named after the *chat-huant*, the screech owl whose call they imitated as a war-cry) were up in arms intercepting communications between Paris and the sea; and all over the country so-called royalist risings were a pretext for brigandage.

Within a prodigiously short time Napoleon justified the hopes placed in him, revealing himself as brilliant a legislator and administrator as he was a soldier. Since his time France has been a kingdom, an empire and a republic, yet even to-day, after the ravages of two world wars, the basic social structure of France is still the one laid down by Napoleon. Authority is still vested in prefects, the ministries are still organised according to his plans, the educational system is still the one he devised, the Code Napoléon still regulates judicial relations, and to belong to the Legion of Honour is still an honour.

Despite his new eminence and the gigantic labours it involved Napoleon remained ever thoughtful of his family. Each member was indeed as much an integral part of him as his Corsican accent. He made Joseph a member of the new Corps Législatif and soon afterwards Ambassador Extraordinary empowered to negotiate the peace with America. (Republican France felt keenly sympathetic towards the young United States, often publicly referred to as " the home of virtue and liberty.") Lucien became Minister of the Interior ; Louis a colonel in the Fifth Dragoons ; Pauline's husband Leclerc received a divisional command with the Army of the Rhine ; Elisa's husband Bacciochi was promoted from Marseille to Paris ; and Letizia's beloved half-brother Fesch, who had resumed his priestly functions after making a religious retreat in Milan, distinguished himself in the negotiations preparatory to the Concordat and was made Archbishop of Lyons by his nephew.

To-day, when youth is often spoken of as if it were a condition peculiar to the mid-twentieth century, it is instructive to remember the extent to which the Bonaparte story is one of youth triumphant. Napoleon was only thirty when he began to rule France ; Ambassador Joseph was thirty-one, Minister Lucien twenty-four, Colonel Louis twenty-one, and even Letizia, sometimes described as if by this time she was already an old woman weighed down by honours and bereavements, was only forty-nine and still energetic as well as beautiful.

Soon after Napoleon became Consul, his seventeen-year-old sister Caroline, who had been attending Madame Campan's famous school at Saint-Germain-en-Laye, married General Murat. Fifteen years older than Caroline, Joachim Murat already had a flamboyant career behind him. His father had intended him for the priesthood, but the boy was far too fond of pleasure for a seminary. At twenty he volunteered for the army and his almost insane bravery made him an incomparable cavalry leader, who enjoyed nothing, except making love, so much as galloping at the head of his troops, sabre in hand. He had met Napoleon when they defended the Convention together at the Church of St. Roch, and Caroline had been in love with him ever since he had arrived, a superb-looking officer, at Marseille bearing news of her brother's first triumph in Italy. Everything about him was superlatively attractive to a romantic schoolgirl. On the night of the 18th Brumaire he had sent four

grenadier guards to Madame Campan's school to reassure
Caroline as to her brother's safety. Hortense de Beauharnais,
who was a fellow pupil, reported that the arrival of four grenadiers in the middle of the night had driven Madame Campan
to complain loudly of this " martial way " of announcing events,
but that Caroline saw in it only further proof of gallantry and
love.

Napoleon was less enthusiastic than Letizia about this
marriage. He valued Murat as a soldier, but thought his exorbitance as a lover would make him a very trying husband for
an inexperienced schoolgirl. This made no impression on iron-
willed Caroline, who was far too much in love not to be all for
exorbitance. (Talleyrand said of her later that she " had the
brains of a Cromwell in the body of a pretty woman.") Even
Letizia had a weakness for Murat at first. His looks reminded
her of Carlo's, he was as stimulating as military music, and
military heroism was romantically fashionable the year Napoleon
won the battle of Marengo, and with it, domination over
Italy.

A month after the marriage of Caroline and Murat Napoleon
moved from the Luxembourg to the royal apartments in the
Tuileries, then still called the Palace of the Government. A
cheering crowd watched his carriage, drawn by six white horses,
approach the Carrousel. The other two consuls, Sieyès and
Ducos, took over the Pavillon de Flore and the Hôtel d'Elbeuf.
Napoleon wanted Letizia to live with him at the Tuileries, and
offered to furnish apartments for her there, but she preferred to
remain with Joseph and Julie. Not only did she dislike Joséphine
and love Julie, but her attitude towards Napoleon's rise to such
exceptional power was becoming ambivalent. Though she
believed he had genius, she feared he was rising too rapidly not
to be in danger of an equally sensational fall. She could appreciate splendour and had a taste for formality, but she did not want
to commit herself to court life, nor to siding exclusively with one
of her children. More than ever she wanted to be free for whichever child might need her most. When Joseph sold his house in

the Rue du Rocher she went to live with Fesch in an equally splendid house in the Rue du Mont-Blanc.

Napoleon's brothers and sisters did not always keep in mind how much they owed to him; on the contrary, they were becoming more and more exigent. Letizia feared that she might presently have to act as peacemaker between them. Her fears were soon justified. The first cause of dissension among her children was the question of Napoleon's successor. As he had no son, his brothers wanted him to choose one of them, or of their children, as his heir. Joséphine promptly read the writing on the wall and began planning a marriage between her seventeen-year-old daughter, Hortense, and her young brother-in-law Louis, in the hope that Napoleon might accept their children as his heirs. Letizia violently deplored this plan, all the more so because Lucien was just then out of favour with Napoleon and she attributed this to Joséphine's influence. In reality it was due to Fouché, who detested Lucien and lost no opportunity to discredit him in his brother's eyes. A tireless, gifted spy, Fouché made much of Lucien's indiscretions as Minister of the Interior and was delighted to be able to reveal that he had written an untimely pamphlet entitled *Parallels between Cæsar, Cromwell, and Bonaparte*, in which he supported monarchism and asserted " Bonaparte must be King."

Napoleon decided to overlook this but send his incorrigibly trouble-making brother out of the country for a while. He then appointed Lucien Ambassador to Madrid, a post which offered plentiful opportunities for making money and love. Lucien's gentle, devoted wife Catherine had died in childbirth four months after Caroline's wedding, and although Lucien was soon courting both the famous actress Mademoiselle George and the equally famous Madame Récamier, his grief was genuine and a change of scene indubitably to his advantage.

Letizia did not view Lucien's departure in this light. As soon as she heard that Fouché had been speaking against him, she drove to the Tuileries and requested an interview with Napoleon. Puzzled by her formality, he at once received her. She found him alone with Joséphine, who was quickly reduced to tears by Letizia's mordant references to Fouché as her daughter-in-law's accomplice. In vain Napoleon tried to interrupt his mother and defend his wife. He always met his match in Letizia. On leaving the room, she turned on Joséphine and said, with the calm that made her rages so terrifying, " Will you please warn your friend Fouché that I believe my arms are long enough to make anyone who slanders my sons regret it."

As he saw Letizia out, Napoleon said, " So far as slandering your sons is concerned, I see you don't read the English papers, which speak ill not only of your dear Lucien, but of me and all the family."

" Possibly," said Letizia, " but whereas I can do nothing about the English, Citizen Fouché is another matter."

Napoleon then reproached her with caring more for Lucien than for himself, to which she truthfully answered, " My favourite child is always the one who is in trouble."

She was to prove this time and again, but she sometimes failed to see which of her children had most to bear.

Within six months of this conversation Lucien was to return from Spain with a fortune, a resident mistress, the Marquise de Santa Cruz, and every prospect of being given a crown by his brother.

ESPITE LETIZIA's objections, Louis married Joséphine's
D daughter Hortense in January, 1802. The long and
stormy marriage of these two young people, the future King
and Queen of Holland, was doomed from the start. Louis was
still in love with Hortense's cousin, Emilie, whom Napoleon
had married off to Lavalette in order to stop Louis from bringing an *émigré's* daughter into the family ; and Hortense had
accepted Louis mainly to reassure and calm Joséphine, to whom
she always showed passionate loyalty. Worst of all, Louis's
formerly charming character was beginning to be affected by
syphilis, for which there was then no certain cure. Letizia was
unaware of this, and soon after the wedding her concern was
diverted from Louis to Lucien.

While visiting a friend at Méréville, Lucien had fallen
violently in love with Alexandrine Jouberthon, a married
woman three years younger than himself. A lawyer's daughter,
she had married a rich broker, Jean-François-Hippolyte
Jouberthon, when she was nineteen, and borne him two children.
By 1801, Jouberthon's business affairs were going so badly that
he sailed for San Domingo, hoping to make a second fortune
there. He left his wife little money, and she was reputed to have
had several lovers before meeting the impetuous and impatient
Lucien, who lost no time in ridding himself of the Marquise de
Santa Cruz and installing Alexandrine in her place at his country
house at Plessis. The rest of the family was immediately informed
of this by Elisa, who, in her husband's absence on duty, had
been living at Plessis, acting as hostess for Lucien and looking
after his two little daughters. She left Plessis on Alexandrine's

arrival, but was kept informed of what went on there by her lover Fontanes, who, after visiting Lucien and his new mistress, wrote to Elisa : " A single glance enables me to see through the masks : the lady is beautiful, as coquettish as she is beautiful, and as avid as she is coquettish. Her reign may prove long and costly." As yet none of the family, not even Lucien himself, had any idea how costly Alexandrine was to prove, and only Letizia felt forebodings. She knew Napoleon had great ambitions for Lucien, whom he considered the cleverest of his brothers.

Napoleon's own position had never been more brilliant. By signing the Treaty of Amiens with England, he had given France peace for the first time in ten years and his popularity was at its peak.

English tourists flocking to France after the peace treaty found pictures of Napoleon everywhere. Tons of earthenware, porcelain, terra-cotta, plaster, ivory, bronze and marble were turned into figurines, busts and statues of the nation's hero. Medallions provided portable iconographies of Bonaparte the Conqueror and Peacemaker. That August, Napoleon was elected Consul for life by plebiscite.

Stendhal summed up what he had accomplished to date : " The dictator's first measures were great, wise and salutary. Everyone recognised the necessity for a strong government, and we had a strong government. Everyone was crying out against the corruption and lack of equity of recent governments, and the First Consul stopped thievery and gave justice the backing of force. Everyone deplored the existence of parties that divided and weakened France, and Napoleon put men of talent at the head of affairs, regardless of party. Everyone feared reaction, and Napoleon checked it with an iron hand . . . Persecution had rekindled the last sparks of Catholicism, and Napoleon protected the Church and restored the priests to their altars . . . He abolished the law of hostages, closed the list of *émigrés* and, by a judicious mixture of mildness and severity, pacified western France. The entire country longed for peace, and Napoleon offered his enemies peace. After this offer was disdainfully refused by England and Austria, he conquered the latter in the admirable campaign of Marengo, then showed reckless generosity to the conquered. . . . Abandoned by its allies, the English Cabinet was at last forced to make peace and recognise the Republic."

One of Napoleon's most popular moves this year was sending an expedition to recover the island of San Domingo (now Haiti), which France had acquired in 1697 and lost during the Revolution, when the negroes, led by Toussaint l'Ouverture, won their independence. San Domingo had prospered as a French possession and Joséphine had repeatedly deplored its loss to Napoleon. Not only soldiers but civilian speculators competed to take part in the expedition. Napoleon needed an impeccably honest commander-in-chief, so he chose his brother-in-law Leclerc. Pauline was at first appalled by the idea of leaving her gay life in Paris for "snakes and savages," but Leclerc did not want to leave her and their baby son Dermide behind, and as both Letizia and Napoleon were firm about a wife's place being with her husband, the resilient creature soon cheered herself with thoughts of striped muslin dresses and creole turbans.

At first all went well. Leclerc landed 20,000 men, conquered the island in forty days and established peaceful conditions. Then an epidemic of yellow fever broke out, killing 37,250 people. In September all the frightened negroes who had joined the French Army deserted, leaving Leclerc with only 2,000 men against 10,000. Pauline showed immense courage, saying gaily that Bonaparte's sister couldn't be afraid, and she refused to leave her husband when he wanted to send her to safety. But it was he who caught the fever and died. A week after his death his twenty-two-year-old widow sailed for France. Of the many men Pauline loved, only her first husband inspired in her a little fear as well as love. Her grief was violent and genuine, and, in accordance with an old Corsican tradition, she cut off her beautiful hair and put it in the coffin, which she took back to France. By a gloomy coincidence, Pauline's first love,

Fréron, who had become prefect of southern San Domingo, also died of yellow fever at this time.

Too ill to attend her husband's funeral, she went to stay with Joseph, now living in the Faubourg Saint-Honoré. Here the family gathered round her, offering every inducement to turn her thoughts away from mourning. Letizia watched her unhappily. She knew enough about Pauline's temperament to realise that unless a second husband was soon found, she would undoubtedly commit one folly after another. But Pauline's were not the most formidable problems confronting Letizia.

Lucien had recently come back from the country to Paris and installed Alexandrine, now pregnant, in a house in what is now the Place du Palais-Bourbon. It was connected with his own house in the Rue Saint-Dominique by an underground passage. Alexandrine gave birth to a son in May, and the next day she and Lucien were secretly married by the priest who baptised the child. Two days later the King of Etruria died and Napoleon, who wanted to make an ally of Etruria in order to control Tuscany and the port of Leghorn, suggested that Lucien should marry the widowed Queen. She was preposterously ugly, but Napoleon had every reason to suppose Lucien would overlook her appearance and welcome a throne. To his surprise Lucien refused, but in a manner that suggested he might change his mind. Napoleon knew of Alexandrine's existence but did not suppose her more important to Lucien than the Marquise de Santa Cruz had been. Shortly afterwards Napoleon appointed Lucien to delimit the senatorships in France's newly annexed territories. Ostensibly delighted, Lucien left for the Rhine with a large suite, including art experts to help him buy Flemish pictures. On his return Napoleon offered him the post of Treasurer to the Senate, and Joseph that of Chancellor. Both refused, saying they did not want to " compromise their rights to the Consular succession." It did not occur to them that rights were not involved, only favours.

Meanwhile a second husband had been found for Pauline, a Roman prince, Camillo Borghese. At twenty-eight the Prince

Borghese was an attractive young man with regular features, large brilliant dark eyes, and immense territorial possessions. Although he wrote his own language incorrectly and spoke bad French, he was enthusiastically in favour of " new ideas." In the summer of 1798 he had thrown his coat of arms into the Roman bonfire where the *Livre d'Or* (the book of the nobility), the cardinals' hats and the record of the Holy See's procedures were already blazing in honour of a brave new world. Then he had danced round the bonfire with the young Prince of Santa Croce. Thanks to his combination of rank and riches, all this was dismissed by the authorities as a boyish escapade. By the time Pauline met the prince her experiences in San Domingo seemed to her to have taken place in another life and she was once more eager for love and gaiety. She accepted the ardent young man, his title and his family jewels, all with equally ingenuous delight, and in August, 1808, Paris newspapers carried reports of the forthcoming marriage. Letizia was relieved that Pauline was to have a husband and pleased that she herself would have an Italian son-in-law.

Since this marriage pleased the Bonapartes, the Borgheses and the Pope, all should have gone smoothly. Yet it did not. Pauline and her prince had either forgotten or never noticed that Napoleon had recently revived the *ancien régime* law imposing one year and six weeks' mourning for a husband. So, legally, Pauline could not remarry until December. Always indulgent with Pauline, Napoleon said she might waive six weeks, but insisted she wait until November. At this point Letizia intervened and encouraged Pauline to marry at the end of the summer. The marriage took place secretly at Mortefontaine in August. The reason for such precipitation was rumoured to be " the ardour of the Italian temperament and the frailty of widows," and it seems likely that, in uncharacteristically urging Pauline to disobey her brother, Letizia was choosing the lesser of two prospective scandals.

Napoleon was so vexed that he did not attend the official wedding in November, and it was unfortunately at this point that he heard of Lucien's secret marriage. This outraged him, since, to his mind, the absence of any convincing evidence of Jouberthon's death, and the illegitimacy of Lucien's son, made this marriage both a *mésalliance* and an immovable obstacle to Lucien's political advancement. In his Memoirs, which show that he had a gift for fiction, Lucien writes : " By her entire approbation and her particular esteem for her daughter-in-law, whom I presented to her, our mother, the true head of the family, gave the lie to those of her children who displayed contrary sentiments." He adds that although Letizia was distressed by Napoleon's opposition to this marriage, she had to some extent anticipated it. She advised him to be calm and show no rancour. " With moderation," she told Lucien, " the Consul's brotherly feelings will return, and his sense of justice, for situated as you are in relation to each other, he knows that he has no right to ask you to marry to suit him, any more than he married to suit you—or me. There is nothing to be said against your wife from the point of view of birth, education or conduct." All of which sounds more like Lucien than like his mother, who is unlikely to have considered bigamy a bagatelle. But she certainly tried to defend Lucien. Napoleon refused to be mollified, so in February 1805, Lucien left for Italy " with hatred in his heart." Thus began the active phase of the almost lifelong quarrel between Napoleon and Lucien which was to cause their mother mortification and misery.

ACCORDING TO BARON LARREY, Letizia now opposed Napoleon, not only in the domestic matter of Lucien's second marriage but in the far graver one of the Duc d'Enghien, whose judicial murder did Napoleon's reputation incalculable harm.

Several conspiracies against Napoleon had previously been defeated, when, on the breakdown of the Peace of Amiens, the English asked all the French *émigrés* whom they were subsidising to assemble at the Rhine preparatory to invading France. Among those who responded was the Duc d'Enghien, grandson of the Prince de Condé and last of his line. Three years younger than Napoleon, the Duc d'Enghien had served in Condé's army until it was disbanded in 1801, when he settled in Ettenheim, near the French frontier, in order to be with his beloved mistress, Princess Charlotte de Rohan-Rochefort. Talleyrand, who played the part of Grey Eminence in this drama and believed, as he later told the Czar, that " treachery is a question of dates," informed Napoleon that the duke was preparing to invade France. After a meeting of the three Consuls, Fouché, Talleyrand and the judge, Régnier, three hundred French dragoons were sent to kidnap the Duc d'Enghien and take him to Strasbourg.

There the duke composed a *Profession of Faith* intended for Napoleon, in which he wrote : " A military career being the only one in which I can henceforth, after all my family's misfortunes, maintain the honour of my name, I give my sacred word of honour that I have never had any aim other than to serve the first power to go to war, and that if any country other than England had been the first to fight, no matter against whom, I should have asked with the same urgency for an honourable military position in its army. I wish to send this declaration of faith with my papers, in order to prevent there being any doubt as to the object of my wishes, my actions, my correspondence : all of which, ever since the peace, have aimed at obtaining my return to a military career."

Napoleon's own intense feeling for the Army might have made him respond to this letter. (Years later, in exile, he told an English officer : " I love a good soldier who has undergone the baptism of fire, of no matter what nationality.") Thanks to Talleyrand, however, he did not receive it until too late. When the Duc d'Enghien was told he was to be transferred to Paris, he expressed satisfaction and said, " A quarter of an hour's conversation with the First Consul will settle everything." He reached the fortress of Vincennes on the outskirts of Paris on March 20th, and was interrogated by a Council of War in the presence of the Prefect of Police. He displayed the courage that was as much a part of him as his coat of arms, and admitted he had fought against France and would do so again if the opportunity presented itself. He was immediately condemned to death and shot in the early hours of the morning. When Alexander of Russia subsequently raised objections, Talleyrand pointed out that France had not asked Russia why no one had been punished for the murder of the late Czar Paul.

Baron Larrey says that Letizia went in tears to Napoleon and begged him to spare the Duc d'Enghien, saying, " You will be the first to fall into the abyss you are digging to-day beneath your family's feet." The *Revue Historique* for May and June, 1879, also states that Letizia was instrumental in carrying out the duke's last request—that his favourite dog and various personal possessions be sent to the woman he loved. Both actions accord with Letizia's character, yet must be apocryphal, unless Fesch, by this time a cardinal and Napoleon's ambassador to the Papal

States, made a most improbable mistake in writing to Napoleon that Letizia had arrived in Rome on *March* 31*st* (only eleven days after the duke's execution) " *after having travelled for eighteen days,*" which was the normal duration of such a journey at that time. Nor is either incident mentioned in the copious Memoirs of Hortense and the Duchesse d'Abrantès, both of whom were at Malmaison at the time. Joséphine did intercede on the Duc d'Enghien's behalf, but Napoleon was determined to " support the revolution " against the forces of reaction represented by the *émigré* army.

It has been alleged that Letizia joined Lucien in Rome only to emphasise her displeasure with Napoleon. But here again the evidence is conflicting. In his Memoirs, Lucien paints a dramatic picture of his departure from Paris, describing how he and Alexandrine threw themselves at Letizia's feet when she cried, " *Au revoir, au revoir, à bientôt à Rome ! * " This, he says, took place on the eve of Easter, 1804 : but on the eve of Easter Letizia was already in Rome, as is proved by the recorded fact that the Pope offered her a special tribunal in St. Peter's for the Easter High Mass. In addition, a letter written by Letizia to a French official in Rome the previous January shows that her stay there was planned long ahead. In this letter she had written : " It is decided that in the spring I shall pay a visit to Italy, where I hope to recover my health and spend several agreeable months, thanks to the beautiful climate and the presence there of a brother and a daughter whom I love." No mention of Lucien—and indeed, he was not in Rome when she arrived there.

Before she left Paris, Letizia persuaded Napoleon to write to the Pope on his brother's behalf, asking him to receive Lucien kindly during the stay he intended making in Rome " in order to study antiques and history." These studies were not merely pretexts. Lucien was in many respects the most artistic of the family and cared passionately for archæology. Far from wishing to interfere with his mother's visit to Italy, Napoleon made her a present of the sumptuous carriage in which she set out accompanied by her friend Madame Etienne Clary (Julie's sister-in-law), by Madame Andelard, a canoness who acted as lady-in-waiting, by her lawyer and man of business, her doctor, a maid, and by Saveria, the faithful Corsican servant who had helped her raise her children.

The journey to Italy was a strenuous one. Writing ten years later, Samuel Rogers, an English banker, writer and poet, said : " The French inn is little improved. In France there are still two classes of society. The first travel from château to château. The last shift as they can. There is still wanting a middle class to command into an inn the comforts and elegancies of life." Letizia travelled under the name of Madame Roccoboni, and although her incognito was respected during the first stages of her journey, there were great festivities at Turin, the handsome, arcaded city where the Holy Shroud is kept. One newspaper announced grandiloquently : " We have formed conjectures that we may not divulge as to the name and family of this lady." In Bologna, birth-place of the great Bibbiena theatre family, the artillery fired a salute in her honour and a Polish cavalry escort was provided—a style of welcome entirely appropriate to this dramatic city of shadowy colonnades, leaning towers and medieval palaces in which the past still seems hermetically sealed.

When she reached the Papal States, Letizia found all the red carpets laid down. At Loreto (the place to which angels transported the Holy House from Nazareth in the thirteenth century), the Papal palace was put at her disposal. Regally escorted all the way to Rome, she went to the Corsini Palace, at that time rented by the French Government. The first important palace built outside the Septimian Gate during the Renaissance, this possessed a stately garden, containing a huge magnolia tree and an army of pines, and was haunted by memories of Catherine Sforza, whom Cæsar Borgia had brought there as a prisoner in golden chains.

The Cardinal Secretary of State immediately called to pay

Letizia his respects, and within twenty-four hours every member of the Sacred College had done the same. Letizia accepted this initial homage with disconcerting equanimity, and since she believed that an honour paid to her was an honour paid to Napoleon, subsequently showed herself quite as strict on points of etiquette as any member of the Sacred College. Fesch wrote to Napoleon :

Your mother arrived in Rome the 10th Germinal (March 31st), Holy Saturday, after travelling for eighteen days without stopping at Lyons or Milan. She was received in the Papal States with the greatest distinction. At Loreto she stayed in the Papal palace.

On her arrival in Rome, His Holiness ordered a tribune to be erected for her in St. Peter's, similar to those of the Queen of Sardinia and the Princess of Meckleburg, so that she might attend Easter Mass ; but as this tribune had to be placed behind those of the above persons, who have been in possession of theirs for a year, she thought it her duty to refuse the proposed honour on the grounds of fatigue.

Yesterday I presented her to the Pope at the Quirinal, accompanied by her daughter [Pauline] and Madame Clary, in full gala dress, and with the greatest ceremony. The Swiss Guards accompanied her to the first ante-room, where she was received by Messeigneurs the gentlemen-in-waiting, and the guard of nobles presented arms. The Pope spoke to her of his attachment to you, and his prayers for your well-being ; he told her he would be enchanted to see her often, and that she must remain in his states as long as she pleased. She took her leave after a long interview.

The Roman nobility call on her without waiting for *ricevimento* days. The Dean of the Sacred College invited all the cardinals to pay her their respects within twenty-four hours. All, even the Neapolitans, hastened to offer her this mark of deference usually reserved for sovereigns.

She bore herself with great dignity throughout these ceremonies, and I believe Rome is really the place that suits her
best. She will be very comfortable here, and I shall do all
I can to make her happy . . .

This Fesch did, helped by Pauline, now one of the most
fashionable Roman princesses. Soon after her arrival, Letizia
moved from the Palazzo Corsini to the Palazzo Nunez (to-day
the Palazzo Torlonia) in the Via Bocca di Leone, a minute's
walk from the Piazza di Spagna. This palace had been bought
by the still-absent Lucien, who, with typical extravagance,
installed a swimming-pool, or a *naumachia* as he preferred to call
it, and a stage for amateur theatricals. (Letizia shared her children's enthusiasm for the theatre. She often invited the great
actor Talma, who was a close friend of Napoleon's, to her house,
and Mademoiselle George, the youthful " Venus of Paris "
who was later Napoleon's mistress, used to recite Corneille in
Letizia's salon and was once given by her an immense stuffed
bird of paradise to be used as a head-dress.) Among the plays
Lucien and his controversial second wife performed here was
Voltaire's *Zaïre*. Lucien created a particularly personal impression as Orosmane, in which role he seemed to be defending
his wife against his brother.

> *Pour Zaïre, crois-moi sans que ton cœur s'offense*
> *Elle n'est pas d'un prix qui soit en ta puissance,*
> *Tes chevaliers frrnçais et tous leurs souverains*
> *S'uniraient vainement pour l'ôter de mes mains.*

When Lucien arrived in Rome, Letizia joined Fesch in the
Palazzo Falconieri, a superb palace, modernised by Borromini, in
the centre of Renaissance Rome. The powerful beauty of Rome,
so in harmony with Letizia's temperament, did not take her mind
off her irremediably amorous children. Her own married life
had been so happy, so fruitful, and so in accordance with
Corsican traditions, that she had to learn to understand her
children's behaviour as one learns a foreign language. This was
not easy for her. Born steadfast and consistent, she had never

heard of the noxious effect of repressions and thought it natural to repress what was not seemly.

The latest matrimonial trouble in the family involved twenty-year-old Jérôme, the youngest and handsomest of her sons. His frivolity had earned him the nickname of Fifi and he was then a naval officer, as happy-go-lucky as he was brave. A few months earlier his ship had anchored off Martinique, the captain had fallen ill, and Jérôme had been given command with the provisional rank of lieutenant. After a practice cruise among the Windward Isles and a visit to Martinique, where he was extravagantly fêted at Joséphine's old home, Jérôme should have returned to France. But as English ships were just then on the lookout for him, he decided to go to North America and to sail from there on a neutral vessel. All the Bonapartes were great travellers, animated by the same instinct that made Mr. Micawber say, " It would be rash not to go on and see the cathedral." While in America, where he spent far more than the generous allowance Napoleon had given him over and above his pay, Jérôme fell in love with an American girl, Elizabeth Patterson, the belle of Baltimore and daughter of William Patterson, president of the city's largest bank.

Full of energy in matters of the heart, Jérôme disregarded the fact that he was under age and so could not marry legally without his mother's consent. He proposed to Miss Patterson through the Spanish Ambassador and was accepted with enthusiasm, to the consternation of the French chargé d'affaires in Washington. This official had no instructions as to how to treat Napoleon's youngest brother—not surprisingly, since Napoleon's youngest brother was supposed to be on the high seas at the time. When the harassed official pointed out that any marriage contracted in these circumstances would be null and void, Jérôme cheerfully told him to mind his own business. Then he said that after all, on thinking it over, he had changed his mind and would not marry just now. The chargé d'affaires's relief was so excessive that he lent Jérôme all the money that improvident young man wanted, thus enabling him to marry Elizabeth

Patterson within a month. The news reached Paris via the English Press.

When Letizia heard of this she was in no mood to sympathise with an irresponsible scapegrace. Public events were filling her with alarm. For although the Duc d'Enghien's execution had horrified many people in France as well as abroad, it had also provoked a widespread desire that Napoleon's position be strengthened. He had already been elected Consul for life two years earlier, and when a member of the Tribunate suggested that he become Emperor the proposition was received enthusiastically. In consequence Letizia was beginning to think that he had been right to tell Lucien that theirs was now " a political family " and individual members must trim their personal wishes accordingly. She understood, too, his desire to establish a " family of kings " and thus federalise Europe. But she was not happy about this new development. After the Senate had voted a constitution of which the first article proclaimed " The government of the Republic is entrusted to an Emperor who takes the title of Emperor of the French," she was attacked by forebodings that made Lucien write from Italy to Joseph :

Our mother is preoccupied by all the changes under way. She believes the First Consul is wrong to want to assume the crown of Louis XVI. She has bad dreams which she confides only to me. She fears lest fanatical republicans assassinate the Emperor. She thinks the republic has more partisans than Napoleon realises.

Letizia had every reason to dread seeing her children caught between the hinges of history. At fifty-three, she could remember both the mountain battlefields where the Corsicans had defied the France of Louis XV, and the glittering Versailles of Louis XVI and a girlish Marie-Antoinette, who bore no resemblance to the haggard, white-haired old woman of thirty-seven immortalised by David on her way to the guillotine. She could remember the stifling atmosphere of civil strife, the hunted sensations of the refugee, the echoes of anonymous denunciations and the sight of severed heads swaying through the air on pikes. She had seen her son take hold of history and bring victory out of disaster, order out of chaos ; she had heard him cheered as a soldier and hailed as a legislator—and she had sat helpless in a box at a theatre while on the stage a stranger announced that this same son had just narrowly escaped assassination. She had plenty of material for bad dreams, and for the fears she succinctly expressed in the words " *Pourvu que ça dure.*"

DURING LETIZIA's second visit to Italy, Lucien took her to see the villa he had bought at Frascati, a fashionable Roman summer resort in the Alban hills where there were several magnificent villas, including that of Pauline's brother-in-law Prince Aldobrandini. Although Frascati is only thirteen miles from Rome, the trip there was a strenuous one. Even half a century later, Alfred de Musset's younger brother Paul could write : " Excursions to Frascati, Albano, Tivoli are veritable journeys, requiring an entire day each. One reaches these green hills only after traversing the desert that for a space of fifteen *milles* contains neither tree nor blade of grass. Scattered about lie the remains of ruined edifices, aqueducts, tombs, and fragments of walls. At sunset our friend Seigneur Tito stopped the carriage and took us through the ravines to a little valley full of young trees. In this oasis we found a grotto containing a layer of fresh earth. Three green oaks grew from the roof of the grotto their leaves outlined against a sky of purest blue. A buffalo was drinking at a fountain. At the sound of our footsteps it turned its head, gave us a sullen look, then continued drinking."

The lower slopes of the hill on which Frascati stands were silver-grey with olive trees, and above these came the dark greens of oaks, pines, cypresses and ilex. On buying the Villa Ruffinella, Lucien had decided to transform the hillside behind it into a kind of Mount Parnassus, with fountains and grottoes populated by statues. According to Diego Angeli's *I Bonaparti a Roma*, this led to " a number of those little quarrels so common between poets and archæologists in every country and especially in Italy." Lucien had to content himself with putting the waste land under cultivation and planting an avenue of myrtles, where he placed the statues he had ordered from Carrara. Once again Letizia listened to lengthy explanations of building projects, such as her husband had enjoyed in the days when he was planning his banqueting gallery. Lucien evidently employed his talents well, since the Pope was so impressed by his agricultural and artistic improvements that he arranged for him to receive his statues free of the usual customs' duties.

In July Letizia accompanied Pauline to take the waters at Bagni di Lucca, a moth-coloured village on the banks of the green River Lima, where Shelley was soon to enjoy sailing paper boats, where Elizabeth and Robert Browning would later spend happy summers with their American friends, the William Wetmore Storys, and where Ouida, the flamboyant Victorian novelist supposed by some people to have Bonaparte blood, was to be buried. The news that Napoleon was definitely to become Emperor had so disturbed Letizia that, while she was at Bagni di Lucca, Fesch wrote to Napoleon without consulting her :

Your mother has gone to take the waters at Lucca. But there are moral rather than physical reasons for her ill-health. I noticed she felt worse every time a courier arrived without a letter for her. She was very much humiliated to learn of the creation of the Empire only through the newspapers, and she has been most distressed not to have received any special message from you for the past three months. She begins to imagine that Your Imperial Majesty prefers any member of the family to her . . . I have done all I can for her . . . but my efforts have been frustrated by the illness of Madame Clary, who always has such a good effect on her . . . She does not know how to reply when some people call her " Majesty," others " Empress Mother," or " Imperial Highness." She would like to know exactly what has been decided. She does not want to return to Rome, and hopes that Your Imperial Majesty will call her to Paris before the end of August, when she plans to leave Lucca.

Public concerns were now banished from Letizia's mind by domestic grief. That summer Pauline's only child, six-year-old Dermide, was seized by a fever followed by violent convulsions, and died within forty-eight hours. Pauline's sorrow left Letizia no time to attend to her own. Soon after the little boy's death came that of Madame Clary. This struck Letizia all the more cruelly because she loved few people outside her family circle. With the death of this dear friend she had passed the frontier beyond which the heart is constantly threatened by time and death, irrevocably on the losing side. Because Letizia controlled her emotions ruthlessly, it seldom occurred to anyone, even her excitable children, that she might be inwardly distraught. Her respect for other people was equalled by the self-respect from which it sprang, and though her emotions gained richness from the restraint she imposed upon them, they often made her suffer. Thanks to the position Napoleon had achieved for his family, she already qualified in the public mind as more—or less—than a human being : an illustrious mother, an inspiringly noble figurehead. Were she alive to-day, she would be interviewed on television as a gold-star mother or offered up as a tranquillising example of a " most unforgettable character," and people would forget now as they did then that behind the slogans was a vulnerable human being.

Still troubled by the quarrel between Napoleon and Lucien, she did not go straight to Paris but stopped in Milan to visit Lucien, hoping against hope to find a letter there from Napoleon expressing the wish for a reconciliation with his brother. The only result was that she did not reach Paris until seventeen days after Napoleon had been crowned Emperor in Notre-Dame. This did not prevent David, who was familiar with her appearance, from including her in the official coronation picture, now at Versailles, from which she still gazes with youthful, passionate eyes, her slender, slightly disdainful elegance in striking contradiction to the rumour that she was a " simple peasant."

With the family in Paris Letizia found Napoleon's wet-nurse, Camilla Illari, whom he had invited to the Tuileries. After

sailing from Corsica in August, Camilla had got into difficulties at Avignon through her lack of French. The parish
priest wrote to the Minister of Public Worship who wrote to
Napoleon, who immediately gave orders that she was to be
given every assistance. She reached Paris in time to attend her
favourite child's coronation, and no one in Notre-Dame understood better than his old nurse Napoleon's whispered aside to
Joseph, " If only our father could see us now." Napoleon
arranged for Camilla to be privately received by the Pope, and
sent her home in a daze, laden with gifts including diamonds
from Joséphine. It was far easier for Camilla Illari, the loving
peasant nurse, to adjust herself to Napoleon's overpowering new
position than it was for those who rose with him. People born
royal adapt themselves to new honours as instinctively as strong
swimmers to the sea, but the Bonapartes had no inherited pattern
of royal behaviour to depend upon, only the genius of one member of their large and assertive family. The difficulties that
resulted from Napoleon's brothers and sisters jostling for rank—
behaving, as he said sardonically, as if he had deprived them of
" their rightful heritage from their father the Emperor "—
made Letizia's role of peacemaker an increasingly exacting one,
and she faced court life and her new responsibilities with a
heavy heart.

LETIZIA NOW HAD HER own house in Paris, the Hôtel de Brienne, in the Rue Saint-Dominique, which she had bought from Lucien for 600,000 francs. She was to be the last private owner of this supremely elegant eighteenth-century *hôtel particulier*, with its pigeon-grey colouring so typical of Paris. After Waterloo she sold it to the French Government and it became, and still is, the War Office. To-day a few rooms retain vestiges of their original decorations—a blue *salon* on the ground floor with charming sculptures of children above the door, a red drawing-room with arabesques painted in yellow and sepia, highlighted with gold, and Letizia's Empire boudoir with gilt bas-reliefs on a yellow background. She arranged to be warned by a bell whenever Napoleon's carriage drove up to her house, in order that she might immediately dismiss whoever was with her and thus have her son to herself.

Napoleon gave his mother the title of *Son Altesse Impériale, Madame la Mère de l'Empereur*, and from then on she was known to the public as " Madame Mère." He also appointed her Protectress of the Hospital Sisters and of the Sisters of Charity throughout the Empire, a position particularly congenial to her since it was natural to her to manifest faith through works. With these titles went an allowance of a million francs a year for the upkeep of the household Napoleon established for her. His choice of personnel showed his determination to combine the best of both old and new régimes. Letizia's *dame d'honneur* was the Vicomtesse de Fontanges, a relative of Joséphine's, whose husband had been in command of San Domingo at the time of the Revolution. Among her other ladies-in-waiting were two of Napoleon's marshals' wives, Madame Davout, Madame Soult and Madame Junot (the former Laure Permon and future Duchesse d'Abrantès). The post of chamberlain was given, at his own request, to the Duc de Cossé-Brissac, who had rallied to the new régime at the beginning of the Consulate. Her master of horse was Colonel Detres, a heroic figure who had been left for dead on the battlefield after receiving nineteen sabre cuts and two bullet wounds. Her equerry was General Marc-Antoine de la Bonninière de Beaumont, formerly one of Louis XVI's pages, now a cavalry inspector and married to Marshal Davout's sister. Monseigneur de Canoviry, Bishop of Verceil, was Letizia's chaplain. The household also included an intendant, a lawyer, a reader, chaplains, doctors and secretaries. (The post of reader to Letizia was no sinecure. They all testified that she kept them hard at work, including Madame de Chantereine, who had been in prison with Louis XVI's daughter, Madame Royale.)

Napoleon provided his mother with a coat of arms (a golden eagle trampling a golden thunderbolt against a blue background, the thunderbolt bearing a silver escutcheon), and with a crown set with precious stones, surmounted by eight pearls and closed by eight semicircles supporting an orb and cross. On official occasions her cloak was similar to Joséphine's in ornamentation, and her livery to that of Napoleon. It has been suggested that grandeur was distasteful to her, but this does not accord with her admonition to the child Napoleone: "Remember that it is better to go hungry than to forgo making a fine appearance." Always able to adapt herself to new circumstances, she was certainly equal to these. In *Un Début dans la Vie*, Balzac wrote of a character named Oscar Husson, the son of one of Letizia's attendants: " It may perhaps be pertinent to mention the reason for Oscar's absurd pride, and observe that he was born in the house of Madame, the Emperor's mother. Throughout his early childhood he was dazzled by the imperial splendour, and his pliant imagination was marked for ever by the stunning pictures of that time of golden festivities."

Golden festivities were robbed of their lustre for Letizia by the continuation of the quarrel between Napoleon and Lucien. She fully understood Napoleon's point of view now and in April she wrote to Lucien :

You have been told of the success of your letter to the Emperor. On the eve of his departure [Napoleon was on his way to Milan to be crowned King of Italy], we talked of you, and I was extremely glad of the good will he displayed towards you. The hope of an early reconciliation between you children comforts my soul. You know I shall have no peace until I have brought that about, but I cannot do so without your help. You have always given me proofs of deference. Now is the time to give me the greatest proof of all. As your mother, I implore you to do this. It is not enough to have put matters in motion, a conclusion must be reached. Take advantage of this favourable moment. Do not miss this excellent opportunity to be reconciled with your brother, and to make yourself, your family and me, happy. If you miss this chance, I have every reason to fear you may never be offered another, and that I shall have to drag out my days in sadness. But I assure myself that this will not be the case and, in the consoling hope of soon hearing that you have embraced the Emperor, I embrace you and your family with all my heart.

A significant point in this letter eludes translation. Letizia addresses Lucien with the intimate " thou " except in one sentence : " I cannot do so without your help," where she uses the second person plural, implying that the co-operation of Lucien's wife was essential. In the early stages of the quarrel Letizia had been moved by Lucien's love for Alexandrine, but even more by his love for the son on whose account he had married her. So now, consistently, she urged him to reflect that Napoleon was ready to adopt Lucien's children and give them royal status if only Lucien would free himself of Alexandrine as a wife (though not necessarily as a mistress, which was what Napoleon in any case considered her), and thus make it possible for him to be given a throne and exercise his undoubted gifts for public life.

That Letizia was not shocked by the worldliness of this proposition indicates that she was a more sophisticated character than is usually suggested, as well as congenitally incapable of imagining parents refusing to sacrifice themselves for their children. The idea of the world well lost for love seemed a pusillanimous one to her resolute nature. Lucien, on the other hand, was a born lover and a tenacious one. Not even Letizia, with whom his relations were far closer domestically than hers with Napoleon, could alter his determination to get his own way.

To Letizia's relief, Jérôme proved more pliant. He and Elizabeth Patterson reached Lisbon from America this same month. Instead of a fatted calf, the prodigal son found port authorities who refused to allow his wife to land. Jérôme sent her on by sea to Amsterdam, while he hurried to Italy to meet Napoleon. He was genuinely in love with his foreign bride, but, since he was as lightminded as he was ardent, all that had happened to him in the remote new world beyond the Atlantic began to seem scarcely real once he found himself back in Napoleon's orbit. Unlike his three elder brothers, Jérôme could hardly remember a time when Napoleon had not been a powerful, glamorous father-figure. He put up no resistance now, to the disgust of Elizabeth Patterson, an ambitious girl who had longed for Europe. She later wrote, " I hated and loathed residence in Baltimore so much that when I thought I was to spend my life there I tried to screw up courage to the point of committing suicide "; and when Jérôme asked her later why she had refused 200,000 francs a year from him and accepted 60,000 from Napoleon she said, " I prefer to be sheltered under the wing of an eagle to being suspended by the quill of a goose."

Letizia wrote to Louis : " I hasten to tell you the reassuring news just received from the Emperor. Jérôme has reached Italy and declared that he is entirely disposed to do as the

Emperor wishes. The Emperor received him like a brother, and has given him back his friendship. He tells me of his satisfaction and happiness. You know mine cannot be complete until I hear that Lucien has been restored to favour, then you will all be the objects of my satisfaction, as you are of my love."

BEFORE NAPOLEON WENT to Italy he suggested that Letizia should stay at the Grand Trianon at Versailles in order to be with Pauline, who was then visiting at the Petit Trianon. Built in 1687 to provide Louis XIV with a retreat from the formality of life in the main palace, the Grand Trianon has two wings joined by a peristyle of green-and-pink marble and a façade of rose-and-white marble. At the beginning of the twentieth century the Grand Trianon inspired Proust's friend, the Marquis de Castellane, to build a pink palace in the Avenue Malakoff. It did not, however, inspire Letizia, who is said to have complained that the rooms were too small and the ceilings too low. Probably the associations of the place were what caused her to dislike it. Although the Trianon's original furniture and objects of art had been auctioned eleven years before and were now replaced by Empire furniture a swarm with Imperial bees, sphinx and eagles, the place still evoked Louis XVI and Marie-Antoinette and their pathetic cry on their accession : "We are too young to reign!" Even the Bourbons, when they returned to France, tried at first to avoid Versailles.

Napoleon did not intend the Grand Trianon as a permanent country residence for his mother. Three months later he wrote to her from Italy that he had bought her the seventeenth-century castle of Pont, on the banks of the Seine, south-east of Paris, and was also giving her 60,000 francs towards furniture. (To this sum he later added 100,000 francs and thirteen pieces of Gobelin tapestry.) She immediately answered :

My extreme weakness, after quite a serious illness, does not permit me to write to Your Majesty myself, as I would have wished, but I do not want to delay in thanking you for this acquisition made on my behalf. I am employing my secretary to tell Your Majesty that I accept this gift, and am particularly grateful for the obliging way in which it is made. This proof of your affection touches me infinitely, for you know that your heart is my most precious domain. On receiving your letter, I sent off my Intendant, and am waiting for his report before making my plans. I shall certainly inhabit this property if possible.

Only the thought of your return will keep me in Paris.

I hope the sum destined for repairs and furnishing will prove sufficient. Everything will be done in accordance with Your Majesty's tastes. I shall, besides, give account of every detail.

Do not be uneasy about my health. My symptoms were alarming at first, but, thanks to Corvisart and my other doctors, soon checked. Exercise and country air will do the rest. I was not able to go to Trianon, the furnishing not being completed.

I need not repeat, Sire, my assurances of an affection that began with Your Majesty's existence and will end only with mine.

Letizia reached Pont on August 25th, 1805, and was received with pomp and ceremony. The inhabitants lined the route, shouting " *Vive l'Empereur !* " and " *Vive Madame !* " and the Prefect of Aube reported : " Her Imperial Highness, Madame, reached her castle at Pont on Sunday at five o'clock in the evening. Compliments were addressed to her by the inhabitants of Nogent. A mounted guard of honour escorted her as far as the limits of the Commune of Pont, where another mounted guard received her. General rejoicing was manifested by illuminations, dancing and fireworks. Yesterday Madame received the local authorities."

Having performed her official duties, Letizia settled into a quiet life that was the despair of her livelier ladies-in-waiting. Her half-brother, Cardinal Fesch, and several other ecclesiastics joined her, and she divided her time between religious observances, walks, needlework, reading and reversi, a card game of Spanish origin to which she was particularly addicted. It was played by four people with a pack of cards from which the tens had been subtracted, and the victor was whoever scored the fewest points. Lucien says in his Memoirs : " Reversi was a family taste that we must have inherited from our mother, who preferred it to any other game and played it to perfection, calculating and knowing the possibilities of all the cards. I remember that our famous Pascal Paoli, who loved the game and played it as well as our mother, often lost to her, and used to console himself for these defeats by saying, ' Signora Letizia has this game in her blood.' "

Daily life at Pont was not exacting. People were free to get up when they chose. Lunch at eleven-thirty was followed by needlework, cards and conversation, after which people dispersed to their apartments or paid calls. After dinner there would be carriage rides along the banks of the Seine. On one occasion Fesch's friend, the Italian poet Gianni, who was so hump-backed that he could fasten his shoes without stooping, took Letizia to visit the shrine of the Paraclete in memory of Héloïse and Abèlard. Letizia's life provides many strange pictures, but none stranger than this one where the stately, still-beautiful Corsican, whose son dominated Europe, stands beside a deformed Italian poet and solemnly contemplates a shrine set up in that typically French landscape to celebrate a form of illicit love far removed from her own emotional range.

Letizia enjoyed listening to music while at the card table, preferably vocal rather than instrumental. This was also true of her servant and confidante Saveria, of whom Madame d'Abrantès writes : " She was an extraordinary woman. I shall never forget the expression of savage sensibility on her face one day at Pont. I was in an old abandoned gallery, where there was a spinet which Mademoiselle de Lannay and I used to play to pass the time. One day I was singing in a low voice, while Madame played reversi, and in this house where everything reminded me of Corsica far more than in my own home, I suddenly recalled a goatherd's song from the mountains that my mother taught me . . . I was singing it softly . . . Saveria, whose room was nearby, heard me. She came silently to me, while I was at the spinet . . . then I heard stifled sobs. It was Saveria, who had wanted to join in, but was choked by tears." Saveria's violent, inarticulate nostalgia for their island home was one of the qualities that made her almost as indispensable as Fesch to Letizia. While the younger generation ranged proudly over Europe, these three created a little Corsica in the French countryside.

When Napoleon said that he wished Letizia to see in the gift of Pont a proof of his desire to please her, he undoubtedly spoke the truth. But he also intended it to stimulate her into spending money on the outward display he considered appropriate to her position as the Emperor's mother. Considering the trouble caused him by his brothers' and sisters' extravagance, it is ironic that he never succeeded in making Letizia spend a franc more than she thought strictly necessary. Her avarice was of the type analysed by Balzac in *Béatrix* : " When avarice has an objective, it ceases to be a vice and becomes the means to a virtue. Its excessive privations become continual offerings, and it reveals at last the grandeur concealed beneath its pettiness." The grandeur in this case was the strength of Letizia's determination to provide for her improvident children and—already— thirteen grandchildren. In her own words : " We Corsicans are familiar with revolutions. All this may come to an end, and then what will happen to children whose imprudent generosity makes them give with both hands, without thought of past or future ? When that happens, I shall be there, and it is better they turn to their mother, rather than to those who may betray or abandon them." Letizia was not a fearless woman, but a woman who mastered her fears.

Justifiably alarmed by her children's capacity to spend and by the way even shrewd Fesch poured money out on his picture galleries, Letizia avoided putting all her financial eggs in one basket and invested in Corsica, Italy, Spain and even London.

She was typically secretive about this. Only by chance did the French minister at Naples discover in 1803 that she had invested 50,000 francs with a local banker who had subsequently failed. Had she told Napoleon, he would have obtained compensation for her, but she preferred to say nothing and cut her losses.

Meantime her imprudently generous children continued to rise in the world like eaglets. In 1805 Napoleon made Elisa hereditary Princess of Piombino, explaining that this state was badly governed and therefore he was entrusting it to his sister, "not from fraternal tenderness but from political prudence." His belief that Elisa would govern well proved justified. Her husband was given command of the troops assigned to protect the coast and communications between Elba and Corsica. In the months that followed, Napoleon made Joseph King of Naples, Louis King of Holland, and Jérôme (who had married Princess Catherine of Württemberg after the annulment of his American marriage) King of Westphalia. Caroline's husband, Murat, became Duke of Berg-Cleves. For the first time Letizia heard herself called by the title that was to become part of her legend : *Mater Regum*, Mother of Kings.

NELSON'S VICTORY AT Trafalgar in October, 1805, gave
England command at sea, but France remained master of
the Continent. Six weeks later, on the first anniversary of his
coronation, Napoleon won the most spectacular of his military
victories, that of Austerlitz, where the French defeated twice
their number of Austrians and Russians in a battle still studied
as a model in military schools the world over. When the thick
white fog enveloping both sides was suddenly pierced by sun-
light, the French Army gave a thunderous cheer and Napoleon
cried, " The sun of Austerlitz has risen." The column in the
Place Vendôme is made of bronze from cannon captured by the
French at this battle.

While Napoleon was away, Letizia saw so little of Joséphine
that he finally wrote to tell his mother that he wished her, when
in Paris, to attend his wife's Sunday dinners, since these were
family reunions and in his absence Joséphine became the head of
the family. But in this matter Napoleon could not control
Letizia. She was much with Fesch at this time, and he fostered
the militantly Corsican qualities that made her ever ready to
fight the world outside for the inner world of blood relatives.
It was Fesch who guided her taste and lent her pictures when she
furnished her Paris house, and who persuaded the museum of the
French School to give her Le Brun's picture of St. Charles
Borremeo, " patron of the Emperor's father," for her chapel.
Even her religion was imbued with family feeling, so it was not
likely she would accept Napoleon's childless and unfaithful wife
as the proper head of the clan.

The prestige of this clan reached its highest point after the victory of Jena, in 1806, gave Napoleon control of the Prussian monarchy, and that of Friedland, in 1807, opened up Russia to him. Two months before his thirty-eighth birthday he had become the most powerful ruler in Europe : Emperor of the French, King of Italy, Mediator of the Swiss Confederation, Protector of the Confederation of the Rhine. When he and Alexander, Czar of all the Russias, met at Tilsit, they did so as equals. This glittering encounter took place in a tent erected on a raft in the middle of the River Niemen. The two Emperors embarked simultaneously from opposite banks and embraced amid the cheers of the assembled armies. A Russian spectator of this interview, David Davidov, reported that Napoleon was " a fabulous being, the most remarkable war captain since Alexander the Great and Julius Cæsar . . . and the greatest politician, law-giver, administrator, and conqueror, who amazed the armies of all Europe."

Two weeks later France and Russia signed a treaty of alliance. The effect in Paris was dramatic. The Polish Countess Hélène Potocka wrote to her husband : " I cannot tell you how lively and animated Paris was yesterday. The Emperor is expected every minute, almost everyone has returned. Yesterday evening, July 24th, the peace was announced by torchlight. The herald-at-arms, followed by scores of torch-bearers and immense crowds, went all over Paris, which was magnificently illuminated for the occasion . . . the Place Vendôme was superb, the streets packed and the Faubourg Saint-Germain was as excited as the Palais-Royal. I drove about in an open carriage with Madame d'Hautpoul and two of the Badens. The warmth and beauty of the night had brought everyone out of doors, and the streets were so full of joyously cheering crowds that carriages could scarcely get through . . . At the Te Deum in Notre-Dame the Empress was graceful and well dressed . . . but the one I looked at most was the Emperor's mother. There she was, that happiest of women, whom no man can ever rob of the glory of having given birth to the most extraordinary man to appear in centuries. How proud she must be ! A great people prostrate before her son, the vaults echoing with acclamations, it is the most wonderful part a woman can play in this world! She is beautiful, still looks young, and no one will say of her, ' What, is that his mother ? ' " The politician and writer Comte Beugnot, who met her for the first time at this period, said that Letizia resembled Raphael's St. Anne.

Letizia was indeed a proud woman, but not, at this stage, as happy as people supposed. In the *Souvenirs* she dictated in old age she says : " Everyone called me the happiest mother in the world, whereas in fact my life was constantly full of grief and suffering. Every time a courier arrived I expected to hear the terrible news of the Emperor's death on the battlefield." She was much moved when, at one of the big military reviews held in Paris at this time, several regiments marched by with flags torn by bullets and blackened by powder and Napoleon bared his head and said, " Salute, gentlemen, it is the glory of France that is passing before you."

Throughout this period when Napoleon was altering the map of Europe, the quarrel between him and Lucien persisted, as did Letizia's desire to end it. Acutely sensitive to her emotions, Fesch had tried to help her by writing Lucien an admonitory letter, which merely drew the bitter reply : " At least have the common sense not to put me on the same plane as Jérôme, and spare me the useless shame of your cowardly advice . . . You had better hide your base sentiments under your purple, and make your way in silence along the highway of ambition."

This time Lucien had gone too far even for Letizia. She wrote to him : " I cannot refrain from telling you that you have treated him [Fesch] very badly. All he said certainly came from the desire to see you happy, and on equal terms with your brothers. He does not deserve to be treated in this way, and you should look for an opportunity to soften the distress you have caused him . . . I am destined to pass my life in sadness and desolation. However, I have done with speaking to you of this matter. In future I shall silently deplore your disgrace and my own."

All Lucien's brothers and sisters were beginning to think him unreasonable, and even his favourite Elisa wrote to him: " Proposals have been made that you would have considered acceptable a year ago . . . to-day you refuse them . . . so long as he [Napoleon] finds family support for his policies, which must be his first consideration, he will not turn to strangers. You should not try to negotiate with the master of the world on equal terms. Nature made us children of the same father, but his achievements have made us his subjects. Although sovereigns, we owe everything to him. There is a noble pride in admitting this, and it seems to me that our only glory should be in showing him that we are worthy of him and of our family . . . Mamma and all of us would be so happy to be reunited, and to make only one family politically. Dear Lucien, do this for us who love you, and for the sake of the people my brother will give you to govern and whose happiness you will ensure."

At this point the Pope's intervention strengthened Lucien's determination to resist his brother. Despite all that Napoleon's sense of political expediency had made him do for the Church, relations between him and the Pope had deteriorated. When the Pope took the unprecedented step of going to Paris to crown Napoleon, he had hoped to recover some of the papal territories in northern Italy conquered by the French. Not only was this hope frustrated, but, since Napoleon needed to safeguard the lines of communication between the Imperial territories in the north and the new Kingdom of Naples, he gradually gained control of still more papal possessions. So the Pope, who was already on friendly terms with Lucien, saw no reason not to stand godfather to his newly-born daughter, thus tacitly approving of Lucien's second marriage.

Obstinately refusing to admit defeat, Letizia persuaded Lucien to take advantage of Napoleon's visit to Italy to meet him there in December, 1802. Joseph, also in Italy, showed tact and energy in attempting to induce a conciliatory attitude in both his brothers. Napoleon and Lucien finally met in many-coloured Mantua, the city where Titans assault Olympus on the walls of the Palazzo del Te. There is a Shakespearean quality about this encounter between the spectacular Emperor whose " reared arm crested the world," and his younger brother who had renounced crowns and coronets for love. Unfortunately Lucien wanted to have it both ways. Reports of the meeting, including those of the protagonists, vary widely. In his Memoirs Lucien makes them sound like actors in a boulevard drama :

LUCIEN: I am determined to do all I can, compatible with honour, to please your Majesty.

NAPOLEON: And political necessity, do you count that as nothing ? You might have been a king, like your brothers.

LUCIEN: And my wife's honour, Sire, and my children's status ?

NAPOLEON: Your *wife* ? You know she is not that and never has been.

Baron Larrey reports that both brothers were exceedingly embarrassed and that when Lucien referred to Alexandrine, Napoleon said, " I repeat that I am sure she has been slandered to me . . . several people have spoken well of her to me, including Mamma, who loves her, she told me, because she makes you happy and is a good mother."

Either way, only a deadlock resulted. Napoleon was obsessed by the need to find a successor, and his fear that he might be obliged to divorce Joséphine made him harshly insistent that Lucien sacrifice inclination to duty. He repeated that, once Lucien had divorced Alexandrine, he would have the same rights to the Imperial succession as his brothers, would be given a throne and could continue to live with Alexandrine, provided she received no royal honours. The interview lasted six hours and at the end of it Lucien offered to give Napoleon his eldest daughter, Charlotte, and to relinquish his rights to the Imperial succession on condition he be given an official position outside France in which his family might share. He then asked for the Grand Cordon of the Legion of Honour " as a gesture of good will."

Waiting nervously in Paris, Letizia wrote : " On the 11th of this month Joseph wrote me from Bologna that he had found the Emperor very well disposed towards you, and that you had gone to meet him. This news gave me great pleasure and contentment, as you will understand. Ever since then I have been, and still am, in the greatest anxiety to learn the result of your meeting, but your silence on a matter of such importance and one on which, as you know, my happiness depends, is beginning to destroy the hopes I had conceived, for I am sure you would not have delayed an instant in telling me had a perfect reconciliation resulted."

Napoleon meanwhile informed Joseph : " I met Lucien at Mantua, and talked with him for several hours. No doubt he has told you of the spirit in which he set out. But his thoughts and language are so remote from mine that I found it difficult to grasp his meaning . . . Lucien seemed torn by conflicting sentiments, without the force to take a definite stand. He seemed to want to send his eldest girl to her grandmother in Paris. If he is still of the same mind, I wish to be informed . . . I have exhausted all the means in my power to make Lucien see reason."

Still as eager for reconciliation as ever her ancestors had been to maintain a vendetta, Letizia continued to plead with her sons. But the quarrel was not to end until nearly eight years later, when the sun that had blazed for Napoleon at Austerlitz was about to set at Waterloo.

THE EMPIRE HAD never been more brilliant, more studded with opportunities for youth, talent and ambition than in the spring of 1808. After concluding his alliance with Russia, Napoleon founded the Imperial nobility by creating thirty-one dukes, approximately five hundred counts and fifteen hundred barons. The rights of primogeniture were restored, and the new nobles could render their titles hereditary by providing their eldest sons with landed property of a value that varied according to rank. Personally Napoleon attached little intrinsic value to the titles he created, but he said they were necessary " to enable France to re-enter Europe." The Revolution had made France a pariah in a continent of monarchies, and what Napoleon did now enabled him to treat crowned heads on terms of equality. It was for this reason too that he insisted upon being crowned by the Pope.

Yet the alliance with Russia did not prove the blessing it had seemed likely to be. By antagonising Turkey and Persia, it undermined French influence in the Orient and involved Napoleon in further wars and annexations. The Continental blockade against England had to be continued, and now resulted in the fatal war with Spain. Portugal, which Napoleon had wanted Lucien to rule, was at this time virtually an English colony. After the French alliance with Russia, Napoleon ordered Portugal to close its ports to English trade, and when it refused Junot marched into Lisbon with 40,000 men. Napoleon's brother-in-law Murat brought a French army into the Spanish side of the peninsula, ostensibly to support Junot. Spain being deplorably governed, the arrival of French troops excited an already overwrought population. A popular uprising at Aranjuez forced King Charles IV to abdicate in favour of his son, Prince Ferdinand. Both appealed to Murat, who responded by marching into Madrid with his army.

Napoleon then summoned the Spanish royal family to Bayonne. After a sordid domestic quarrel, Prince Ferdinand returned the crown to his father, who promptly turned it over to Napoleon. The proceedings took on the aspect of a baroque game of musical chairs when Napoleon passed the Spanish crown on to Joseph, who accepted it with alacrity, thus vacating the throne of Naples which Napoleon bestowed on Murat, to the delight of Caroline, who thus became Queen of Naples. Four of Caroline's five brothers were kings, but she was the only one of Letizia's daughters to become a queen.

Napoleon had not expected any resistance from a country as poverty stricken and appallingly governed as Spain, but within a few weeks 150,000 peasants and partisans rose in arms against him. Eleven years later, in exile, he said : " The greatest fault I committed was the Spanish expedition. I was led into this by the belief that in order to safeguard the French throne, the Bourbons must be driven from Spain. I thought them more powerful than they were." This war marked the beginning of the end of his empire. It also marked a subtle change in Napoleon's character. Stendhal thought that prosperity had gradually altered and weakened his nature, that he had been wrong to be so astonished by his own success, and that he should have had more contempt for his fellow rulers. From then on he drank in flattery, thought nothing impossible for him and could not bear to be contradicted. Soon any criticism seemed like insolence, or worse, stupidity. Because he chose men badly, he soon found that actions succeeded only when he himself carried them out.

Still foremost among his preoccupations was the problem of the succession, into which a new factor had now been introduced. Two years earlier Napoleon had come to suppose that, since Joséphine had borne her first husband two children, it was he who was sterile. Then, as the result of a brief and casual

163

affair with Eléonore Denuelle, a young woman employed by his sister Caroline as a reader, a son was born to him. There was no doubt as to his paternity, so when his favourite nephew—Napoleon-Louis Charles, the son of Hortense and Louis—whom he had wished to adopt, died of croup the following year, Napoleon began to think not of choosing another heir, but of begetting one. Letizia, almost as stricken as Hortense by the death of the bright and promising Napoleon-Louis, longed more than ever for Napoleon to have children of his own and told Madame d'Abrantès : " I only hope the Emperor will have the courage this time to do what not only France but all Europe anxiously expects of him. His divorce is now a necessity."

Finally convinced of this, Napoleon said wearily, " Politics have no heart, only a head," and told Joséphine that he and she must part. The Pope was the only public figure to object officially to the divorce, but by that time Napoleon had had enough of the Pope. When the latter excommunicated him, Napoleon told Murat, " He is merely excommunicating himself." In July, while Napoleon was away fighting the Austrians at Wagram—the battle which the Viennese watched from their spires and rooftops—the Pope was seized at the Quirinal by French troops and removed first to Grenoble, then to imprisonment at Savona, near Genoa. When Napoleon heard of this he wrote to Fouché : " I am angry that the Pope has been arrested, it is a piece of folly . . . but it can't be remedied ; what is done is done."

On the evening of December 14th, 1809, Letizia, Louis and Hortense, Caroline and Murat, Jérôme and Catherine, Pauline and Joséphine's son Eugène, assembled at the Tuileries to hear the announcement of the divorce. Joseph was in Spain, Lucien and Elisa in Italy. The palace was illuminated and everyone wore court dress. Both Napoleon and Joséphine were obviously in a highly emotional state. Although Napoleon indulged in extramarital love-affairs, he was by nature uxorious, and had Joséphine not betrayed him so cruelly in their first years together he would probably not have been able to bring himself to leave her. Even as it was, they had become close friends and accomplices, and the naturally affectionate Joséphine now loved him more dearly than he still loved her. Napoleon's voice faltered when he said, " God knows how much this decision costs me . . . I have nothing but praise for the attachment and tenderness of my beloved wife . . . she has embellished fifteen years of my life." Tears prevented Joséphine from reading to the end of her declaration : " The dissolution of my marriage will not change my feelings. The Emperor will always have in me his best friend . . . we are both proud of the sacrifice we are making for the country." Next day their marriage was dissolved by the Senate.

Despite Letizia's conviction that Joséphine had brought this on herself, she was disturbed by their grief. But it did not shake her belief that in future Napoleon would care more for " his own family " than he had done since his marriage. She had written to Lucien that he ought not to be obstinate at a moment when Napoleon's sentiments for his family were " already quite different." Fortunately for Letizia, she could not foresee the character of Napoleon's second wife.

NAPOLEON'S FIRST marriage had been prompted by romantic passion ; his second was a matter of politics. At one point he had wanted to marry the Czar's young sister, Anne, but according to contemporary gossip Joséphine helped wreck this project by telling the Prince of Mecklenburg that Napoleon was impotent. Repeated to the Czar's mother, this made her hesitate to come to a decision. Napoleon always loathed delay, and during this delay Austria offered him the Emperor's eighteen-year-old daughter, the Archduchess Marie-Louise, great-niece of Marie-Antoinette. The offer came purely from fear. The Comte de Narbonne, who was in Napoleon's confidence, had pointed out to Prince Metternich, recently Austrian Ambassador in Paris, that Austria's survival depended upon her securing the alliance with France that would otherwise be accorded to Russia. The Emperor Francis therefore felt that since it was useless to defy Napoleon, it would be best to placate him.

Three months after Napoleon's divorce the little archduchess set out for Paris in a state of terror. It was only five years since she and her brothers and sisters had had to flee from Vienna to Hungary in order to escape the " Corsican Ogre " after the Austrians had been defeated by him at Ulm. Now she was to be the ogre's bride. The marriage took place on April 1st, scarcely an auspicious date, though this was not immediately apparent. A lymphatic and sensual girl, she was delightfully surprised by Napoleon and found him charming. For his part, Napoleon saw in Marie-Louise a suitable mother for his children and guarantor of his dynasty. His hopes for children were increased when, this same year, his lovely Polish mistress, the Countess Walewska, bore him a son. Even before Marie-Louise became pregnant, he had decided to bestow the title of King of Rome upon his future heir, thus revealing how deeply his active imagination was involved with dreams of renewing the dynasty of the Cæsars.

Letizia wished to care for her Habsburg daughter-in-law as much as she did for Joseph's and Jérôme's wives, but this proved impossible. She described Marie-Louise with arid truthfulness as insipid in both looks and speech, though with a certain facility for expressing herself on paper. This is not contradicted by Napoleon's declaration that Marie-Louise was virtue itself, orderly, truthful and, unlike Joséphine, asked for money only when she needed it. He never spent an entire night with her.

When Napoleon decided to repudiate Joséphine his brothers and sisters had hoped he might marry Lucien's daughter Charlotte and thus consolidate the family's power. (Such a marriage would have been permissible and not, at that time, unusual.) Ever since Napoleon and Lucien met at Mantua, Letizia had been expecting Charlotte in Paris, yet again and again Lucien obstructed the plan he had himself suggested. Consistently bewildered by his inconsistency, Letizia sent her secretary to Italy to ask Lucien the reasons for this delay. As might have been anticipated, except by her, they were specious. She had asked, he said, for two of her granddaughters. Always literal, she pointed out that this was no reason for failing to send even one of them. To this Lucien replied that since Napoleon had divorced Joséphine he felt they ought to "be able to come to an arrangement," and that if ever he, Lucien, sacrificed his private life it would be "in order to prove his attachment to his family," but that the ties he had formed were insoluble until death. After which inconclusive exchange, Lucien sent his eldest daughter to her grandmother. She reached Paris in March and Letizia immediately wrote to Lucien :

Lolotte has arrived in good health. As soon as her clothes

are ready I shall present her to the Emperor, and I know in advance that she will be warmly welcomed. I will write you next day. Pray heaven I may at the same time be able to tell you of the only thing my happiness lacks—your reconciliation.

Once again Letizia was disappointed, so much so that she took the extreme step of writing to Lucien's wife : " You know how many misfortunes your marriage has caused our family, and you will realise their extent by what I am asking you to do. The Emperor wants you to divorce, and only you can persuade Lucien to agree to this, or, if he refuses, ask for a divorce yourself. You will thus avoid the disgrace threatening him, your children, and everyone belonging to you, and will confer happiness on your husband and children. Do not hesitate between a lifetime of bitterness and grief, which is what awaits you if you remain obdurate, and the prospect of a happy future in which your children will be acknowledged by the Emperor and enabled to take their places upon thrones . . . Finally, if you have any respect for a mother who has always known how to make sacrifices for her children, you will do this for me, and I assure you I shall never forget it."

This was signed " your mother," as was Letizia's letter to Lucien saying that the family's future depended on him : " The time for arguing is over, my dear son, what you have told me cannot alter the situation . . . your obstinacy is shortening my life and happiness . . . this is the last time I shall ask you." Letizia never wrote heedlessly, and so rarely expressed even the most natural and innocuous forms of self-pity that from her this amounted to an irrepressible cry from the heart. Her distress was so extreme that Pauline, who was staying with her, wrote to Cardinal Fesch in Italy : " Try to make Lucien listen to reason. The Emperor's mind is made up. If Lucien refuses to come to Paris, he will not be permitted to stay in Rome. The Emperor is ready to receive him back with open arms. He will give him the rank due to him, and ensure his wife and children a brilliant future . . . We cannot consider ourselves as ordinary private people. So if Lucien will not return to us, we shall have to sever all connexions with him. As for you, my dear Uncle, I beg you not to see any more of his wife. She alone is responsible for our misfortunes. If she had any pride she would behave differently. Be firm with Lucien. It is his duty to make a sacrifice for his mother and all his family."

None of these pleas affected Lucien, and from Letizia's point of view the dispute was soon to take a turn for the worse.

FOURTEEN-YEAR-OLD Charlotte's visit to Paris was not a success. Although she responded to her beautiful grandmother's love and had inherited the Bonaparte devotion to family, she was what the Italians proudly called " a true Roman Bonaparte "—which meant that she sided fervently with her father and stepmother against her uncle. She was more than ready to ridicule the French court, and her letters home, read of course by the censor, were as full of lese-majesty as *A Yankee at the Court of King Arthur*. They were also full of gossip : " The Queen of Naples [her Aunt Caroline] behaves very oddly. Her husband has left for Naples and she did not accompany him, which Grandmamma thinks very bad. The worst of it is that she spends every minute of the day with a certain Meternik [Metternich, who was Caroline's lover], an ambassador who is quite young. [He was thirty-six]. This attracts a lot of notice. Princess Pauline is so ill that she does not even busy herself with amusements. In general the Grand Duchess [Elisa] and the Queen of Naples grieve Grandmamma by their conduct. When I think how different they are from Mamma ! " Her father did not allow her to stay in Paris long, and no sooner was the Roman rebel back home than she flung herself into Lucien's arms, saying, " Ah, my dear little Papa, how wise you are not to wish to go up there. I am sure America would be better ! "

For Lucien had now decided to make a new life in the New World. He asked the English Minister for a passport to Cagliari, the King of Sardinia for permission to embark, and in August he sailed with his wife, their children, his wife's nephew and a daughter by her first marriage, a secretary accompanied by a wife and son, an almoner, a doctor, a tutor, a painter and twenty-three servants. Lucien's idea of "retiring into private life" involved no parsimony. His plans, however, soon went awry.

Instead of being allowed to land at Cagliari, the party was besieged by English ships and Lucien declared a prisoner of war. Always confident in the power of words, he "explained his position" at length and asked for a passport to Plymouth, meaning to sail from there to America. His captors listened politely. Then, jubilant at having Napoleon's notoriously dissident brother in their hands, they took him to England, where he spent the last four years of his brother's reign as an English country gentleman, like many other *émigrés*, including the future Louis XVIII and the future Charles X. His interest in agriculture appealed to the English, as did his literary productions. Byron was particularly appreciative of his grandiloquent epic on the subject of Corsica's liberation from the Moors. As for his financial worries, these were relieved by Letizia, who now had good reason to be glad she had invested money abroad.

Having done all she could for Lucien, Letizia turned to his brother Louis, who was in a far more miserable state. Obstinate, touchy and ravaged by syphilis, Louis had been outraged when his refusal to maintain the trade blockade against England drove Napoleon to deprive Holland of territorial independence. He promptly abdicated and rushed from Holland in the hope that Napoleon would implore him to return. Instead of which Napoleon merely wrote to Letizia : " I hasten to tell you that the King of Holland is taking the waters at Toeplitz in Bohemia. As you must have been very uneasy at his disappearance, I am not losing a moment in telling you this to reassure you. His conduct is such that only illness can explain it." Letizia felt for both her sons in this instance. Once when Napoleon was complaining of his brothers' incompetence, as he often had reason to do, Letizia said, " My son, you are right and wrong : right if you compare them with yourself, because you are incomparable, a marvel and an indefinable phenomenon. But you are wrong if you compare them with the other kings to whom they are superior, kings who have revealed such stupidity that it is as if they had a veil over their eyes and fell on purpose to be replaced by my children." When Napoleon laughed and said, " Signora Letizia, are you too flattering me ? " she retorted, " You are unjust to your mother. A mother does not flatter her son. You know, Sire, that in public I treat you with all possible respect because I am your subject ; but in private I am your mother and you are my son and when you say ' I wish this,' I may say ' And I do *not* wish it.' "

From Bohemia, where he assumed the name Saint-Leu (that of his country estate near Paris), Louis wrote to the three people he considered most devoted to him—his mother, his brother Jérôme and Decazes, a civil servant who served Letizia as secretary for a time and achieved the singular feat of pleasing Louis, Hortense, Letizia and Louis XVIII. Thoroughly unbalanced by now, Louis told Letizia he wanted to live with her in the South of France, but that since Napoleon forbade this (Louis had never asked him) he had requested permission to stay in Germany. He asked Jérôme if Napoleon would allow him to live at Saint-Leu, and by the same mail begged Decazes to find a purchaser for Saint-Leu.

With one of her poignant displays of calm, Letizia wrote Louis : " I repeat what I have said in previous letters, that I will not abandon you. But it seems to me that after taking the waters you ought to do what I have suggested, namely come to Saint-Leu or to Pont where I will wait for you and we can decide what had best be done . . . your health is what is most important. I shall always be with you." Unfortunately not devotion, common sense or doctors could help Louis. Two years later paralysis attacked his upper limbs, and he could write only if a pen were tied to his fingers.

Letizia's dearest hopes were fulfilled in March, 1811, by the birth of Napoleon's son, Napoleon-François-Charles-Joseph. Wild rejoicings welcomed the ill-fated King of Rome, a city the boy was never to see. Stendhal, then twenty-eight, noted in his journal : " I was in bed with Angéline. The cannon woke us at ten. It was the third shot. We counted the twenty-second with transports of joy. At our nineteenth shot, which was the twenty-second for people outside, we heard applause in the street. Even in the most solitary places, such as the Augustin Museum, there was applause. My wigmaker told me that in the Rue Saint-Honoré people applauded as if at the appearance of a favourite actor. It is a great and happy event." All over Europe bells pealed, cannon roared, cities were illuminated, torchlight processions were succeeded by Te Deums, and peasants left their work to shout " Long live the King of Rome ! " Napoleon said of his new-born son : " I envy him, for glory awaits him, whereas I had to pursue it. I shall have been Philip, he will be Alexander. He will have only to stretch out his hands to hold the world." Joséphine sent Napoleon a loving note in which she said, " My sacrifice has not been in vain."

Letizia's joy in the happiness of one child was soon cut short by the grief of another. A month after the birth of Napoleon's son, Elisa's baby, Jérôme, died. Although not a punctilious wife, Elisa had inherited the Bonaparte passion for children and was overcome by her loss. Letizia wrote to her son-in-law Bacciochi : " I am incapable of offering you the least consolation, since I need consolation myself, but nothing gives it to us in this world." Almost alone among her direct utterances, this brief expression of pain enables us to understand Michelet's description of her in his *History of the Nineteenth Century* : " Madame Letizia, in her Italian portraits, like the one before my eyes, is grandly beautiful. She is mysteriously and indefinably tragic. One cannot take one's eyes off her. The mouth is disdainful, capable of hatred, full of the bitter honey found only in Corsica. The eyes—black, fixed, wide open—are equally enigmatic. Their gaze is directed inwards, at some dream or passion. This gives her the strange air of a fortune-teller or a Moorish sibyl, descended from the Carthaginians or Saracens whose tombs are near Ajaccio."

Sibylline powers would have afforded Letizia no comfort had

she possessed them on the occasion of the King of Rome's baptism, which took place on June 9th, 1811. Seen in retrospect, there is a sunset splendour, sublime or ridiculous according to one's viewpoint, about this last majestic ceremony intended to consecrate the durability of the great empire so soon to fall. The royal cortège, similar to that of Napoleon, was not due to assemble until five o'clock in the afternoon, but by midday the route was already lined by crowds. All the sovereigns wore elaborate court dress with an abundance of velvet, ermine, diamonds, diadems and plumed hats. Effervescent cheering greeted the baby when he appeared in a carriage drawn by eight horses. He was held on the knees of the Comtesse de Montesquieu, for whom Napoleon had revived the *ancien régime* title of " Governess of the Children of France," and over his white lace robes glittered the scarlet ribbon of the Legion of Honour. The Parisians particularly relished this hint that there was to be nothing Austrian about their little king. When the cortège reached Notre-Dame the baby was wrapped in an ermine coat with a long train carried by the Duc de Valmy (Napoleon's old companion in arms, Kellerman). At the font he was held by his godmother, Letizia, and by the Grand Duke of Würzburg, acting as deputy godfather for the Emperor, Francis. After the baptism, Napoleon, who was so radiant with joy that Madame d'Abrantès said he reminded her of the line " *les cœurs de lion sont les vrais cœurs de père*," took his son in his arms, kissed him tenderly three times and held him up for everyone to see. Whereupon, although they were in church, there was an irrepressible outburst of applause. It was very unlike Napoleon's own unostentatious baptism in Ajaccio forty-one years earlier.

Once the cheers and tumult had died away Letizia was free to leave Paris for a long-planned visit to her youngest child, Jérôme, King of Westphalia. After taking a cure with Pauline at Aix-la-Chapelle (the beautiful grey city of statues that was to become much-bombed Aachen), Letizia set out for Jérôme's palace, Napoleonshöhe. Now that Napoleon was committed to an increasingly perilous destiny, Joseph struggling to avoid his inevitable abdication in Spain, Lucien still a prisoner in England, and Louis a self-exiled invalid, Jérôme was a unique source of pleasure to her. Despite its partly political inception, his second marriage was proving a most happy one. Although Princess Catherine of Württemberg had come to her husband as reluctantly as Marie-Louise to Napoleon, she had fallen passionately in love with the handsome, gay, witty and affectionate Jérôme, and, being a woman of fine emotional quality, was to show him unfailing love and loyalty for the rest of her life. Letizia was, from the first, devoted to her, and Catherine said that her mother-in-law " had the same gift for inspiring respect as the Empress of Russia."

As is often the case with self-indulgent natures, Jérôme liked giving pleasure to others almost as much as to himself, and he was instinctively adept at those gestures that are the small change of the heart. Letizia was surprised and touched to discover that he had taken the trouble to send to Paris for furniture and hangings similar to her own, in order that she might feel at home in Westphalia. This initial discovery set the tone for the entire visit, which was to be one of the happiest times of Letizia's middle years. There was no end to his and Catherine's desire to make much of her. They arranged trips to points of interest, hunting expeditions, a state entry into Cassel with a military guard of honour and all the authorities in ceremonial dress, a gala with cantatas by Blangini, and a military review displaying twenty battalions of infantry, two regiments of cuirassiers, and two of light cavalry, nineteen hundred men in all. They enjoyed themselves so much that she let herself be persuaded to prolong her visit into October.

Avarice forgotten, she showered pearls on Catherine—her own portrait set in pearls, a pearl-edged parasol with a pearl-encrusted gold and enamel handle, and a superb pearl necklace. She also gave her daughter-in-law sympathy and understanding, for after Letizia had left, Catherine noted : " This separation was very painful to me. At her age and in the times in which we

175

live, it is very difficult to foresee the moment when we shall meet again. The separation was doubly painful because Madame Mère was a most delightful companion for me. She has great wit and vigour. As I am often alone, I found her a great resource. Besides, a woman often feels a need to pour her heart out to another woman." The noblest and most appealing of Letizia's daughters-in-law, Catherine was too loyal to add "especially when a woman adores a husband as charming and unfaithful as Jérôme."

From the gay pageantry of this musical-comedy world, Letizia returned to Paris and the lengthening political shadows soon to banish gaiety from her life for ever.

LETIZIA WAS AT HER castle at Pont when Napoleon left to join the Grand Army for what was to prove the disastrous campaign against Russia. In order to cheat her impatience for news she went to Aix-en-Savoie (to-day's Aix-les-Bains) to take the waters. There she found Cardinal Fesch, Pauline, Julie and her sister Désirée (now married to Marshal Bernadotte), the Duchesse d'Abrantès, the Duchesse de Raguse and the ex-Empress Joséphine. Most of the visitors at this fashionable spa had relatives at the wars in Russia or in Spain, and the atmosphere of febrile excitement foreshadowed that of the Duchess of Richmond's famous ball, where the guests were to maintain their gaiety so stubbornly that, at the last, many officers had no time to change into uniform but fought at Waterloo in evening dress.

Her brother's company was particularly precious to Letizia since he and she had recently been separated by an incident equally painful to both of them. Before leaving for Russia, Napoleon had ordered the Pope, his prisoner since 1809, to be transferred from Savona to Fontainebleau, and when Fesch courageously objected to this Napoleon banished his uncle to his diocese of Lyons. It says much for Fesch's good heart that he made no attempt to draw Letizia into the quarrel but wrote her from Lyons : " To-day, the solemnities of Easter being over, I am writing to express the pain I felt at leaving you and the happiness that was restored to me when I saw my church again. This happiness will be unclouded if you continue to enjoy good health and do not forget me. Do not add to your troubles by brooding over the reasons for my leaving Paris. I have laid them at the foot of the Cross. God will be my strength, I put all my trust in Him."

Fesch has been described as a materialistic Italian cardinal with exclusively worldly ambitions. But the more one studies him the more complex he appears. That he was capable of deep and sustained emotion is shown by his relations with Letizia. As she protected his childhood, so he protected her old age, and in seventy years of close friendship neither ever failed the other. His artistic sensibility might have served him better in Renaissance Italy than in Revolutionary France, since he had a passion for painting and the capacity to recognise talent even when the possessor exasperated him, as was the case with Chateaubriand, at one time his secretary. He also had a sense of the value of compromise that could verge on the humorous : in 1805, when Napoleon wished the Pope to arrest the English poet, Coleridge, then Rome correspondent for the *Morning Post*, it was Fesch who saved the Pope from embarrassment and Napoleon from making a blunder by smuggling the poet out of Rome disguised in the uniform of the French Legation. It was this ability to compromise that had made it possible for him temporarily to abandon the priesthood ; but there is no compelling reason to believe that because he lacked fanaticism he also lacked sincerity in his faith. Certainly no such lack in him troubled Letizia, and it was with regret that she left him and returned to Paris.

After receiving a visit from Marie-Louise and going to visit her little grandson at Saint-Cloud, Letizia returned to Pont where she remained until the end of October, devoting most of her time to letter-writing. She was now the centre of a postal web that linked her with Joseph in Madrid, Julie at Mortefontaine, Lucien in England, Louis in Graz, Elisa in Florence, Pauline in Aix, Caroline in Naples, Jérôme and Catherine in Westphalia, Fesch in Lyons and Napoleon wherever she could reach him by courier. Thanks to this industry, each of her eight children knew what was happening to the other seven. She also acted as their business adviser, rendering them countless practical services, and kept up a continuous correspondence with Corsica, where she and Fesch were now all-powerful. The Prefect, Arrighi, was a cousin of theirs and never appointed even a minor official on the island without first consulting them.

When Letizia returned to Paris in October she found the capital in an uproar as the result of a conspiracy hatched since Napoleon left for Russia. An unemployed general named Malet, of proved dishonesty and eccentricity, had celebrated his release from prison by spreading rumours that Napoleon had been killed. He followed this up by adorning the City Hall with a poster announcing :

The Emperor was killed on October 7th at the head of his army.

The Senate invests General Malet with command of the armed forces and authority to do all the situation requires.

The Imperial Government is destroyed ; the young Bonaparte is declared illegitimate ; Marie-Louise's marriage is annulled ; conscription is abolished ; and the Pope restored to his estates.

A provisional government is set up at the Hôtel de Ville.

There will be a peace congress.

The preservation of honours and public functions is guaranteed, as is the inalienability of national property.

All the signatures to this fanciful document were forgeries, except that of Malet ; nevertheless, it was momentarily as effective as a conspiracy would be to-day if its instigators controlled the Press, radio and television services. High-ranking civil servants showed a total lack of initiative, and neither the Prefect of Paris nor the Minister of the Interior resisted when arrested. Nevertheless, Malet was soon unmasked and Letizia wrote to Louis : " You have read in the papers of the riot, or rather the farce, that took place in Paris on September 23rd. I was not yet back. The culprits are paying for their folly with their lives and all is calm and tranquil in the capital, as throughout the Empire."

While Letizia wrote these deliberately confident words the Grand Army, with its complement of green-coated Württembergers, Portuguese in plumed shakos, white-cloaked Poles, Italians, Croats, Dalmatians, Prussians and Austrians, was being smothered under the Russian snows. Stendhal, who took part in the retreat from Moscow, wrote: " The Russian campaign turned me against snow, not on account of the perils I underwent, but because of the hideous spectacle of human suffering and ruthlessness. At Wilna breaches in the hospital wall were stopped up by the frozen bodies of the dead. How, with these memories, can one take any pleasure in snow ? "

Still unaware of the turn history was taking at the other end of Europe, Letizia divided her time between the little King of Rome, Julie, who was ill, and Louis's sons whom Hortense had sent from Saint-Leu to visit their grandmother. Letizia was deeply attached to these children and the younger boy, the future Napoleon III, considered her a superlatively romantic figure. This lull in Letizia's life was not to last long.

When Napoleon learnt that after his rumoured death no one had proclaimed his son as his successor, he was so appalled that he immediately set off for home. His two weeks' journey across a now largely hostile Europe was one of the most perilous even he ever made. He reached Paris on December 18th, 1812, and for the first time Letizia saw him at grips with a disaster as mighty as any conjured up by Corneille in the tragedies Napoleon had so often declaimed to her when he was a boy in Corsica with the world before him and Providence his guide.

DURING THE NEXT THREE months Napoleon worked harder than ever, and Letizia had every reason not only to admire her son's fortitude in adversity but to believe he would again prove triumphant. Then, on March 30th, Marie-Louise took the oath as Regent—Letizia would undoubtedly have done far better in this capacity—and a fortnight later Napoleon took command of the army for what was to be his last campaign in Germany. Not everyone on the Allied side hoped for Napoleon's downfall. In September, Byron wrote to Thomas Moore: " What say you to Bonaparte ? Remember, I back him against the field, barring catalepsy and the Elements. Nay, I almost wish him success against all countries but this—were it only to choke the *Morning Post*, and his undutiful father-in-law, with that rebellious bastard of Scandinavian adoption, Bernadotte."

Nevertheless, the Allies were victorious all along the line, and, wanting to avoid a winter campaign, proclaimed that they were not making war against the French people but against Napoleon's authority outside France. This proved effective. In December the Legislative Assembly voted against fighting on except for independence and territorial rights. But it was too late for such limited action. France was completely surrounded now that the English had the upper hand in Spain, from which Joseph had finally been driven. The Allies began crossing the Rhine just before Christmas, 1813. Joseph's brother-in-law, Bernadotte, who had gone over to the enemy, invaded Holland and Belgium and entered France by the Escaut valley. Blücher and Schwarzenberg crossed the Rhine between Basle and Coblenz. Napoleon had 70,000 men against the enemy's 260,000, and, as he was to say himself, only General Bonaparte could save the Emperor now.

It did not occur to Letizia to leave Paris and she wrote vigorously to Fesch : " I have spoken to the Emperor as you desired. He told me to urge you to remain in Lyons as long as there is no danger and if the enemy approaches and it seems likely the city will fall, you are to retire, but to remain in your diocese doing good. I am glad to learn that Louis is with you. The Emperor asked me why he did not come to Paris immediately. Tell him I expect him, and that his brothers should arrive this evening. My dear brother, this is no time to cling to etiquette. The Bourbons lost all through not knowing how to die fighting."

Paradoxically, this campaign that ended in Napoleon's defeat was one of the most brilliant he ever fought. First he marched on Blücher's army and drove it back to Chalons, then he turned on Schwarzenberg and drove him back to Chaumont. Astonished and dismayed, the Allies decided to ask for a truce, and on February 23rd, Prince Wenceslas de Liechtenstein was sent to Napoleon to negotiate terms. Nothing came of this. The French peasants were actively behind Napoleon. Maddened by Allied looting and by fear lest a Bourbon restoration rob them of the *émigré* and Church land for which they had paid, they armed themselves with scythes, pitchforks and shotguns and acted as snipers. In Lorraine a Russian column lost 3,000 men without encountering one French soldier.

Men who saw Napoleon at this time reported that he seemed to have recovered all the genius of his youth, and he himself said he had " donned once more the boots he had worn in Italy." He was uplifted by two desires : to prevent France being driven back within her pre-Revolutionary frontiers, and to safeguard his son's future. He had just recaptured Arcis-sur-Aube from the Austrians when he made the mistake of writing to Marie-Louise : " I have decided to make for the Marne so as to drive the enemy farther back from Paris." This letter was intercepted by the Cossacks. Blücher sent a translation of it to

Schwarzenberg, then forwarded the original to Marie-Louise with a bouquet of flowers. Guided by this letter, the Allies changed their plans.

The final blow to Napoleon's hopes came partly from a Corsican vendetta. His distant cousin and enemy, Pozzo di Borgo, who had served Paoli and then left Corsica with the English, was now one of the Czar's diplomats. When the Allies learnt that Napoleon intended to attack their army in the rear, Pozzo di Borgo urged the Czar to make for Paris at all costs : " While you go on thinking in terms of battles you run the risk of being defeated, because Napoleon will always be able to fight better than you and because his army, although dissatisfied, will always be inspired by honour, and will fight to the last man as long as he is at hand. No matter how much his military might has been shaken, it is still great. But his political power has been destroyed. Times have changed . . . You should attempt to end the war by political means . . . Touch Paris with a finger and the colossus Napoleon will come tumbling down." Talleyrand was already in secret correspondence with the future Louis XVIII, and exercising his influence over the Czar in favour of a Bourbon restoration. There was even treachery within Napoleon's family, for Murat and Caroline had come to terms with Austria in the hope of retaining their throne. They promised Austria 30,000 men to help drive the French out of Italy.

Yet comparatively few people realised what was happening. It is difficult for us, accustomed to telephones, radio and television, to imagine how long it took so short a time ago for news to spread. The atmosphere retained more secrets than now, and no television screen could replace personal contact, word of mouth or handwritten word transported by feet, hooves or sailing-ships.

Thus in March, when Napoleon was fighting desperately only eighty-five miles east of Paris, Letizia was sufficiently in the dark to write Elisa a letter devoted almost entirely to domestic matters : " I congratulate you on what you tell me of your daughter's disposition and education. Please talk to her often

183

of her grandmother and of my love for her . . . The King of Rome, about whom you specially inquired, is in excellent health. He is a great joy to the Emperor and to all of us." Only at the end does anxiety break through : " I see with distress that more fighting is coming, and the moment is near when the Emperor will again be in danger. I think I was born only to suffer." The day after she wrote this the Duc d'Angoulême arrived in Bordeaux and Louis XVIII was proclaimed King there.

By March 28th Paris was so obviously threatened that the Regency Council met to decide what was to become of Napoleon's wife and son. Napoleon had already told Joseph, now Lieutenant-General of the Empire : " If you receive news of defeat or of my death, send the Empress and the King of Rome to Rambouillet . . . I would rather my son were dead than brought up in Vienna as an Austrian prince." Clarke, the Minister of War, urged them to leave Paris since he saw no chance of defending the city with the 50,000 men who remained ; but Talleyrand, who hoped to be tutelary ruler should the child succeed his father, swore that only the presence of Marie-Louise and her son would prevent revolution in Paris. After two rounds of voting it was settled that mother and child should leave Paris as quickly as possible. As the meeting broke up, Talleyrand said to Rovigo : " It is not incumbent on everyone to be swallowed up in the ruins of this edifice."

Awakened by the frenzy of packing that filled the Tuileries that night, Napoleon's son realised something of what was happening and began to protest : " I don't want to go, and since Papa's away I'm the master here." It was as if he had a premonition that his short ration of happiness was already consumed. He called again and again for the father he would never see again, and was carried screaming out of the palace where he had been born to greatness and tragedy.

At nine o'clock next morning ten large green carriages marked with coats of arms were drawn up in the Cour du Carrousel. The guards presented arms as Marie-Louise and

Madame de Montebello entered the first coach. The King of Rome occupied the second one with his beloved governess. The child wore a miniature National Guardsman's uniform which he loved, as he did everything connected with his father's soldiers. Then came Letizia, the pregnant Catherine, Jérôme, and a crowd of officials and courtiers. The procession was completed by a baggage train, a platoon of mounted grenadiers, three squadrons of chasseurs and two pickets of lancers. The first time Letizia was a refugee she had been a fiery young bride, capable of galloping over mountains and of fighting for the baby she carried ; the second time she had been the widowed mother of eight children ; now, the third time, she was a grandmother of sixty-three, her living hostages to fortune scattered all over Europe.

The sky was overcast, the atmosphere oppressive. Passersby, including Stendhal, watched in morose silence as the procession clattered out of the Tuileries towards the still rural Champs-Élysées and Napoleon's Arc de Triomphe, which had been begun eight years ago and was still incomplete. They crossed the Bois de Boulogne and made a halt at Versailles. Thirty-two years had passed since Letizia first visited Versailles with Carlo and was disturbed by the doomed Queen's expression. Marie-Louise and the King of Rome reached Rambouillet at five in the afternoon ; Letizia, who had stopped to look after the exhausted Catherine, not until late in the evening.

Meanwhile Joseph had stayed behind and issued a proclamation to the people of Paris : " The Regency Council has provided for the safety of the Empress and the King of Rome. *I remain with you.* Let us take up arms to defend the city . . . the Emperor is marching to our rescue." This was true, but Joseph lacked both the means and the ability to plan a well-coordinated defence, and when the battle for Paris began, at six in the morning of March 30th, Napoleon was still a hundred miles away. That same morning the refugees at Rambouillet were awakened by a message from Joseph that the Russians had reached the outskirts of Paris. Rambouillet was no longer safe. They immediately set out anew, but their coaches were delayed by muddy roads. Twilight fell before the mighty ship of Chartres Cathedral appeared to them on the horizon, and night before Letizia and Marie-Louise found shelter in the Prefect's house. They were not allowed to rest long. At midnight there was a clattering of carriage wheels and horses' hoofs and Joseph arrived to tell them that Paris had fallen. Letizia's first question was, " Did we at least fight well ? "

That afternoon a courier reached Chartres with the news that the Senate had repudiated Napoleon and the Czar refused to treat with him. (Stendhal said later that had Talleyrand not remained in Paris, against Napoleon's orders, so as to act as host to the Czar, France's entire future, and probably that of all Europe, would have been altered.) Joseph had brought instructions for the fugitives to move south, towards the Loire. They thought of making for Tours, but as General Clarke reported typhus there, they chose Blois instead. They slept at Châteaudun on March 31st, and at Vendôme on April 1st, unaware that the Allies had entered Paris that morning. A local landowner, Monsieur de la Chesnaye, wrote an account of their passage : " The Imperial family consisted of the Empress and her son, the King of Rome, of Joseph and Jérôme Bonaparte and their mother, Letizia. The Arch-Chancellor, Cambacérès, accompanied these illustrious personages, who reached Vendôme on Friday, April 1st, in the coaches that had been used on December 2nd, 1804, for Napoleon's coronation. These coaches, the richest and most magnificent ever seen, were displayed in the Place Saint-Martin. The Empress and her son stayed with the Marquise de Soisy, who moved out so as to give them the entire house. Joseph, King of Spain, was received at the College. Jérôme, King of Westphalia, lodged with Madame de Paris. Letizia their mother stayed with Monsieur Lemoine de la Godelinière . . . The travellers left Vendôme next morning for Blois." Again the roads were muddy and this short journey took nine hours.

The Old Guard who had endured so much for Napoleon

were still ready to die for him, but the marshals and senators whom he had enriched were not, and on April 4th, he was forced to abdicate, ostensibly in favour of his son, in fact to make way for Louis XVIII. Still mindful of his family, Napoleon wrote at once to Joseph that they must all disperse : " Let the King of Westphalia go to Brittany or to Bourges . . . I think Madame had best join her daughter [Pauline] at Nice ; Queen Julie and her children should go somewhere near Marseille ; it is natural that King Louis, who has always loved the Midi, should go to Montpellier . . . recommend the most strict economy to everyone." He also told Marie-Louise to divide two million francs among the family for their immediate needs.

On Good Friday the Czar's aide-de-camp, General Schouva-loff, arrived in Blois and advised Marie-Louise to proceed with her husband's family as far as Orléans, where she would be met by Prince Esterhazy and the Prince de Liechtenstein, who had orders to escort her to her father at Rambouillet. The Emperor Francis invited Letizia to accompany Marie-Louise, but she refused indignantly, saying she would never voluntarily separate herself from her children. On parting from her mother-in-law, Marie-Louise said, " I hope you will always retain benevolent feelings towards me." Literal-minded and formidable Letizia replied : " That will depend on you and your future conduct." They never met again, and Letizia was mercifully unaware that Napoleon's son was from this moment to be lost for ever to his father's family.

IV

Transformation

1814-15

. . . dans un cadre ovale dédoré, sous une vitre moisie, une tête blême sur fond noir. . . . Elle ressemble à Lui, elle a les mêmes yeux impératifs et les mêmes cheveux plats en mèches collées : son expression d'une intensité surprenante a je ne sais quoi de triste, de hagard, de suppliant . . . et l'on dirait d'une morte effrayée de se trouver dans la nuit, qui aurait mis furtivement la tête au trou obscur de cet ovale, pour essayer de regarder à travers la brume du verre terni ce que font les vivants et ce qu'est devenue la gloire de son fils. . . .

PIERRE LOTI, describing a portrait of Letizia in
Le Livre de la Pitié et de la Mort

Toujours lui ! Lui partout !
Tu domines notre âge ; ange ou démon, qu'importe !
Ton aigle dans son vol haletant nous emporte !
L'œil même qui te fuit te retrouve partout.
Toujours dans nos tableaux tu jettes ta grande ombre.
Toujours Napoléon, éblouissant et sombre,
Sur le seuil du siècle est debout !

VICTOR HUGO : "Lui," from *Orientales*

How far is St. Helena from the field of Waterloo ?
A near way—a clear way—the ship will take you soon.
A pleasant place for gentlemen with little left to do.
(*Morning never tries you till the afternoon.*)

KIPLING : *A St. Helena Lullaby*

ON EASTER SUNDAY churches all over France omitted the *Domine salvum fac imperatorem* from the service. Letizia had a mass said privately for Napoleon and his son. Next day she left for Italy with Fesch, who had come to fetch her despite many obstacles. In February, after being warned that a party of Austrians had been specially detailed to seize him, he had fled from Lyons to Montpellier, where the bishop sheltered him. By chance he met there his niece Elisa, who had been expelled from her Italian principality by the Austrians. She told him of the fall of Paris, and after this news he could think of nothing but Letizia's safety and welfare.

The Mayor of Orléans raised no objections to supplying them with passports. Slightly less inaccurate than the passport with which she had left Corsica, Letizia's read:

Age : 64 [she would be 64 in four months' time].

Height : 1 metre 50.

Hair : greying.

Forehead : rounded.

Eyebrows : chestnut.

Eyes : brown.

Mouth : well-made.

Chin : rounded.

Face : oval.

Complexion : clear.

Peculiarities : none.

As they left Orléans under the escort of a colonel of the Gendarmerie, she said sadly : " It is not all over yet, alas." That same day Napoleon was notified that the Allies had accorded him the sovereignty of the island of Elba : " Their Majesties the Emperor and Empress will retain their titles and rank for their lifetime. The Emperor's mother, brothers, sisters, nephews and nieces will retain the title of princes of the family wherever they reside." At the same time, Napoleon was told that he might take 400 men with him for his garrison. Immediately this news spread, the Old Guard began quarrelling among themselves. They all wanted to go to Elba. The violence of their reaction was such that 600 instead of 400 were allowed to share Napoleon's exile.

This six hundred, a symbol of fidelity in the midst of betrayal, set out from Fontainebleau four days after Letizia had left Orléans. With them went six of Napoleon's favourite horses. They marched out as if on parade, drums beating and the forbidden tricolour flag flying. In the same invincible spirit they crossed a France now hostile to them and flying the white flag of the Bourbons. Such is the power of fidelity, even over the unfaithful, that everywhere their attitude imposed respect. In many places the peasants gathered to cry " *Vive l'Empereur !* " as they marched by. The first time someone shouted " Down with the tricolour ! " the colonel halted his troops and demanded, " Who is coward enough to insult the Guard ? " No one answered. Questioned about their destination, they said, " We don't know the place we're going to, but we're going to join the Emperor and that's enough for us."

At one stage of their separate journeys into exile, Letizia and Napoleon almost met. While he was under escort at Roanne, on the Loire, a Benedictine almoner brought him the news that Letizia and Fesch were awaiting a safe-conduct at Saint-Symphorien, only ten miles away. Napoleon asked the almoner to tell them that he would look down at Saint-Symphorien as he went by : " That will be my farewell to my mother." This mute farewell was not, however, to be their last. In the coming year mother and son were to share fresh perils, and to part at last amidst the ruins of the Empire.

Letizia and Fesch reached Italy soon after the Pope, who had been liberated by Napoleon when Murat treacherously occupied the Papal States with the Allies' consent. Their encounter at Cesana was one of the most ironic in the gigantic game of musical chairs being played anew all over Europe. Fesch requested an audience, which was immediately granted. He told the Pope of his wish to retire to Rome with his sister and was generously assured that they would be welcome. They reached Rome on May 12th and went to the palace in the Via Giulia which Letizia had left ten years earlier to go to Paris for Napoleon's coronation.

DETERMINED TO JOIN Napoleon in Elba, Letizia's next move was to accumulate funds by selling her house in Paris. She did not believe that the allowance granted the Imperial family by the Treaty of Fontainebleau would ever be paid (she was right); nor did she think that, considering what had happened at Pont, looted by order of Jérôme's brother-in-law, her property would be respected for long. The new French Minister of War, General Dupont, offered her 600,000 francs for her house in the Rue Saint-Dominique. She promptly asked for 800,000. Dupont said she would be sorry if she stuck to that price. She not only stuck to it but obtained it, and when Dupont complained that he could not afford to buy the furniture and decorations, she had these packed up and sent to Rome and Elba.

Her next moving encounter in Rome at this time was with Lucien, whom she had not seen for ten years. His Roman property was intact and the Pope now made him Prince of Canino " in recognition of his attachment to the Holy See." Letizia was pleased that he should be thus honoured, and she suggested that he adopt his father's coat-of-arms, which he did; but he could no longer claim the lion's share of her sympathies as the least fortunate of her children. On the contrary, he and Pauline were, as Roman princes, the only two safe from political persecution.

Now that the disaster she had anticipated had come, it was difficult for her to get news of " all the kings she had borne," let alone help them. Joseph had moved to a house on the shore of the Lake of Geneva, but as soon as he began receiving visitors,

Letizia Bonaparte

Letizia and Napoleon Bonaparte

The Empress Joséphine

The Empress Marie-Louise

The King of Rome, son of Napoleon and Marie-Louise

Letizia Bonaparte, Madame Mère

The Reunion of the Sovereigns at the ball given by the City of Paris on December 4th, 1809, to celebrate the marriage of Jérôme Bonaparte and Princess Catherine of Württemberg.

Left to right: Joachim Murat, King of Naples; Frederick Augustus, King of Saxony; Jérôme Bonaparte, King of Westphalia; Frederick, King of Württemberg; Louis Bonaparte, King of Holland; Napoleon Bonaparte, the Empress Joséphine; Letizia Bonaparte, Madame Mère; Julie Bonaparte, Queen of Spain; Hortense Bonaparte, Queen of Holland; Caroline Murat, Queen of Naples; Catherine Bonaparte, Queen of Westphalia; Pauline Bonaparte, Princess Borghese.

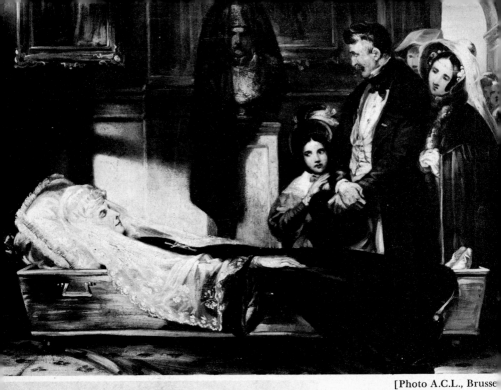

Letizia's death-bed

Letizia Bonaparte in 1833

Talleyrand, so often Joseph's guest in the past, declared this was a cover for spying and persuaded the Canton of Vaud to expel him. Harmless Julie was driven from Vichy, where she had been taking the waters with her sister Désirée, now Crown Princess of Sweden. Even Louis aroused suspicion in Switzerland by paying a courtesy call on Marie-Louise when she went through Baden on her way to Aix-en-Savoir. Jérôme was isolated in Ekensberg, an isolated castle in Württemberg, together with Catherine, who, unlike her sister-in-law Marie-Louise, had bravely defied her father when he exhorted her to leave her husband and " come to the bosom of her family which could never receive a Bonaparte." The domineering King of Württemberg did not reflect that his grandchild would be irreparably a Bonaparte and he was outraged when Catherine replied that she owed her husband seven years of happiness and would certainly not abandon him in misfortune. While shut up in Ekensberg, Catherine and Jérôme received a visit from Elisa, who, although pregnant, was attempting with characteristic energy to reach Vienna and complain at court about the Austrians' seizure of her Italian property. Elisa's intrepidity appealed to Letizia, who had admired the good sense with which the most Napoleonic of her daughters ruled her little principality and enjoyed with Pauline a visit to the beautiful royal villa near Lucca, with bosky gardens where Elisa had kept a tame Corsican eagle. Only Caroline and Murat still clung at any price to the crowns Napoleon had given them.

As often in the gravest moments of Letizia's life, her most frivolous daughter proved the tenderest and most helpful to her. Napoleon had not been a month in Elba before Pauline paid him a flying visit on the pretext that she was on her way to Naples. As faithful as a sister as she was volatile as a mistress, Pauline did all she could to cheer her adored brother by assurances that the family remained loyal to him. She then wrote to Letizia : " I have suffered so much that I need to recover myself near you, dear Mamma. Tell me when you intend to join the Emperor at Elba. He seems to desire that extremely, and bade me tell you so. I hear with sorrow that Elisa has been to Vienna. Yet she wrote the Emperor that she wished to go to Elba . . . I hope Joseph will go to see the Emperor as he promised. It would be very bad of him otherwise. We must not leave the Emperor alone. It is now that he is unhappy that we must show our attachment to him."

Letizia's request for permission to visit Elba was speedily answered by General Bertrand, who confirmed Napoleon's eagerness to see her. Captain Tower, an Englishman in command of the frigate *Curaçao*, who brought Letizia letters from Elba, offered to fetch her at Civita Vecchia and take her to her son. She accepted joyfully, but Colonel Sir Neil Campbell, the English Commissioner to Elba whose portrait can be seen in the elder Vernet's famous picture " Les Adieux de Fontainebleau," put a stop to this plan, saying that although Captain Tower had acted in good faith, naval regulations forbade him to take foreign passengers without special authorisation. Complications gathered round the projected visit like barnacles on a rock. Messages went to and fro between Elba and the mainland. Napoleon mobilised his tiny fleet. *L'Abeille* brought Fesch dispatches. A small reconnoitring vessel came to fetch the servants and luggage. The brig *L'Inconstant* was ordered to Piombino so that Letizia might have the shortest crossing possible. At last, ten weeks after her arrival in Rome, she was able to start on her voyage into the beginning of her son's long night.

Calling herself Madame Dupont (the French equivalent of Smith or Brown, and seldom can anyone have suited the name less), Letizia set out in a berlin drawn by six horses and escorted by four of the men Lucien employed to protect his land. With her were her chamberlain, Colonna, and two of her ladies-in-waiting.

At Pisa the Austrian commander courteously offered her an escort of four hussars, but at Leghorn the Austrian Count Stahrenberg was so alarmed by the rumour that Leghorn and Civita Vecchia were Bonapartist enrolment centres that he demanded she leave at once. There was nothing Letizia would have liked better than to leave the port of Leghorn at once, but *L'Inconstant* had not yet arrived and it would have been futile for her to sail in a small vessel inadequately armed against the Algerian pirates infesting the Mediterranean. At this point Sir Neil Campbell offered himself as an escort. He noted in his diary:

July 26–28 : Landed at Leghorn, and remained to await the expected arrival of Madame Mère.

July 29 : Arrived Madame Mère and suite in two carriages, with six horses to each. She came from Rome, and travelled under the name of Madame Dupont, accompanied by M. Colonna, lately Préfect at Naples, which office, however, as a Frenchman, he was obliged to resign when that Government declared war on France.

July 30 : Received a visit from M. Colonna and M. Bartolucci, an Italian resident in Leghorn and formerly member of the municipality under the French. They requested a passage for Madame in a man-of-war. Among the reasons alleged for this appeal were the disappointment of a passage in another of His Majesty's ships, Napoleon's corvette being absent at Genoa, and these seas being infested with Algerian pirates. I promised to speak to the captain of the corvette attached to my mission, who accordingly acquiesced.

M. Colonna paid me a complimentary call to thank me on the part of Madame, and to say that a visit would be very acceptable. Promised to attend in the evening.

July 31 : Visited Madame, in company with Captain Battersby of H.M.S. *Grasshopper*. She got up, as if with difficulty, some seconds after our approach, and made us sit down upon chairs close to her. M. Colonna, her agent M. Bartolucci, and two ladies, entered and sat down soon afterwards. I addressed her as " Madame " and " Altesse." She was very pleasant and unaffected. The old lady is very handsome, of middle size, with a good figure and fresh colour . . .

August 2 : Embarked on His Majesty's brig *Grasshopper*, Captain Battersby, with Madame Letizia, M. Colonna and two *dames d'honneur*, and landed at Elba the same evening. In leaving the inn at Leghorn to walk to the boat, M. Colonna took the arm of Madame with his hat off all the way. Captain Battersby and myself took the arms of the two ladies with our hats on. Crowds followed us and, on quitting the shore, a number of persons hooted, and whistled, and hissed.

Captain Battersby and two of his officers, M. Saveira a passenger, and myself, all dined with Madame on deck. A couch was arranged for her, from which she never stirred during the whole voyage, except once to look out for Napoleon's house, when she mounted upon the top of a gun with great activity.

In this picture of the elderly woman scorning her infirmities and climbing on to a gun " with great activity " to catch a first glimpse of her exiled son's house, we see once more the lineaments of the dazzling adolescent who galloped over the Corsican battlefields among her kinsmen in arms.

THE ISLAND OF ELBA resembled Corsica and Sardinia with its spectacular mountains, wild forests, sandy beaches, eagles'-nest villages and aroma of oranges, lemons, pines, honeysuckle, rosemary, aloes and eucalyptus. This characteristic fragrance was what Letizia noticed first, since it was dark when she arrived and little could be seen of the port but a few flickering lights.

As the *Grasshopper* entered Portoferraio harbour there was no sign of Napoleon. The harbour-master, one of Napoleon's valets, and various officials arrived in a small boat to explain that Napoleon had waited all day for his mother, then, presuming there had been an unforeseen delay, had gone to the hermitage of the Madonna at Marciana in the mountains. They could not tell her, since they did not know, that he was expecting a secret visit from his faithful Polish mistress, the Countess Walewska, and that he had gone to make arrangements for her reception in this out-of-the-way spot. Sir Neil Campbell suggested that Generals Bertrand and Drouet be summoned to welcome Letizia. When Colonna asked her for orders she appeared, according to Sir Neil, " gravely agitated and mortified at no one coming to meet her," and gave her assent to sending for the generals " with great violence." Only when they arrived would she go ashore. The Old Guard were waiting to receive her at the wharf, a carriage drawn by six horses took her to Napoleon's Mulini palace on a cliff top four miles from the harbour, mounted torch-bearers escorted her up the steep streets thronged by cheering Elbans, and she once more had the pleasure of hearing Italian spoken all around her.

Next morning Napoleon returned. His delight at seeing his mother compensated her for the mishap over her arrival. It also astonished the English present, and according to André Pons de l'Hérault, an eyewitness said: " One would have to imagine an ardent young man who, after a cruel separation, finds himself in the presence of his beloved, to form an idea of the ineffable joy his mother's arrival aroused in the Emperor. He gave orders, contradicted them, said yes then no, without knowing what he was doing."

The Villa Mulini was a charming house, its pink façade and green shutters overlooking a typically Mediterranean garden planted with palms, cypresses, box, arum lilies, wild geraniums, figs and olives, vines and maize, acacias and broom, sheltered by a low wall from which the cliff dropped sheerly into the sea. House and garden were enclosed by the walls of a fortress built in the middle of the sixteenth century by Cosimo I, the Medici who transformed Portoferraio from a fishing village into a naval station, renamed it Cosmopoli, defended it against the French and the Turks, and introduced a seafaring population from Sicily and Genoa. Named after the mills that surrounded it until demolished in 1808, the villa had started as a four-room cottage built by Giovanni-Gastone dei Medici for his gardener in 1724. When Elba became French seventy-seven years later, this cottage was enlarged to accommodate artillery and engineering officers. To-day the enlarged villa with its red-tiled floors, pale-green walls, *trompe l'œil* ceilings, its Empire furniture, drapery and chandeliers, its Napoleonic bees and Egyptian motifs, its faded Elban flag, and the bookcase crammed with Napoleon's leather-bound editions of the *Moniteur Universel*, serves both as a museum, always crowded in the tourist season, and as a centre for Elban archæological studies. A plaque on the wall commemorates Napoleon's sojourn in this " august and sovereign house."

There was nothing august or sovereign about it when Letizia came to Elba. Still in the hands of workmen, the villa smelt of new paint and mortar, and Napoleon was doing little more than camp out there. He still believed his wife and son would soon be joining him, so had ordered another story to be added to the house. Deprived of outlets for his energy, he not only supervised the execution of these plans but contributed to the work, often wielding a pickaxe and sharing the workmen's lunch of hard-boiled eggs and bread. It distressed Letizia to find him preparing a room for Marie-Louise, its ceiling decorated with symbols of conjugal fidelity : two doves separated by clouds " but united by a bond that becomes closer the farther they draw apart." He did not know that his wife and son had reached Vienna the very day he moved into the Villa Mulini, and he clung to the notion of their arrival all the more desperately after he learnt of Joséphine's death at fifty-one (precisely the age at which he himself was to die). He wept at the news and shut himself up in his study. Joséphine had been his romantic love, and he did not believe she would have abandoned him in misfortune.

Since the Villa Mulini was still in the builders' hands, Napoleon had taken for Letizia the Casa Vantini, a house on one of the staircase-streets just below the fortress. It is only a few steps' walk from the little church of the Misericordia, where, to-day, the sacristan will show visitors the Emperor's death mask and a cast of his hand, both treasured in a black and gold coffin that is a copy of the one at Les Invalides in Paris.

Letizia was to be happy in the Casa Vantini with its Empire furniture and the *trompe l'œil* tent that struck a fashionably martial note. The local officials were presented to her, and every Sunday she held a levee after Napoleon's ; but for the most part her life was quiet and domestic. During the daytime she read, wrote letters and worked at her tapestry ; in the evenings she and Napoleon walked or drove together, dined and afterwards played reversi, when he would tease her by cheating as he had done years ago. " The Emperor," she noted, " is always busy trying to render my stay here agreeable." He need not have made much effort. Nothing could have been more agreeable to her than being free for the first time in twenty-one years of fearing for her favourite son's life on some far-flung battlefield.

A<small>T</small> <small>ELBA</small> <small>NAPOLEON</small> could never be busy enough for his own needs. He had talked beforehand of the delights of rest and retirement, but within three days of his arrival he had begun riding all over the island, inspecting local defences, visiting the tin mines that had been a feature of Elba since the Etruscan days, and planning the reorganisation of his tiny kingdom as thoroughly as if it had been a great empire. He asked questions about the salt ponds and the tunny fisheries, decided to plant more vineyards, build roads, pave the towns, provide more water supplies and add to the fortifications. The Old Guard worked with the local labourers on these projects, and on building a hospital and, of course, a theatre. The Bonapartes found it hard to imagine life without drama, even over and above that which their own lives provided. But all this only reminded him of what he considered his lasting achievement : " the construction of the Louvre, the public granaries, the Bank of France, the Canal de l'Ourcq, the Paris water-supply ; the drains, quays and many improvements in the capital." His brothers and sisters applied their exuberant artistic instincts to their private lives and houses, their objects of art, their novels, poems, and archæological studies. Napoleon spent his on cities. Nevertheless, he persisted in trying to fill his time in Elba. He formed a cabinet headed by the faithful General Bertrand, Grand Marshal of the Palace, and entrusted the military command of Portoferraio to Cambronne, whose army consisted of the Old Guard, 800 local recruits and 200 men labelled " miscellaneous." It was most unlikely that this tiny world would long hold a man to whom recently realms and islands were as plates dropped from his pocket.

In August Napoleon took Letizia to Marciana Alta, a quiet Medici village on a hilltop overlooking the Gulf of Procchio. One can still rent the whitewashed, red-tiled bedroom that Letizia occupied that summer. The superb view over the Mediterranean is unchanged and a plaque on the house commemorates her stay :

NAPOLEON THE GREAT
Received appreciated hospitality
In this dwelling
The property of the brothers
The chevaliers Giuseppe and Giovanni Paolo Vadi
Their grandfather Corbona Vadi
Being then mayor of Marciana
From the 21 to the 24 of August 1814
and
LETIZIA RAMOLINO HIS AUGUST MOTHER
From August 25 until September
The Commune of Marciana
Announces this to posterity
1894

Letizia was still there on September 1st, when Napoleon left her in order to welcome a woman and child locally rumoured to be Marie-Louise and the King of Rome. They were his Polish mistress Marie Walewska and Alexandre, the child she had borne him four years earlier. Accompanied by her brother and sister, she and Napoleon stayed at the hermitage of the Madonna. The hermits who usually lived there vacated rooms for Madame Walewska and Napoleon had ordered a tent to serve as dining-room between the Hermitage and the chapel. A certain amount of romance of the " Napoleon did not emerge from the tent . . . until morning " kind has been woven around an encounter intended principally to settle the future of the little boy, who was to prove far more fortunate than his half-brother, the King of Rome. Whether or not Letizia was aware of this meeting is not known as she made no recorded comment, but it is in any case unlikely to have shocked her. Despite the austerity of her personal standards, she never complained of her children's sexual appetites unless they threatened the interests of the family as a whole.

Letizia spent money with such uncharacteristic lavishness in Elba that Napoleon contributed nothing to her household expenses, telling Bertrand that to let her pay all her own bills was the sole way to restrain her. Not only did she spend lavishly, but as the French Government never paid the income promised to Napoleon, she gave a sum Baron Larrey estimates at 500,000 piastres towards the upkeep of the Old Guard. When old soldiers reached Elba and found no place for themselves in the small garrison, she insisted on seeing them before they left and giving money to each one. In October she sent one of her ladies-in-waiting to Rome for her diamonds ; these she offered to Napoleon, who, much touched, refused to accept more than a buckle for his sword-belt. Among the people on whom she showered gifts at this time was a young girl named Rosa Mellini, daughter of a retired Elban colonel. Letizia liked her so much that she asked her to be one of her ladies-in-waiting. Rosa accepted joyfully and remained with her, acting as daughter, friend, confidante and secretary, for the rest of Letizia's life. From now on most of Letizia's letters were dictated to Rosa.

No sooner was Letizia known to be in Elba than Corsicans began flocking to her in hope of employment. " Madame," says Pons de l'Hérault, " was Corsican in the complete sense of the word. Her accent, her habits, her memories, everything evoked her early years, and one sometimes asked oneself if she had ever left Corsica." Even so, she could not assist all her compatriots, and she wrote to Lucien : " I am very sorry not to have been able to place Tavera, but there was nothing available. Every day we have to refuse someone. You cannot imagine how many people are arriving here." With this she sent Lucien a present of "fishes' eggs, very good with figs." She also gave him her best mahogany bed, just delivered from Paris, and asked him to buy her a house in Rome, which she hoped to use as the family headquarters.

At the end of October Pauline reached Elba, to the joy of her mother and brother. Napoleon gave her the rooms he had prepared for his wife, since he was now aware that Marie-Louise had taken the one-eyed Austrian General Neipperg as a lover. Neipperg had made her acquaintance in Dresden in 1812, when she and Napoleon were there as conquerors, and after Napoleon's defeat Metternich had encouraged the affair on the shrewd assumption that once she had a lover Marie-Louise would completely forget her husband. Pauline was surprised to find in these rooms some of the Borghese furniture that her husband had sent from Turin to Rome by sea. A storm had driven the ship into Elba, and as Napoleon was just then short of furniture he had requisitioned it, saying, " Like that, it remains in the family." So did the symbols of conjugal fidelity, which were scarcely more appropriate to Pauline's bedroom ceiling than they would have been to that of Marie-Louise.

Letizia had brought Napoleon devotion, companionship and moral support. Pauline, whom Stendhal called " *la divine Princesse Borghese*," introduced gaiety into his exile. Always fond of pleasure, she exaggerated this taste in order to provide amusement for Napoleon. Her beauty and her charm drew everyone to her, and she immediately made a friend of anyone her brother singled out. No local festivity, village concert or peasant dance was too insignificant for her. She gave balls and receptions, engaged singers, organised amateur theatricals, superintended rehearsals and designed costumes ; and although she teased and petted Napoleon and made him laugh, even against his inclination, just as she had done when she was a child, she also yielded to him in every way and treated him with the most tender and tactful respect. She never failed to curtsy to him precisely as she would have done at the Tuileries, and she made dozens of small sacrifices that from such a coquette were heroic—changing out of a newly-arrived evening dress because Napoleon disapproved of it, and refraining from wearing her beloved diamonds lest their magnificence humiliate the Elba ladies. In all this Pauline was aided and abetted by Letizia, who was never again to be as light-hearted as when she shared Napoleon's exile.

D ESPITE LETIZIA'S AND Pauline's efforts to lessen the tedium of his exile, Napoleon became increasingly restless. Elba could not absorb the energies of a man who had dreamed of creating the United States of Europe and a vast eastern empire, who had planned a canal to join the Mediterranean to the Red Sea—and, above all, a man who had acquired the habit of seeing his dreams come true. He no longer believed that his wife and son would join him; nor did he expect the French Government to pay the income it had promised him, though both the Czar and Lord Castlereagh had protested about this. Lord Castlereagh had also agreed with Talleyrand at the Congress of Vienna that Napoleon ought to be deported still farther from Europe, perhaps to one of the Azores islands or to St. Lucia or St. Helena. This proposal was discussed all over Europe, and news of it soon reached Napoleon and added to his fevered restlessness.

Meanwhile French public opinion had been veering in his favour. The abrogation of the Continental blockade was ruining French manufacturers and, despite the Bourbons' promises, *émigrés* were returning to seize lands for which the owners had paid. The censorship had been re-established; torture was restored by the royal courts in Piedmont; the university in Paris temporarily closed; royalist priests said expiatory masses for the crimes of the revolution; and twelve thousand officers of the Grand Army were retired on half pay while twenty thousand royalists were promoted for their services against Revolutionary France. As a result, revolutionary passions revived and ex-soldiers forgot their hardships, remembered their glory, and began to long for the Little Corporal. A popular song of that year began :

> *Conservez bien la croix d'honneur,*
> *A dit l'Empereur à ses braves,*
> *Le prix, créé par la valeur,*
> *N'était pas fait pour des esclaves.*
> *Je vois un avenir honteux*
> *Se montrer pour ma belle France,*
> *Et lorsque je quitte ces lieux,*
> *Un roi revient sans qu'on y pense.*

(Take care of the cross of honour, the Emperor told his soldiers, its value was created by valour, it was not made for slaves. I foresee a shameful future for my beautiful France, and as I leave here a king slips back.)

Bonapartists meeting in the street would ask each other, " Do you believe in Christ ? " and get the reply, " Yes and in the Resurrection."

Much of this was reported to Napoleon on the night of February 13th, 1815, by a visitor who came to Elba disguised as a sailor in a small felucca. This was Fleury de Chaboulon, a former State Auditor and Sub-Prefect, who had been living in retirement since the Restoration. He left for Naples the following night and Napoleon immediately began to plan his incredibly audacious return to France. The curtain was about to rise on the Hundred Days, which Balzac called " a fairy-tale play in three months."

THREE DAYS LATER Sir Neil Campbell mentioned to Napoleon that he had to make a trip to Leghorn and Florence on official business. (He was also going to visit his Italian mistress.) Napoleon expressed the hope that Sir Neil would be back by February 28th, in time for the ball Pauline was giving that evening. Sir Neil assured him that he would do his utmost to be present. After this exchange of courtesies, Napoleon knew that he had twelve days in which to prepare his escape from Elba. The moment Sir Neil sailed, Napoleon ordered Drouot to refit *L'Inconstant* and equip her with twenty-six cannons. This brig and six smaller vessels composed his entire fleet.

Letizia was not told of his plans until the day before he sailed. In her *Souvenirs* she says :

One evening when we were at Portoferraio, the Emperor seemed to me gayer than usual. He suggested Pauline and I play a game of écarté [a card game for two players]. A minute later he left us and went and shut himself up in his study. Noticing that he did not come back, I went to his room to call him, and the chamberlain told me he had gone into the garden. I remember it was one of the mildest spring nights we had had ; the moon was shining brilliantly among the trees, and the Emperor was alone, walking with hasty steps along the alleys of the garden. Suddenly he stopped short and, leaning his head against a fig tree, exclaimed, " Yet I must tell my mother." At this I went to him and said, with the liveliest impatience, " What is the matter with you this evening ? I can see you are much more absorbed by your thoughts than usual."

His hand on his forehead, the Emperor hesitated a moment, then replied : " Yes, I must tell you, but I forbid you to repeat what I am going to confide in you to any-one, not even to Pauline." He smiled, embraced me, and went on, " Well, I must tell you that I am leaving here."

" To go where ? "

" To Paris. But above all, I want your advice."

" Ah ! Allow me to forget for a moment that I am your mother." I reflected, then added, " Heaven will not permit you to die by poison, nor in an activity unworthy of you, but with your sword in your hand. Go, my son, fulfil your destiny, you were not made to die on this island."

Few scenes in Letizia's stormy life are more moving than this exchange with her son in that moonlit garden by the Mediter-ranean. She had been happy in Elba, had begun to hope that Napoleon was genuinely reconciled to their life in this homelike place. Yet when he offered her a chance to detain him she refused to allow herself to act possessively and did precisely what she asked his permission to do : forgot for a moment that she was his mother, considered nothing but the imperative needs of his nature and genius, and gave his plans the encourage-ment of the one person for whose opinion he had unqualified respect.

On the morning of Sunday, February 26th, Napoleon held his usual levee. He then attended nine o'clock mass with Letizia and Pauline. At eleven a small boat arrived, carrying a courier. His miniature army of 1,100 (600 of the Old Guard, with the Corsican battalion and some Polish and Elban volun-teers) assembled at two in the afternoon. Napoleon appeared in his legendary green uniform with the famous grey redingote, and when he announced their embarkation for that evening the soldiers broke ranks and flung themselves into one another's arms and at his feet, shouting " *Vive l'Empereur !* " The Elbans joined in with " *Viva l'Imperatore !* " and " *Evviva Napoleone !* "

Letizia and Pauline watched in tears. Napoleon had already instructed them to wait at Portoferraio until he could send a ship to take them to France. In his farewell speech to the National Guard, he said : " I entrust the defence of the place to you. I cannot give you a greater proof of confidence than by leaving my mother and sister in your care." He also had a private conversation with his mother's chamberlain, in which he begged the latter not to let Letizia out of his sight and said he counted on Colonna to look after her. Meanwhile Letizia had taken aside Napoleon's faithful valet Marchand, commended her son to his care, and given him a comfit box (Napoleon always carried aniseed-flavoured liquorice) decorated with her portrait, saying, " Let the Emperor use this in future in place of the one he has now. If misfortune overtakes him, do not abandon him." Here she broke down and put her hands over her eyes. This Marchand who described Letizia as " perfect in her noble simplicity," played an important part in Napoleon's life. Fidelity ran in his family. His mother, who was cradle-rocker to the King of Rome had accompanied the child to Vienna, and Marchand unhesitatingly accompanied Napoleon both to Elba and to St. Helena. After Napoleon's death all the Bonapartes showed Marchand gratitude, and in 1869 he was made a count by Napoleon III.

At four o'clock the troops were served with soup, and at five o'clock the call to arms sounded. At seven they marched out of the fortifications, quickly and without music, to the quay where they embarked in small boats moored alongside. Two hours later Napoleon embraced his mother and sister and drove to the harbour with General Bertrand in Pauline's small carriage drawn by four horses. The town had been lit up and lanterns swayed all along the ramparts. The churches were packed, and at the landing-stage the local authorities, civil and military, were waiting to wish Napoleon well. As he came aboard the brig *L'Inconstant* his soldiers began to sing the Marseillaise. The singing spread from ship to ship, was taken up on shore, and travelled through the town and all the way up to the citadel, where Letizia had already resumed her habit of waiting impassively for news from alien battlefields.

AFTER NAPOLEON HAD sailed, Letizia wrote Lucien a letter intended to deceive anyone who might intercept it. She sounds as wary as an author unwilling to reveal the plot of his next book : " I leave here in three days, weather permitting. The Emperor has gone with all his men, but I do not know his destination. I hope to see you at Civita Vecchia, also Louis. It is essential that you tell me if there is any reason why I should not come to Rome, if so I will go farther. I chose Rome on account of my extreme desire to see you, Louis and my brother."

Next day she was on the terrace at dawn. At noon an English corvette was signalled on its way from Leghorn with Sir Neil Campbell, who had kept his promise to return in time for Pauline's ball. When he heard of Napoleon's escape he hurried to confront Letizia and Pauline and furiously assured them that, since the Mediterranean was full of Allied ships, Napoleon must by now be a prisoner. His anger increased at the sight of Letizia's outward composure, maddening courtesy and obstinate insistence that she had no idea of her son's whereabouts. It would have been difficult for Sir Neil Campbell to hinder Napoleon's escape, since, according to Samuel Rogers's *Italian Journal*, the English Commissioner's position had been vaguely defined as merely " a sort of policeman " who might not even call on Napoleon uninvited. This did not lessen Sir Neil's fury. Frustrated by Letizia's impassivity and Pauline's impertinence, he became, says William Hazlitt, " not a little nettled at their want of English plain dealing and sincerity in not betraying their son and brother into his hands, out of the love which he [Sir Neil] bore to his native country."

His attitude was so threatening that Pauline, fearing he might take her as a hostage, decided to follow her brother's example. Thanks to a French officer, she was able to hire a felucca in which she escaped at two in the morning three days later. She landed at Viareggio, where the customs officers, immediately subjugated, hastened to give up their rooms to her. She would have done better, however, to remain with Letizia, since the Austrians presently put her under house arrest in Viareggio and thus deprived her of her last opportunity to see her beloved brother again.

A week after Napoleon's departure, Letizia wrote to Lucien triumphantly :

It is a pleasure for me to give you news of our dear Emperor's departure from this town and arrival at the Gulf of Juan, near Antibes.

The Emperor left Portoferraio at nine o'clock in the evening of the 26th ; on the morning of the 27th he saw an English corvette between him and the Continent ; at midday he saw a French corvette in the direction of Corsica. It was going to meet the fleet and exchanged words with the Emperor's brig. The sight of all these warships made him uneasy, but he was fully prepared to put up a fight and his lucky star preserved him from fear and peril. So much so that in the evening he compared the day with that of Austerlitz.

At five in the morning of the 28th, the Emperor saw to the north of him the vessel he had noticed the previous evening, but at ten o'clock it vanished. The wind was favourable, my dear son, because they covered four and a half *milles* [8 miles] an hour. At ten o'clock that same morning the Emperor had the tricolour cockade fastened to his hat, and the troops did the same amid cries of " *Vive l'Empereur !* " The transport ships, which had remained far behind, caught up with him at dawn on March 1st. This delighted him. At last, my dear son, the fleet dropped anchor in the Gulf of Juan and the troops disembarked.

The local inhabitants received the Emperor with joy. [A customs officer who saw them come ashore reported that during the afternoon the military band repeatedly played the popular air " *Où est-ce qu'on peut être mieux que dans le sein de sa famille?* " (Where can one be better than in the bosom of one's family?)] Couriers were sent to every department to announce the day of resurrection, and proclamations were dispatched. The Emperor counts on the loyalty of the troops scattered all over France, especially as he met a courier *en route* from Paris to the Prince of Monaco who assured him he would be received with open arms by the French Army and people. The Emperor left Lyons at midnight on March 1st. He is well, and I am overjoyed.

Equally though differently dazzled was Byron, who wrote to Thomas Moore on March 17th : " Making every allowance for talent and most consummate daring, there is, after all, a good deal in luck or destiny. He might have been stopped by our frigates—or wrecked in the Gulf of Lyons, which is particularly tempestuous—or—a thousand things. But he is certainly Fortune's favourite, and

> Once fairly set out on his party of pleasure,
> Taking towns at his liking and crowns at his leisure,
> From Elba to Lyons and Paris he goes
> Making *balls* for the ladies and *bows* to his foes.

" You must have seen the account of his driving into the middle of the royal army, and the immediate effect of his pretty speeches. And now if he don't drub the Allies, there is ' no purchase in money.' If he can take France by himself, the devil's in't if he don't repulse the invaders, when backed by those celebrated sworders—those boys of the blade, the Imperial Guard, and the old and new army. It is impossible not to be dazzled and overwhelmed by his character and career."

Napoleon's progress across France by the highway known

to-day as the Route Napoléon was indeed dazzling and over-whelming. In inviting his soldiers to follow him he had said, " Victory will march rapidly. The eagle, with the national colours, will fly from steeple to steeple up to Notre-Dame "— and that was precisely what happened. On March 7th Louis XVIII summoned the Chamber of Peers and the Chamber of Deputies to an extraordinary session. Napoleon's name was not mentioned in the convocation, but ambiguous references to ill-will and treachery indicated that momentous events were under way. In Vienna, early that same morning, Metternich received a despatch from Genoa reporting Napoleon's dis-appearance from Elba. Six days later the Allied Governments declared him an outlaw and public enemy. On March 19th, the King fled from the Tuileries to Belgium.

Next day, which was the King of Rome's fourth birthday, about two thousand travel-stained troops, each man wearing the tricolour cockade, marched into Paris by the Boulevard Mont-martre. Their cries of " *Vive l'Empereur* " were echoed by those of the populace, who rushed to link arms with them. Growing larger every minute, the procession was constantly and vocifer-ously invited to halt at wine shops, where great cans of wine were freely distributed for toasts to the Emperor and the Old Guard. Among the well-known figures who crowded to their windows to see Napoleon's troops enter the capital were the actresses Mesdemoiselles George and Mars, each of whom carried a huge bouquet of violets, which so struck the public imagination that from then on these flowers have been con-sidered a Bonapartist emblem. The crowds pressed on down the boulevards and the Rue de la Paix to the Place Vendôme, where they waited for further orders.

At half past six shouts came from the direction of the Tuileries. These grew thunderous when a small escort galloped into the Cour du Carrousel, followed by Napoleon's carriage. The crowd pressed around him so ardently that he was scarcely able to alight. A lapel torn from his coat was instantly divided among his adorers. When he reached the bottom of the grand staircase his officers insisted on carrying him into the palace on their shoulders. The Emperor was home again. He had marched from the Mediterranean to the Tuileries, without firing a shot, in barely twenty days : a phenomenally short time from a military and political viewpoint, but an exhaustingly long one for the elderly woman waiting for news in Elba.

Now it was Letizia who grew restless. The ship Napoleon ordered to go for her was held up and at last she had to resign herself to sailing on the *Joachim*, sent from Naples by Caroline. This took her to the Palazzo Portici, just outside Naples, which was the Murats' favourite residence. Ten years later Lady Blessington described this palace : " It comprehends a magnificent prospect of the bay, being only divided from the sea by a garden filled with the finest trees, plants and flowers. No palace that I have ever seen so completely realises the notion I had formed of an Italian one . . . This residence owes all its comfort and elegance to the good taste of Madame Murat, ex-Queen of Naples . . . The present sovereign and his family [the restored Bourbons] are said to have been hardly able to recognise their ancient abodes, when they returned from Sicily . . . Ferdinand is reported to have said that Murat was an excellent upholsterer, and had furnished his palaces perfectly to his taste . . . The bedroom, bath, boudoir and library of Madame Murat are faultless specimens of Parisian elegance and comfort . . . One of the *salons* particularly attracted our attention. The ceiling and walls were covered with panels of the most beautiful china of the ancient and celebrated manufactory of Capo di Monte, of which specimens are now become so rare. The panels have landscapes and groups finely painted, and are bordered with wreaths of flowers the size of Nature, of the richest and most varied dyes, in alto-rilievo ; among which, birds of the gayest plumage, squirrels and monkeys . . . We were shown two portraits of Murat . . . An air of braggadocio characterises both, conveying the impression of a bold captain of banditti,

dressed in the rich spoils he had plundered . . . but the countenance is remarkable for an expression of good humour . . .
Murat and his wife are remembered with kindness, if not
lamented, by the Neapolitans."

In this sunlit palace Letizia found the ambitious Caroline
surrounded by her four handsome children and determined to
regain her mother's good opinion and prove her renewed
loyalty to Napoleon. Always direct, Letizia reproached her
daughter with ingratitude and treachery, and when Caroline said
that she had acted under her husband's influence, Letizia
retorted: " If you could not control him, you should have
opposed him. But what sort of struggle did you make ? Whose
blood was shed ? Only over your dead body should your
husband have been able to strike your brother, your benefactor
and master." (This conversation was later described by Napoleon at St. Helena.) Caroline's assurances of remorse and of
Murat's determination to make up for his momentary defection
—on March 30th he called upon the Italians to rise against the
Austrians—brought about a partial reconciliation between
mother and daughter, encouraged by Fesch, who had reached
Naples three days earlier in search of his sister. In moments of
crisis Fesch's first thoughts were always for Letizia.

Joseph had already left Switzerland and rallied to Napoleon,
while Jérôme hastened to Naples in order to accompany his
mother and uncle to Paris. They all three sailed on the *Joachim*
in April, but the wind was so unfavourable that, after tossing
for eighteen hours, they were driven back into port. The
Melpomene, sent by Napoleon from Toulon, was sunk by the
English just outside the Bay of Naples. Ten days passed without
another ship coming to the Bonapartes' rescue, and with every
day their danger from the Austrians increased. On May 9th
they heard gunfire at sea, and from a hill-top Jérôme saw a
French and an English vessel in combat. By skilful manœuvring
the French ship, the *Dryade*, got within shelter of the coastal
defences and landed General Belliard at the fortress town of
Gaeta, north-west of Naples.

The orders that the general brought from Napoleon arrived too late to prevent Murat, now his brother-in-law's only ally, from attacking the Austrians as rashly as he had previously supported them, thus ruining Napoleon's plan to conciliate Austria and lessen the number of enemies he would have to face simultaneously. Deserted by his troops, Murat fled from Naples, disguised as a sailor. Caroline and her children were later seized by the Austrians and taken to Trieste.

Jérôme telegraphed to the *Dryade's* commander to wait at Gaeta, and he and his mother and uncle drove up the coast, past the Grotto of the Sibyl and the Elysian Fields, a twelve and a half hour journey through wild, bandit-infested country. They sailed on May 13th, only just in time to elude the Austrians.

While the *Dryade* was off the coast of Corsica, the captain sighted an English vessel pursuing them and decided to put in to Bastia. As soon as the townspeople heard that the Emperor's mother was aboard the *Dryade*, cheering crowds flocked to the quayside. A salute of honour was fired as Letizia came ashore on the governor's arm, and the streets were lined by the National Guard and decorated with hastily improvised arches of leaves and flowers. According to Jérôme's Memoirs, he was receiving local notabilities at the house of their cousin, the Duc de Padone, when news came that the English ship had disappeared. The wind being favourable, they quickly re-embarked, to the consternation of the local ladies who were already planning what to wear for the ball Letizia was to have given that evening. As the *Dryade* moved out of harbour, Letizia saw the austere fourteenth-century citadel, the tower of St. Mary's church and the Dragon's jetty for the last time. She was sixty-four and would never see Corsica again.

The wind forced them into the Gulf of Juan and they landed on May 22nd at precisely the spot where Napoleon had landed nearly three months earlier. They spent the night in Antibes, full for Letizia of memories of the home Napoleon had given her when he was first promoted general. Many waters had flowed through the river of that garden since she washed her children's clothes there and slapped Pauline for stealing the neighbours' figs.

Letizia and Fesch travelled up through Fréjus, Brignoles, Aix, Avignon, the Pont Saint-Esprit and Montélimar towards Lyons. Impetuous Jérôme hastened ahead, leaving them to return together as they had left, two wary Corsicans in a land temporarily dominated by their clan. As Fesch was still Archbishop of Lyons, they were welcomed there with pomp as well as enthusiasm. When they reached Paris on June 1st, they discovered they had just missed the Ceremony of the Champ de Mai, an impressive piece of pageantry suggested to Napoleon by Lucien, who had arrived from Rome as the Pope's emissary to solicit the evacuation of the papal territories occupied by Murat. Letizia heard with joy that Joseph had acted as peacemaker between his two brothers and that Napoleon had greeted Lucien enthusiastically, making him a French prince and giving him as residence the Palais-Royal, always hitherto allotted to the younger branch of the reigning family. At the Champ de Mai an open-air mass had been celebrated in the presence of thousands of Parisians and 20,000 delegates from the provinces, after which Napoleon had publicly sworn fidelity to the Empire. Joseph, Lucien and Jérôme stood beside him, all in uniform, typifying family solidarity. New flags were distributed to the Grand Army and 40,000 soldiers declared their allegiance in a thunderous " *Nous le jurons.*" Listening to resounding accounts of this, Letizia could believe that her nightmares were over and, as she had written to Lucien from Elba : " He is well and I am overjoyed."

LETIZIA ATTENDED a special session of the Chamber on June 7th to hear Napoleon address the Legislative Assembly and receive oaths of loyalty from the Senators and Deputies. An eyewitness, Mademoiselle Cochelet, describes the occasion in her *Mémoires sur la Reine Hortense et la Famille Impériale* :

Towards four o'clock there was the sound of a door opening, and all eyes turned to the tribune adorned for Madame and Queen Hortense, who were arriving followed by their ladies-in-waiting.

The Emperor's mother must have been one of the most beautiful women who ever existed. She was at this time about sixty-five, and still striking on account of the regularity of her features and the atmosphere of nobility that emanated from all her person. I remember she wore a high-necked lace dress, its long sleeves lined with orange satin, and a toque with white plumes, which was decorated, as was her bodice, with superb diamonds. Her beautiful black eyes, with long lashes and delicately arched eyebrows, were as brilliant as those of a young woman . . . Queen Hortense's fair hair and complexion and her graceful movements were in striking contrast with the classical gravity that was her mother-in-law's dominant physical characteristic.

(Until extreme old age Letizia retained enough coquetry to use a white liquid cosmetic, corresponding to to-day's foundation make-up, that suited her admirably but gave her neuralgia.)

On her arrival from Elba, Letizia had refused to meet Hortense, whom she blamed for having remained in Paris during the restoration and accepted the title of Duchesse de

Saint-Leu from Louis XVIII. Napoleon had already told Hortense what he thought of this, but he also knew that she was fundamentally devoted to him, so he persuaded his mother to change her mind, pointing out that Hortense had been obliged to consider her children's interests, had done all she could for the family, and had undoubtedly behaved far better than Caroline. Letizia received Hortense only to please him, but for the first time a genuine affection sprang up between them, an affection which was to be strengthened by Hortense's attitude after Waterloo and to last the rest of their lives.

Despite the fervour with which Paris had welcomed him back, Napoleon was in a melancholy mood. Some spring of energy seemed broken in him. He thought constantly of his son, who was still a prisoner in Austria. Méneval, his former Secretary of Portfolio, had recently seen the child in Vienna, and reported that when asked if he had any message for his father, the little boy pulled him aside and whispered, " Tell him, Monsieur Méva, that I still love him dearly." For the first time Napoleon was drawn to the past rather than the future, and when Letizia accompanied him to Malmaison she realised that the unfaithful but warm-hearted Joséphine had been a better wife than the voluntarily absent Marie-Louise.

On Sunday evening, June 11th, Letizia and Napoleon presided over what was to be their last family dinner. Not all her children were present—never once had she and Carlo had an opportunity to share a meal with all their children—but it was a joy to her to see Joseph, Napoleon, Lucien and Jérôme united in amity. Of all the family only Louis, sulking in Florence, was absent from choice, but he was represented by his sons, eleven-year-old Napoleon-Louis and seven-year-old Louis-Napoleon, who were brought in by their mother Hortense, at the end of dinner.

Napoleon showed particular tenderness to both his nephews as if this were the only way in which he could express his love for the child in Vienna.

Next day Napoleon left to command the Grand Army,

already marching to defy the rest of Europe. Once more Letizia could do little but wait and pray. His immediate aim was to stop the Allies from completing their preparations. Wellington's army at Antwerp and Blücher's on the Rhine totalled 210,000 men, all to be concentrated in the Namur region. Napoleon planned to get there first and prevent their joining forces. His own army of 124,000 men crossed the Sambre at Charleroi on June 15th. That same day the Prussians were warned of his approach by a royalist deserter, General Count de Bourmont. Next day Napoleon defeated Blücher at Ligny, but without completely crushing the Prussian Army. Then, leaving Grouchy with 30,000 men to pursue Blücher, he rounded on the English. Meanwhile Wellington had taken up a strong position on the Mont-Saint-Jean plateau, south of the village of Waterloo, barring the route to Brussels.

When the battle of Waterloo (which Wellington called " a damned close-run thing ") started on Sunday, June 18th, Napoleon was worn out by an agonising attack of hæmorrhoids which had started two days earlier. There had been a violent storm the previous evening, so the ground was still a morass, and the soldiers were hampered by the mud that clung to their boots. In order to give them some respite, and above all to allow the ground to get dry enough for artillery manœuvres, Napoleon held off action until midday. This inevitable delay was fatal to the French, since it gave the Prussians time to join forces with the English Army. At two o'clock Bülow attacked the right wing of the French Army with 30,000 men. This first assault failed and Napoleon flung his cavalry against the English centre. For three hours they fought with no decisive result. Towards evening, completely paralysed, they had to give up. Napoleon's remaining cavalry managed to repulse the Prussians and the Guard made a last effort against the English. Two-thirds of the Guard had been shot down when a second Prussian corps appeared and routed the main French army. What was left of the Old Guard, three battalions under Generals Christiani, Cambronne and Roguet, formed a square and fought on alone.

A number of *cantinières*, women as fearless in battle as had been Letizia herself, rallied to the Guard for this celebrated " last quarter of an hour." Among them was the typical figure of fifty-year-old Marie-Tête-de-Bois (Wooden-headed Mary), considered by the veterans as a regimental mascot. An ugly, good-hearted creature who smelt of pipe tobacco, wine and brandy, she had survived seventeen campaigns and carried her six-months-old baby through the retreat from Moscow without either of them so much as catching a cold. Her soldier husband and trumpet-major son had been killed defending Paris, and, determined to serve the Emperor once more, she had marched with the army to Waterloo and chosen to remain with the Guard to the end. She was distributing brandy to the wounded when a bullet hit her full in the face. A dying grenadier said teasingly, "You don't look too good, Marie." She answered: "Possibly. But anyway I'm the daughter, widow and mother of soldiers. *Vive l'Empereur!* "—and on this she died. It was during this fatal stage of the battle that Cambronne immortalised his name with his famous oath. When the enemy called on him to surrender he yelled " *Merde!* " a word still known to every French schoolchild as " *le mot de Cambronne.*" Like Marie Tête-de-Bois and many other old soldiers whose names have faded away, Cambronne believed that " the Guard doesn't surrender, it dies."

An English account of the debacle is provided by Fanny Burney, who was in Brussels at the time. She wrote to her husband: " The maimed, wounded, bleeding, fainting, arrive still every minute . . . Jérôme is said to be killed [Jérôme fought heroically but, although wounded, was to live another forty-five years] . . . The Imperial Guard is almost completely annihilated. They fought like demons. Napoleon cried out continually to them, the prisoners say, ' *A Bruxelles, mes enfants! A Bruxelles!* ' They were reported one day to be actually arrived here. I never saw, never, indeed, felt such consternation . . . Murat is dead of his wounds." (Murat was not present at Waterloo.)

Rumours swayed both sides. The writer and politician Benjamin Constant, who was in Paris on the day of Waterloo, noted in his journal that a great victory was reported and a hundred cannon fired in celebration, which increased the shock when the news of defeat arrived. Napoleon reached Paris on June 21st and in conversation with Constant (a former opponent who had now rallied to him) said : " If I abdicate to-day, in two days' time you will no longer have an army. These poor fellows do not understand your subtleties. Is it credible that metaphysical axioms, declarations of rights, harangues from the tribune, will stop an army disbanding ? To reject me when I landed at Cannes, that I can conceive possible ; to abandon me now is what I cannot understand. A government cannot be overthrown with impunity when the enemy is only twenty-five leagues away. Does anyone imagine that the foreign powers will be won over by fine words ? If they had dethroned me fifteen days ago, there would have been some spirit in it ; but as it is, I am part of what strangers attack, so I am part of what France is bound to defend. In giving me up, she gives up herself, she avows her weakness, she acknowledges herself conquered, she courts the insolence of the conqueror. It is not the love of liberty that deposes me, but Waterloo ; it is fear, and a fear of which your enemy will take advantage."

Fear indeed abounded. Constant noted in his journal : " The end is approaching. A complete debacle. No more army, no more cannon, no more means of defence . . . the Chamber cold, not knowing how to save itself . . . the Emperor sent for me . . . He is still calm and full of spirit. I think he will abdicate to-morrow. The wretches who were eager to serve him when he crushed liberty are abandoning him now that he is establishing it." Among those abandoning him were Talleyrand and Fouché, a pair described by Chateaubriand as " Vice leaning on the arm of Crime." On June 22nd Napoleon abdicated for the second time in favour of his son, though he had no illusions as to who would immediately succeed him.

Letizia's only comfort during these apocalyptical days, many hours of which she spent restlessly pacing the gardens of the Palace of the Élysée on Hortense's arm, came from the way Joseph, Lucien and Jérôme stood by their brother. On June 26th Lucien wrote to Pauline : " By now you will know of the new misfortunes of the Emperor, who has just abdicated in favour of his son. He is going to the United States of America, where we will all join him. He is calm and full of courage. I shall try to get to my family in Rome, so as to take them to America . . . If your health permits [Pauline was seriously ill] we shall see each other again . . . Adieu, my dear sister—Mamma, Jérôme and I embrace you warmly." The following day Napoleon's son was officially proclaimed Napoleon II, as ineffectually as Louis XVI's imprisoned son had been proclaimed Louis XVII. Meanwhile the Allies were bringing Louis XVIII back to France, " in the baggage train," said those who did not want him.

After abdicating, Napoleon went to Malmaison. The famous roses, of which Joséphine had had two hundred and fifty varieties planted and tended by hand-picked English and Scottish gardeners, were in bloom, and their scent reminded him of the days when his ships had searched all over the world for rare plants for his wife. Now the world was closing in on him, and even at Malmaison his situation was so precarious that the faithful Comte de la Bédoyère, whose loyalty was to cost him his life, tried to reassure Letizia by insisting Napoleon have a bodyguard. Young Audiffredi, a relative of Joséphine's and formerly one of the Emperor's pages, slept fully armed outside Napoleon's bedroom door. (Refused permission to accompany Napoleon to St. Helena, this boy returned in despair to Martinique and died at eighteen.)

By the afternoon of June 29th Napoleon was ready to leave for the west coast port of Rochefort and so to America. The last survivors of the Old Guard left in tears, and Hortense, who knew that her stepfather had kept little ready money for himself, sewed her diamond necklace into the lining of his clothes. Shortly before his death Napoleon was to give this necklace to

Marchand, saying, " When you arrive in France it will enable you to live in comfort until you receive the legacy I have left you."

Napoleon was finally alone with Letizia when a valet knocked at the door and announced that a National Guardsman had arrived to say good-bye to the Emperor. It was the great actor Talma, an old friend who could not be turned away and thus witnessed part of a scene as moving as any in the classic tragedies he had so often performed before mother and son. In his Memoirs Talma wrote : " Of what a beautiful tragic scene was I a witness. What a spectacle, this separation of Madame Mère and her son ! Although it forced no outward signs of emotion from the Emperor, yet the expression of his fine features, and his attitude and unspoken thoughts were eloquent."

It was thirty-seven years since Letizia and Napoleon first parted, when he had sailed as a child from Corsica to the country he was to rule and from which he was now to be for ever exiled. She hoped to join him in America, but many an obstacle stood between them and yet another strange new world, and now she could not restrain her tears. But all she said at the last was " Farewell, my son," and he " Farewell, Mamma." Letizia must have wept over her husband's death and on many another occasion, but of the six times when she is recorded as having done so, four were for Napoleon and one for Napoleon's son. Both her pride and her grief were summed up in him, and in later years she said, " My life ended with the Emperor's fall."

V

Night : Italy

1815-36

Je prévois déjà tout ce qu'il faut prévoir.
Mon unique espérance est dans mon désespoir.

RACINE : Bajazet

La noble dame, en son palais de Rome,
Aime à filer ; car, bien jeune, autrefois,
Elle filait en allaitant cet homme
Qui depuis l'entoura de reines et de rois.
Près d'elle, assise, est la vieille servante
Qui, nouveau-né, le reçut dans ses bras.
Au bruit de leurs fuseaux elles disent : Hélas !
Que la fortune est décevante !

BÉRANGER : Madame Mère

How far from St. Helena to the Gate of Heaven's Grace?
That no one knows—that no one knows—and no one ever will.
But fold your hands across your heart and cover up your face,
And after all your trapezings, child, lie still !

KIPLING : A St. Helena Lullaby

AFTER SAYING GOOD-BYE to Napoleon, Letizia fell ill, so was still in Paris when Louis XVIII returned to the throne and Talleyrand headed yet another Ministry. Fesch wrote to Pauline : " The Emperor supports his misfortunes with incredible composure. Madame will stay in France with me until her children have reached the destinations assigned them by Providence. Lucien has gone to London to obtain passports for the rest of the family . . . you must be at great pains to live economically. At present we are all poor." Like Balzac's Bonapartist Colonel Chabert, he knew " our sun has set, and we are all cold now."

Fesch dined with Letizia every evening and Hortense and Julia were constantly in attendance on her. For some inexplicable reason this displeased Louis XVIII's odious mistress, Madame de Cayla, a former schoolfellow of Hortense and Caroline. She complained to Monsieur de la Rochefoucauld of the Bonapartes' " effrontery," an attribute on which she was certainly an authority. She reported Letizia as having said that since the Duchesse d'Orléans (mother of Louis-Philippe) had remained in Paris, there was no reason for her not to do likewise —most improbable words from Letizia, who was far too proud of her own family to base her conduct on that of the Bourbons. Moreover, but for illness, Letizia had every reason to leave France. Her former secretary, Decazes, was now Prefect of Police, and perhaps because he knew the strength of her character, set his spies on her. Even more trying, from her point of view, was Fesch's taking it into his head that he would be allowed to remain in his diocese. Letizia settled the matter by asking for passports to Italy for them both. She received these with a letter from Metternich offering her a military escort out of Paris.

Accompanied by Prince Schwarzenberg's cuirassiers, Letizia and Fesch set out on the road to Burgundy at four in the morning on July 20th. They stopped to rest at Bourg-en-Bresse, where Letizia heard mass in her room. When they left the crowd that had gathered around their carriage cried " *Vive Madame Mère !* " Next they made for Geneva, where they expected Hortense to meet them, but they were refused permission to enter the city. Letizia told the Allied official who turned them away : " Despite your sovereign's rage against the Emperor Napoleon, I am prouder to be his mother than if I were the mother of the Emperor of Russia or of your Emperor or of all the Kings in the world."

Geneva being barred to them, they went round by Prangins, where they stayed in Joseph's empty house before going on to Italy. At this period the word Italy still represented a unity that was merely geographical, since the country was divided into seven distinct states. The Kingdoms of Naples, Tuscany and Sardinia, and the Papal States had all recently been restored to their pre-Napoleonic rulers ; the Duchy of Parma was entrusted to Marie-Louise ; Modena had been given to an Austrian arch-duke ; and the Lombardy-Venetian Kingdom was restored to Austria, whose influence thus dominated the peninsula. When Letizia reached Bologna on July 31st, the cardinal asked the Grand Duke of Tuscany to allow them to settle in Sienna. This request proved embarrassing all round. The grand duke was Marie-Louise's uncle, had been a guest at the Tuileries and was on cordial terms with Letizia and Fesch, but as his secretary of state, Fossombroni, insisted that the presence of " these two individuals " was politically undesirable, the grand duke felt obliged to refuse them permission for more than a " provisional sojourn."

Sienna, which they reached in August, was the epitome of medieval Italy with its dusky palaces and labyrinth of flagged alleys. They lodged at the Locanda del Sole, a palace built for Catherine Piccolomini, sister of Pope Pius II, and to-day occupied by the Bank of Italy. Here too they found themselves in trouble. The day after their arrival one of Letizia's servants went to a café to read the Florentine gazette and not only complained loudly that all the news was stale but sang Napoleon's praises. Since Letizia and Fesch were under police surveillance, this increased their undesirability as residents. Legend also has it that Letizia came to the window of the Locanda del Sole and applauded a group of local women who had gathered below to sing songs in favour of Napoleon. It is most unlikely that they would have dared to do this, and the French historian Masson denies it. In any case, Letizia's servant had given the Secretary of State sufficient excuse to inform Fesch that " the complexity of the present circumstances " forced the grand duke to conclude that the travellers had best continue their journey south after taking such rest as they needed. They left Sienna after mass on August 13th and slept at Radicofani, a gloomy and desolate spot.

Next morning as they drove past Lake Bolsena, the largest volcanic lake in Italy, they noticed scattered tree trunks marking the places where Napoleon had ordered parts of the forest to be cut down in order to dislodge the bandits who had taken up headquarters there. From Etruscan Orvieto they went to Montefiascone, where they spent the night, and on August 15th, Napoleon's forty-sixth birthday, they came into the wild stretches of the campagna and saw the dome of St. Peter's on the horizon. Entering Rome by the Porta del Popolo, they drove unnoticed to Fesch's palace beside the Tiber. Here they were left in peace, since the Pope proved a magnanimous host and urged them to stay in Rome, despite the hostility his offer aroused in many of Fesch's fellow cardinals.

It was here that Letizia learnt how Napoleon had given up the attempt to sail for America, which would have cost sailors' lives, and entrusted himself to the English, who were deporting him to St. Helena, a small island in the Atlantic one thousand two hundred miles off the coast of West Africa. He reached St. Helena in October, after over two months at sea, and although the place was described to Letizia as " an extinct volcano, where twelve hundred Indian and Chinese slaves ministered to five hundred Europeans and men seldom reached the age of fifty or even sixty," she wrote to the Allied authorities asking permission to join her son. This plea was never answered, but a letter in which she repeated it reached Napoleon in May, 1816, and brought him the first news he had received of his family since leaving Europe. From now on Rome was to be Letizia's home, the Rome Byron described a few months later as :

The Niobe of nations ! there she stands,
Childless and crownless, in her voiceless woe.

THE ROME IN WHICH Letizia now found herself more tolerated than welcomed was a curious mixture of the cosmopolitan and the provincial. Of its population of 180,000, foreigners tended to group themselves around the Piazza di Spagna, known locally as the English Ghetto (English being a portmanteau word for all foreigners), ecclesiastics in the Borghi, and the working classes in Trastevere. The rare hotels accepted clients only for a night or two, so visitors rented furnished apartments, which were plentiful. There were four famous cafés : the Greco (still flourishing to-day), where artists gathered; the Inglese, which was decorated with archæological panels by Piranesi and attracted rich Anglo-Saxons ; the Ruspoli, centre of fashionable youth ; and the Veneziano, which was popular with poets, archæologists and the clergy. Except for the puppet show in the Palazzo Fiano courtyard, theatres were dirty and un-inviting. Entertaining took place almost exclusively in the palaces of the aristocracy, and the Church dominated everything. One of the best ways to know what daily life was like in this cardinal-ruled world, so brilliant on the surface, so provincial underneath, is to read Stendhal's vivid *Promenades dans Rome* and *Rome, Naples, et Florence*.

Everywhere she looked Letizia was reminded of her exiled son. The rule of the French in Rome was over, but since the sixteenth century no pope had made such an impression on the city as had Napoleon during his fourteen years' reign over Italy. The idea of a new Imperial Rome had been deeply rooted in him, and he had engaged artists who understood how to transplant his ideas into buildings and statuary. The Piazza del Popolo had been cleared and made into the architectural delight that is still one of the great spectacles of Rome. The Pincian hill had been transformed into public gardens with marble balustrades, fountains and terraces. The Tiber now possessed embankments. Only the mighty palace Napoleon had planned for his son remained imaginary. Ironically, Rome was to be the Bonapartes' great place of refuge. Even to-day, when the head of the house is a French prince, the majority of the "Napoleonites" are Italian.

The first of Letizia's children to escape the Allies was Joseph. At Rochefort he had offered to impersonate Napoleon in order to give the latter time to flee to America. When Napoleon refused to accept this sacrifice, Joseph decided to go to America himself. He still believed that the rest of the family would eventually foregather there. He sailed on July 25th with a passport in the name of Monsieur Bouchard, on the American brig *Commerce*. During its trip the *Commerce* was twice accosted by English ships, but as all the passengers' passports appeared to be in order and the captain was unaware of Joseph's identity, nothing prevented him from landing in New York, where he took the name of Comte de Survilliers.

In November Letizia wrote to him : " I am taking advantage of the opportunity offered by Mr. Cox, the American Consul in Tunis, who is going home, to send you news of us. You can imagine the joy it gave me to know you are in America, safe from the vexations and persecutions of the enemies of our family . . . In Rome I spend my days occupied by my children, and preoccupied by their misfortunes. Send me your news, and may it please God to let me embrace you before I die. You have heard of Murat's sad end."

Tracked by royalists after Waterloo, Murat had taken refuge in Corsica. There he fell into a trap laid for him by agents of Ferdinand IV of Naples and Sicily, who persuaded him to make an attempt to regain his kingdom. Murat sailed for Ajaccio with 250 men in early autumn, was thrown on to the coast of Calabria by a storm, and speedily arrested by the police who had been awaiting him. He was court-martialled on October 13th and shot that afternoon. At forty-eight he faced the firing squad with the same bravery he had shown as a youth on the battlefield, and, with the same ingenuous vainglory, admonished his executioners to " spare the face."

Letizia also told Joseph that Lucien had reached home in September, after having been interned for two months in Turin by the King of Sardinia ; that Pauline was ill in Rome ; that the Prince Borghese was staying in Florence ; and that she herself was without news of Joseph's family, Jérôme, Caroline and Elisa. She concluded : " Louis is here, his health is passable. The Cardinal has accompanied me throughout this time. He is well and prays for you constantly. He is devoted to you and joins me in wishing you all the happiness you could desire. Adieu, my very dear son, remember your tender mother and be assured she carries you in her heart."

Like Napoleon, Joseph and Elisa were never to see Letizia again. Early in 1816 *Le Moniteur* published the text of a law which deprived all the banished Bonapartes of the protection of French embassies, legations and consulates everywhere ; it also forbade them to travel in France or any Allied country without a permit from an inter-allied committee that met in Paris and might take as long as three years to come to a decision. This " proscription," in the ancient sense of the word, applied not only to Napoleon's mother, brothers, sisters, brothers-in-law and sisters-in-law, but to his aunts, uncles, nephews and nieces. To-day our universal servitude to passports, permits, visas and currency regulations makes it difficult for us to understand how outrageous such a ban then appeared to be. Even in 1800 it had been possible for a reputable English guide-book to announce that it was " strongly inclined to believe that English families travelling for health may, at this moment, reside in any City of Italy with as little risk of inconvenience attributable to war, as they could before the invasion of BONAPARTE."

The police surveillance to which all the Bonapartes were now subjected often had ludicrous results. For example, the French Chancellory in Rome sent a special memorandum to Paris informing the Foreign Office that Letizia had sold her house in the Rue Saint-Dominique. This was scarcely a top secret, since the French Government itself had bought the house through official channels a year earlier and it was already occupied by the Ministry of War. Such pettifogging vigilance encouraged the Bonapartes to use private channels for their correspondence.

Letizia's first direct news from St. Helena was given her by Mrs. Skelton, wife of the former under-governor there. Both Lieutenant-Colonel Skelton and his wife saw much of Napoleon between his arrival in October, 1815, and their departure in May, 1816. They dined with him frequently, and never missed an opportunity to show him respect and kindness. In the *Mémorial de Sainte-Hélène*, Las Cases noted that although Napoleon's arrival deprived the Skeltons of their house at Longwood, and eventually put an end to their employment at St. Helena and sent them back to Europe where they had scant means, they were the only couple on the island to show the exile unvarying regard and courtesy. As soon as Mrs. Skelton reached Europe she wrote to Letizia. Fesch immediately answered : " You cannot imagine the joy your letter gave my sister and myself. This is our first news from Longwood . . . your letter gives us the assurance that he was well up to May 13th. Has he received our letters ? Will we be able to keep in touch with him ? Would you be so extremely kind as to let us know when you have news from St. Helena ? Would it be possible for you to tell us if we may send him anything, books or anything else ? " But Lieutenant-Colonel Skelton had no more news from St. Helena.

All Letizia's thoughts were now dominated by Napoleon. Henceforth she always wore mourning and led so quiet and restricted a social life that it was difficult for ambitious spies to make a profit out of observing her. Nevertheless, they did their best with inventions and surmises. The Bonapartes were forbidden to write to Corsica, and in April, 1816, it was rumoured that Letizia was " supplying Corsican agents with millions to foment trouble." The French Ambassador, Pressigny, complained to the Cardinal Secretary of State, who called on Letizia.

It has been recorded that she told him : " I do not possess millions, but kindly tell the Pope, in order that my words may be reported to King Louis XVIII, that if I were fortunate enough to have the amount charitably attributed to me, I should not use it to foment trouble in Corsica, nor to obtain partisans for my son in France—he has plenty of those already —but to arm a fleet to rescue the Emperor from St. Helena." Whether or not she said this, she undoubtedly thought it, and the fact that such a story has survived indicates the strength of her personality.

The next year the Cardinal Secretary of State found himself constantly nagged about fictitious Bonaparte activities by the new French Ambassador, the implacable Comte de Blacas d'Aups, a man whose death Stendhal wished for, and whom Chateaubriand described as " the undertaker of the monarchy." A former *émigré*, Blacas was far more royalist than the King and suspected even the most distant and innocuous of Napoleon's relatives of conspiratorial designs. In 1817, he was brought to the verge of apoplexy by a rumour that the Princess of Wales (Caroline of Brunswick) intended to stay with Lucien and his family at Canino during her forthcoming visit to the Papal States. Though she did not stay with Lucien this time, she did visit him, and, since Lucien was now a Roman prince, there was nothing Blacas could do about it except rage. Nor could Blacas plague Pauline, who, since the Pope had shown approval of her loyalty to her exiled brother, was once more the darling of the *salons*. The cardinals might be less eager than in the past to pay their respects to Napoleon's mother, but every distinguished English or American visitor to Rome clamoured to meet her, or indeed any member of the proscribed but apparently fascinating family.

More seriously exasperating to Blacas than the Bonapartes' social resurgence was the Santini affair, which brought Letizia into correspondence with Lord Holland, a gifted, humane and powerful Whig peer who had received his political training from his uncle, Charles Fox. Giovanni-Natale Santini was a

Corsican who had served with the light infantry in the Grand Army. Fanatically devoted to Napoleon, he had accompanied him to St. Helena and longed to shoot Sir Hudson Lowe. Instead of which, however, Santini succeeded on his return from St. Helena in getting Lord Holland to speak in the House of Lords on Napoleon's behalf. At the same time a pamphlet on the treatment of Napoleon entitled *An Appeal to the British Nation* and signed by Santini but composed by a colonel who had served under Murat, was published simultaneously in English and French and ran into edition after edition. This caused repercussions all over Europe. Lord Holland had already opposed a move to confine Napoleon more strictly, saying, " To consign to distant exile and imprisonment a foreign and captive Chief, who after the abdication of his authority, relying on British generosity, had surrendered himself to us in preference to his other enemies, is unworthy of the magnanimity of a great country ; and the treaties by which after his captivity we bound ourselves to detain him in custody at the will of Sovereigns to whom he had never surrendered himself, appear to me repugnant to the principles of equity, and utterly uncalled for by expedience or necessity." To-day, knowledge of concentration camps and totalitarian states makes it hard for us to understand the widespread indignation about the relatively mild treatment accorded this caged conqueror, but widespread it was, and sincere.

Letizia wrote at once to Lord Holland :

Napoleon's mother does not know how better to express her gratitude to you than by telling you of the astonishment with which she read in Lord Bathurst's reply that none of Napoleon's family had entrusted letters for him to the British Minister. Such effrontery proves how great an impression your motion has made, and the benefit the Emperor may derive from it.

I have written to my son several times through commercial channels, and among others, through the banker Torlonia, who assured me the letters were handed to English nobles who generously offered to give them to the Minister.

But I can remember the name of only one of them, Lord Lucan, who promised my brother and myself that my letters would be given to Lord Castlereagh in person by his eldest daughter, to whom he would send them on his arrival in Paris. Since the New Year I have entrusted other letters to General Mathew.

Feeling, moreover, that the Emperor might not be permitted to write, I addressed some letters to Madame la Comtesse Bertrand, all of which have remained un-answered.

However, Providence, which unveils lies, allowed a lady who was in Rome last February, connected, it was said, with an Under-Secretary of State and, if I am not mistaken, of the name of Hamilton, to tell Captain Tower [captain of the ship on which Letizia had gone to Elba] that she had read letters from me to my son that had been brought to her in her country house. Having realised the use the Ministers made of my letters, which never reached the Emperor, I would have refrained from offering them further subjects for amusement if a mother could forgo all hope of com-municating with an unhappy son. Lord Bathurst's motion has decided me to try by every means to get news to my son.

Permit me, therefore, I beg you, to send the enclosed letter to Lord Bathurst. Will it be more fortunate than the previous ones? Or do they wish to force a mother to address her son in thoughtlessly harsh terms? I would rather my son supposed me dead than that he should doubt my love and the extent to which I feel his situation and long to see him again.

To leave the Minister no excuse, I have written two letters, so that he may choose which he will send if you do not think it possible to send both.

My lord, your noble character relieves me of the necessity to tell you of my eternal gratitude, but I cannot conceal from you that the only happy days I have known since my son's captivity are those animated by the hope I place in the power of your virtues.

May Lady Holland find here the assurance of feelings worthy of her heart ; and may she not cease to take an interest in my son.

(Lady Holland did all in her power to alleviate Napoleon's captivity with letters and gifts, which included a bust of his son, an ice-box and six shipments of books. In his will he left her a gold snuff-box given him by Pope Pius VI and a note expressing his " esteem and affection " for her.)

Letizia did not forget the faithful Corsican soldier whose constancy had proved so effective. Santini had gone from London to Brussels, then to Munich, intending to make for Rome. But he was arrested at Como, taken to Milan and imprisoned in a fortress at Mantua. Letizia appealed to Metternich :

An afflicted mother grasps every opportunity of alleviating her misfortunes, and I was rejoicing in advance at the thought of receiving news of my son when I heard of Santini's arrival in Milan, coming from St. Helena and on his way to Rome. Your Highness can imagine my renewed distress at finding myself deprived of such a consolation . . . The letters he was bringing us have been read in England, also by the Governor of Milan. So there could be nothing in them to disturb the peace, and the arrested man is far too prudent to have said anything provocative. What could he tell me, except how my son is ? And could his telling me this enable me to alter my son's situation? . . . Will Your Highness allow me, in the name of humanity, to beg him to set this man free, so that he may continue his journey : a man whose only fault is fidelity to his master, and whose journey to Rome had as its only aim that he might enter my service and give me news of my son.

Like most of her appeals this was unanswered and Santini remained a prisoner until Napoleon's death. But the Bonapartes never forgot him. Thirty-three years later, in 1850, when

Night: Italy

Letizia and all of her children except Jérôme were dead, Napoleon's nephew, son of Louis and Hortense, then Prince-President of France and shortly to become Napoleon III, decorated Santini and appointed him guardian for life of Napoleon's tomb in Paris.

Now that she had settled in Rome, Letizia needed her own establishment. In 1818 she bought the Palazzo Rinuccini, a dignified seventeenth-century palace of three stories topped by a balustraded terrace. It is in the centre of the city at the corner of the Corso and the Piazza Venezia, on the site of the Septa Julia, where the enfranchised citizens of Imperial Rome came to cast their votes. When Letizia lived there it was called the Palazzo Bonaparte and faced a projecting wing (demolished in this century to provide an approach to the modern Victor Emmanuel monument) of the castellated Palazzo Venezia. The *appartamento nobile* on the first floor where Letizia lived contained nine rooms. The decorations, stucco and painted doors were all of the eighteenth century, and she made few alterations beyond installing some Venetian mosaic floors and exquisite white marble chimney-pieces decorated with cherubs and swags of fruit and flowers. The main entrance to the palace was surmounted by a marble eagle with outspread wings, and Canova's gigantic statue of Napoleon stood at the foot of the Grand Staircase. (The plaster model for this later decorated the Duke of Wellington's London house.) The walls of the vast tiled ante-room were decorated with frescoes of Law and Justice in chiaroscuro, and war trophies beneath tablets bearing the name Bonaparte. On the ceiling of Letizia's bedroom can still be seen a painted angel with a cornucopia shedding darkness over the sky, while a cherub with a poppy in its left hand makes a gesture of silence with its right. Here she hung the portrait of her husband which Napoleon had commissioned from Girodet (now in the Ajaccio museum), David's portrait of Napoleon, and a marble bust of the King of Rome. Here, later, she was to keep the bed on which Napoleon died and the little silver night-lamp that had lit his last moments and was to light her own. Busts and portraits of all her children populated her rooms. The second floor of the palace was at the disposal of her children and grandchildren. The third floor was occupied by her attendants and servants. Lady Morgan, who complained emphatically of the dirty and neglected state of the Roman palaces, said that the only exceptions to this rule were the palaces of the ambassadors and of the Bonapartes, which were distinguished by comfort, orderliness and elegance.

During the First World War the Palazzo Bonaparte was bought by the Misciattelli family, and it was here that the late Marchese Piero Misciattelli prefaced and edited a remarkable collection of Letizia's letters, many of them hitherto unpublished, from the family papers of the Baronne de Beauverger, née Clary. The marchese restored the palace and gave the rooms the look they had worn in Letizia's time. His widow, the Marchesa Misciattelli, shares her husband's enthusiasm for the Emperor's mother and, thanks to this, one can still see Letizia's surroundings much as they were during the last eighteen years of her life.

By the time Letizia moved into her last home she knew the whereabouts of each of her scattered clan. Julie and her children were in Frankfurt, hoping to join Joseph in America, a plan that Julie's ill-health was to defeat; Hortense and her children were in Switzerland, where she had bought the charming little Arenenberg castle (to-day a Bonaparte museum and an agricultural college); Jérôme, Elisa, Caroline and their families were in Austria—Jérôme and Elisa in Trieste, Caroline in Frohsdorf. Lucien wanted to join Joseph in America but was refused passports. Again it was Pauline who of all the children was Letizia's mainstay and comfort. Napoleon once told General Montholon : " My mother is a woman of great orderliness and virtue. But like all mothers she loved her children unequally. Pauline and I were her favourites, Pauline because she was the loveliest and most full of grace, I perhaps because she had an

instinctive feeling that I should make our family great." Their
stay at Elba had created a special bond between mother and
daughter, and although Pauline still seemed to live for pleasure,
she understood the depth of her mother's attachments. One day
when they were walking on the Pincian hill she said to the
Duchesse d'Abrantès : " You see my mother lamenting over my
brother's misfortunes . . . well, this grief won't kill her, she will
suffer a long while and her unhappiness will be more terrible
than the Emperor's."

Pauline had recently bought a charming little palace (now
the seat of the French Embassy to the Vatican) near the Porta
Pia. She named it the Villa Paolina, since Letizia forbade her
to call it the Villa Bonaparte, explaining that in a city with
gardens so magnificent as those of the Pamphili, Boncompagni,
Borghese, Patrizi and Albani palaces the name of Bonaparte
must not be given to a villa with a " small, plain " garden. It is
through chance remarks like these, with their indications of
fierce pride, that one realises how mistaken is the image of
Letizia as a simple peasant, dazzled by her children.

Pauline was now separated from Prince Borghese, but
Roman society did not hold this against her. Lady Morgan,
the Irish novelist who met Letizia through Pauline, wrote :
Among all the villas of the Borghese family, there is but
one habitable and enjoyable, where English neatness, French
elegance and Italian taste, are most happily united. This
is the Villa Paolina Bonaparte Borghese, laid out, adorned,
and furnished by the Princess. Whoever has passed a
spring morning in this beautiful *retreta*, and partaken of one
of the Princess Borghese's weekly *déjeuners*, has seen the
interior of a *Roman villa* under an aspect that forms a curious
solecism in Roman habits and Roman hospitality . . .
the day before we left Rome, we breakfasted at the Villa
Paolina, with a circle composed of British nobility of both
sexes, of the Roman princes and princesses, German
Grandees and American Merchants—a singular congress.
The collation was of sweetmeats, ices, light wines, coffee ;

and the principal amusement, looking at the elegant apartments of the Villa, sauntering in the gardens, and visiting some antiquities within their walls . . . it is the most hospitable house in Rome . . . and possesses all the *agréments* which wealth, rank, taste and high cultivation can bestow . . . In her circles a great proportion of the conclave may always be found; for since the days of Pope Jean, no lady was ever so attended by Cardinals as the beautiful Pauline. Lucien and Louis Bonaparte, though they have fine palaces, live exclusively in the bosom of their family. But by far the most distinguished and interesting of that family is the venerable mother of Napoleon. Retaining great remains of the most brilliant beauty, dignified in adversity as she was moderate in prosperity, her thoughts and feelings have now but one object—the prisoner of St. Helena; whose pride she reproved in the days of his glory, whose fall she laments, more as the child of her affections than the sovereign of a mighty empire. We saw much of this venerable lady (though in general she received no company), and fancied we could trace in her energy and force of character the source from whence her extraordinary son derived his talents . . . Shortly after Bonaparte's elevation to the Imperial throne, meeting his mother in the gardens of Saint-Cloud, half playfully, half seriously, he held his hand to her to kiss. She flung it back indignantly, and presenting her own in the presence of his suite, said, " It is your place to kiss the hand of her who gave you life." We observed the pictures of all her handsome children in the room she occupied (where we generally found her spinning, with her prayer book beside her); there were four of them kings when they sat for her, with the Emperor, their brother, at their head; viz., the Kings of Spain, Holland, Westphalia and Naples (her son-in-law Murat). " You see," she said one day as I was looking on Napoleon's picture, " when my son Bonaparte sat for me, I made him lay aside his crown "; which was the case.

Except for visits to her children, Letizia's most frequent outings were to the Palatine hill. Here she would walk in silence beneath stone pine and ilex among the flower-grown ruins of the palaces of the Cæsars. What remained of Domitian's palace was occupied by an eccentric and highly fashionable Scotsman, Charles Andrew Mills, who had built there a sham Gothic house decorated with the Tudor rose, the Scottish thistle, and the Irish shamrock, a monstrosity that was not demolished until 1927. From the Palatine hill Letizia often went to the Colosseum, its corridors then open to the sky, the walls and arches covered by grass, pomegranate trees growing from the parapets, the only sounds those of hundreds of birds and the chants of pilgrims come to kiss the cross that stood where the Christian martyrs had died. Jérôme described her at this time as : " Thin, with black eyes full of fire, the pure type of Corsican still found in the mountains of the island in families who have never intermarried with other races. She always wore a severe black merino dress and an Empire-style turban . . . Everything in her palace revealed that one was in the presence of great sorrow, of august memories slowly being transformed into mute and proud resignation."

Her pride was as durable as her grief, and she turned instinctively to scenes of grandeur and stories of glory on the same scale as her conquered son's past victories. When she heard that her grandson in Vienna had been given the title Duke of Reichstadt she said : " My grandson will never bear a finer name than his father's. The title of Duke of Reichstadt has no resonance, but the name of Napoleon Bonaparte will always reverberate to the ends of the earth and the echoes of France will repeat it."

HITHERTO LETIZIA'S attitude towards Napoleon's exile had been what anyone who had studied her character would have expected. Now a new element was introduced, one that linked her Roman old age in the shade of the Vatican with her Corsican childhood in a world of ballads, spells and omens, where the saints were on friendly terms with older deities and Balaam's ass was neither more nor less real than St. George's dragon or the Trojan horse. This change came into her life, almost imperceptibly at first, as the result of Fesch's increasing piety, which encouraged her own. No one accused him of worldliness now. He fasted excessively and was constantly adding to his religious observances, and every Friday he would set out barefoot and in penitent's grey garb to carry a crucifix to the cross in the Colosseum. (Madame de Staël described one of these processions in her novel *Corinne*.) A belief, older than Christianity, in miracles and portents, began to stir in him and he communicated it to his sister, who, in her despair at being without news of Napoleon, was thus put into a state of mind in which she could listen to the vaporising of Madame Klein-muller, a most dubious clairvoyante who may have been a spy in the pay of Metternich.

This charlatan soon convinced Letizia and Fesch that Napoleon was no longer at St. Helena, with deplorable results. In May, 1818, Fesch received a letter from General Bertrand telling them of the death of Napoleon's *maitre d'hôtel*, Cipriani, as " the result of the unhealthy climate of this country where few men reach old age. Therefore we have felt, and feel every day, the need of a minister of our religion. You are our bishop, and we desire that you send us a Frenchman or an Italian. Please choose a cultivated man, under forty, with a mild character and not anti-Gallican." Bertrand also asked them to send a doctor and a French or Italian cook, preferably a man who had already served the Bonapartes. Instead of jumping at this opportunity to send Napoleon men of proved competence and loyalty, Letizia and Fesch ignored an application from the distinguished doctor, Foureau de Beauregard, who was familiar with Napoleon's constitution and eager to go to St. Helena, and sent instead a quack named Antommarchi, whose medical experience consisted mainly in having prepared dissections in Florence, an ignorant young priest, Vignali, and an old Corsican abbé, Buonavita, who had served in Spain, Mexico and Paraguay, been Letizia's almoner at Elba and was now almost speechless from apoplexy. Antommarchi was such a fool that he allowed Sir Hudson Lowe to convince him that Napoleon was feigning illness from political motives even when he was dying either of cancer or of perforation of the pylorus by a peptic ulcer.

This ludicrous choice was the result of Letizia's and Fesch's belief that Bertrand's letter must be a forgery since Napoleon had left St. Helena. Why send gifted priests and doctors to St. Helena when Madame Kleinmuller had seen Napoleon in a vision being transported out of exile by angels ? Five months after receiving General Bertrand's letter, Letizia told her daughter-in-law Catherine that she knew Napoleon was on his way to Malta. The following February, Fesch wrote to Las Cases : " We are assured that three or four days before January 19th, the Emperor received permission to leave St. Helena and that, effectively, the English are taking him elsewhere . . . Everything about his life is miraculous, and I am inclined to believe in yet another miracle. His existence is prodigious . . ." Months later Fesch was still writing in the same vein : " Although the gazettes and the English always insinuate that he is still at St. Helena, we have reason to believe this is no longer so, and although we do not know where he is, nor when he will appear, we have sufficient proof to hope we shall soon be told this with

certainty. There is no doubt that the gaoler of St. Helena forces
Count Bertrand to write as if Napoleon were still there." Incredible as this may sound now, similar beliefs were widespread.
Napoleon's energy had filled the world with such rousing martial
music that the ensuing silence seemed unnatural.

Joseph, meanwhile, was involved in a plan to rescue his
brother which had been conceived at Champ d'Asile, a colony of
French refugees in Texas. The leader was Charles-François
Lallemand, one of Napoleon's most devoted officers, who had
got in touch with Jean Lafite, an adventurous French pirate who
had a fleet of ninety vessels. When Lucien heard of this he
thought it would be an excellent plan for him to go to America
and combine with Joseph and Napoleon in attempting the con-
quest of Mexico. He was refused a passport, however, and confined to his estate at Canino for a short while. But the conspirators in America were so sure of success that a house was
built and furnished for Napoleon in New Orleans, at the corner
of Saint Louis and Chartres Streets, and an especially rapid
vessel, the *Séraphime*, was constructed at Charleston and just ready
to sail when news came of Napoleon's death.

For all her conviction that supernatural powers were pro-
tecting her son, Letizia did not neglect mundane channels of
appeal. When the three Allied sovereigns met at Aix-la-Chapelle
in August, 1818, she wrote to each of the three : " An inexpressibly afflicted mother has long hoped that the meeting of
your Imperial Majesties would restore her happiness." (It was
possible for Letizia to refer to herself unselfconsciously as an
inexpressibly afflicted mother because, despite the fortitude that
prevented her from bemoaning trifles, when it came to tragedy
she was both natural and logical enough to pity herself precisely
as she would have pitied someone else in a similar situation. She
was a literal Christian, who endeavoured to love her neighbour
as, not more nor less than, herself.)

It is impossible that you will not discuss the Emperor's
prolonged captivity, and that your greatness of spirit, your
authority, and the recollection of past events will not urge

you to deliver a prince who shared your interests and friend-ship.

Would you allow a sovereign who threw himself in his enemy's arms, confident of magnanimity, to persist in the torment of exile ? My son might have taken refuge with his father-in-law, the Emperor ; he might have relied on the great character of the Emperor Alexander ; he might have turned to His Prussian Majesty, who, finding himself appealed to, would have remembered his former alliance. Can England punish him for the trust he showed in her ?

The Emperor Napoleon is no longer to be feared ; he is an invalid. Even were he in good health, and possessed of the means Providence formerly put into his hands, he abhors civil war.

Sire, I am a mother and my son's life is dearer to me than my own. Pardon the grief that makes me take the liberty of sending Your Imperial and Royal Majesties this letter.

Do not render useless the move of a mother protesting against the long cruelty exercised against her son.

In the name of Him who is essentially good, and whom Your Imperial and Royal Majesties represent, take it upon yourselves to put an end to my son's torments, to restore his liberty. I ask it of God, I ask it of you who are His lieutenants on earth.

Reasons of State have their limits and posterity, on which immortality depends, admires above all else the con-queror's magnanimity.

No answer came to this and Letizia said, " I knew they would kill him." Such moments of lucidity only drove her back all the more hungrily to the clairvoyante's cloudy assurances. Both her good judgment and her resistance to tragedy began at last to show the ravages of time.

WHEN THE EMPEROR of Austria visited the Papal States the following year, Letizia's palace was the only one not illuminated in his honour. Its darkness was remarkable in a city so gifted for display, and the story began circulating in Roman drawing-rooms that the Emperor had sent his chamberlain to ask Letizia if she would receive his daughter Marie-Louise. "You amaze me, Signor Ambassador," Letizia reportedly answered, "and you insult my daughter-in-law by imagining that she is travelling about instead of remaining with her husband, a martyr at St. Helena. The lady you refer to cannot be my daughter-in-law, but must be some adventuress taking our name in vain, and I do not receive adventuresses."

Of more concern to Letizia than faithless Marie-Louise were her three other daughters-in-law, Julie, Catherine and Hortense, all separated from her by frontiers and regulations. She kept up as steady correspondence with them all as with her own children. Among the latter, it was Elisa who seemed to have adapted herself best to their altered situation. She was able to satisfy herself with domestic happiness and wrote Letizia from Trieste that her home life was "perfect." Then suddenly, in July, 1820, she caught malarial fever and died. She was only forty-three and this was Letizia's first taste of the sorrow that comes from outliving one's grown-up children, of the sense of revolt with which the deaths of the young fill the old, giving them a catastrophic feeling of time displacing itself. She wrote to Elisa's fourteen-year-old daughter, Napoleone (an eccentric, fiery character, whose subsequent attempt to help her cousin, the Duke of Reichstadt, to the French throne was used by Rostand in his famous play *L'Aiglon*) : " You have reason to feel your loss, but it is not irreparable ; your mother is praying for you and will obtain for you graces that will console you in your present affliction and support you in the future . . . I wish I could be with you to guide you in the world with my experience, and according to the principles that should govern all the children of my family . . . " When Napoleon heard the news he said, " Death, which seemed to have overlooked our family, now begins to strike it."

Despite the rigorous common sense Letizia applied to all else, she continued to rely on supernatural intervention where Napoleon was concerned. In July, 1821, Pauline wrote to Planat de la Faye (one of the Emperor's former officers who became Jérôme's secretary and was able to obtain permission to go to St. Helena only when Napoleon was dying) : " All the letters Madame and the Cardinal have received during the past two years are considered forgeries : forged signatures, forged letters invented by the English Government to create the belief that the Emperor is still at St. Helena, while the Cardinal and Madame say they know pertinently that His Majesty has been removed by the Angels and taken to a country where his health is very good, and they have news of him. This witch [the clairvoyante] makes use of every political event to further her ends. Everyone in Madame's household has been won over, beginning with Colonna. Madame and the Cardinal wanted to make me and my brother Louis share their beliefs, but seeing that we both tried by every means to remove their blindness and ended by mocking their credulity, I must keep silent about the scenes, the quarrels, and the coldness that resulted."

A few days later, the Abbé Buonavita arrived in Rome with a letter for Pauline from Napoleon, written on March 17th. By this time mother and daughter were on such strained terms (it is their only recorded quarrel) that Pauline told Planat :

They wanted to keep the Abbé Buonavita's arrival from me. He was in Mamma's room when I went to say good-bye as I was going to Frascati, and I was refused admittance.

Fortunately, I learnt from the doorkeeper that the Abbé was there. I went up. Mamma said nothing to me. So I was obliged to tell her that I knew and that I wanted to see the Abbé and have news of the Emperor. She told me she was expecting the Cardinal, and that the Emperor was furious with me for having received English people. [What Napoleon said when he heard this of Pauline was " All the better ! It means that amount of enemies won over."] I met Lord Anglesey at Madame's house. His wife is charming and gives me proofs of friendship. He is a man of fifty-five, ugly, but loves the Emperor and his family. My uncle scarcely leaves the duchess.

Mamma and my uncle do not believe that the Abbé Buonavita left the Emperor at St. Helena. They said, " We do not believe a word of it, the Emperor is no longer there, we know better." My grief is extreme.

I threw myself at Mamma's feet, I explained the intrigue and I begged her, for honour's sake, to send this woman away, but she became furious with me, saying she was free to see whomever she wanted. She is encouraged by my uncle and Colonna . . . Finally, after a terrible scene between us, Mamma began to be shaken, but the scene was so violent that I have quarrelled with the Cardinal for life. It is very fortunate that the Abbé had a letter to give to me in person, otherwise everything would have been concealed from me.

Letizia realised the folly of having listened to the clairvoyante. Thus her quarrel with Pauline was ended and her courage restored.

On MAY 5TH, 1821, THE day of Napoleon's death, a "decently dressed individual" came to the Palazzo Bonaparte and requested an audience with Letizia. The doorman asked if he had an appointment, and since he had not, refused to admit him. The visitor then insisted so vehemently that the doorman gave way. In the ante-room the stranger was again questioned, again refused admittance, and again insisted so passionately on seeing Letizia that Colonna, hearing voices raised, went to the door and finally admitted him.

"Madame," the stranger said to Letizia, "at this very moment His Majesty is freed from his sufferings and is happy." Whereupon he thrust his hand inside his jacket and drew out a crucifix which, for a moment, Letizia thought was a dagger. He continued solemnly : "Your Highness, kiss your son's Saviour. You will see this son who has caused you so much grief again, in many years, and his name will echo through all the cities of the world."

Madame de Sartrouville, Letizia's reader, was there at the time and says that Colonna told her the visitor resembled Napoleon uncannily in bearing and voice, but that, although they searched all over Rome after he vanished, they were never able to discover a trace of him.

Official news of Napoleon's death did not reach Rome until July 16th. Everyone around Letizia conspired to keep the news from her and a letter of hers to Jérôme shows that she was still unaware of it two days later. When at last she had to be told, she gave a scream that echoed through the palace, flung her arms around Napoleon's bust, and fainted.

FOR THE NEXT TWO weeks Letizia remained crushed and numb. She scarcely wept or spoke and refused to see anyone. Fesch answered the letters that came from her children and grandchildren. Lucien hastened to her from Viterbo and Louis from Florence. But none of them could help her this time. " Unlike me," she once declared, " they have never been able to understand the humiliation into which the Emperor's fall plunged them."

The French Embassy feared that the Pope, who obstinately refused to forget that Napoleon had re-established Catholicism in France, might allow a memorial service to be celebrated in one of the more important Roman churches, a basilica or, worst of all, the Sistine Chapel. After much agitated discussion and running to and fro, the Cardinal Secretary of State, Consalvi, notified the French Embassy that no such service would take place. Once this was settled, Fesch persuaded Letizia to accompany him to Lucien's villa in the near-by Alban hills to escape the heat. Before leaving, she wrote to Lord Castlereagh asking in the name of all mothers to be granted possession of Napoleon's body : " My son has no more need of honours ; his name suffices for his glory ; but I need to embrace his remains." This letter of hers also contained the remarkable phrase, " inexorable history is seated on his coffin." Like all her pleas, this one was unavailing.

One of the first intimates to whom she wrote was Hortense : " Your letter brought me some comfort as my heart was touched by your sentiments of attachment to him for whose sake I desired my existence to be prolonged. I have no further satisfactions to expect in this world, except to see my other children and grandchildren. Since fate has willed it that the family be dispersed, let me at least have news of you as often as possible."

Napoleon's death did not modify the Allied Governments' fear that his family was plotting a Bonaparte restoration. Public reaction to his death fanned this fear. In Paris young men wore black armbands, mourning odes and dithyrambs were widely circulated, shops displayed trinkets, statuettes, and coloured prints recalling Napoleon's achievements, while a group of officers headed by Lafayette demanded that his body be brought home. Any play about the Grand Army was sure of a success, and when *Napoleon at Schoenbrunn and St. Helena* was put on at the St. Martin's Theatre, a hundred and fifty old soldiers were engaged as supers, and the actor who played Sir Hudson Lowe had to be protected by an escort when he left the theatre. Nor was this intense emotion confined to France. Hero-worship flared from one end of Europe to the other. The Irish, naturally, shouted " Long live Napoleon ! " but even in London Napoleon's former antagonists, such as Napier, showed genuine grief, and public placards invited all those who " admired talent and courage in adversity to mourn his premature death." In Italy, Manzoni, the most famous poet of the time, composed a resounding ode to Napoleon ; and Stendhal was repeatedly asked both in England and in Italy for first-hand stories of the fabulous Emperor. Even in Russia peasants hung coloured prints of the " Farewell at Fontainebleau " in their hovels. Like Victor Hugo, though in a very different way, the Allied Governments began to feel it was a case of " *Lui, toujours lui.*"

Nevertheless, the Allies were mistaken in suspecting Napoleon's brothers and sisters of political conspiracy. Their appetite for epics had been finally sated. The potential troublemakers were still in the nurseries and schoolrooms, where a new generation of Bonapartes was growing up, a generation of children who idolised the memory of the uncle most of them had never seen, and who considered their sequestrated cousin in Vienna the legitimate ruler of France. Las Cases's *Mémorial de*

Sainte-Hélène became their Bible, as it was to be that of Stendhal's Julien Sorel. This extraordinary masterpiece was published simultaneously in French and in English in 1823. In it Las Cases, the aristocratic chamberlain and former *émigré* who had constituted himself Napoleon's shadow and accompanied him to St. Helena, provides an intimate picture of a man of genius, in which history, legend and reportage are mingled with dazzling effect. Letizia, who had been in touch with Las Cases ever since his return from St. Helena in 1817, when she had put her fortune at his disposal, was inexpressibly moved when she read the words in which Napoleon had described her to Las Cases : " One of the most beautiful women of her time . . . She would have given all she possessed to prepare my return from Elba, and after Waterloo would have lived on dry bread without a murmur to help restore my fortunes . . . Madame was a heroine who thought only of her children and family, of duty and honour."

The effect of such a book on her excitable grandchildren is easy to imagine, and current events soon heightened their conviction that they had a special appointment with history. Letizia's invalid son Louis was undoubtedly sincere when he told Cardinal Consalvi that the Bonapartes were far too grateful for the Pope's hospitality to engage in any conspiracy ; but Louis's ebullient sons had been tutored by a Colonel Armandi who was, unknown to his employer, an ardent Carbonaro.

The Carbonari were members of a secret society that originated in Naples and aimed at freeing Italy from foreign rule and obtaining constitutional liberties. Young nobles and educated bourgeois formed the majority of those who rallied to the red, blue and black banner, and the movement soon spread to France, where it had links with Freemasonry and alarmed the authorities. Particularly alarmed was the French Ambassador to Italy, who reported home : " The Roman Carbonari and those of the Italian peninsula draw new hope and audacity from the reunion here of the Bonaparte family. They use those names, so rightly proscribed, to rally all the passions and discontent fermenting in

Italy. It is useless to dissimulate that, given the Pope's great age [he was 81], it is most important for the future peace of the peninsula to isolate all individual members of the Bonaparte family whose accumulated riches might contribute to popular uprisings, even if they themselves are not personally esteemed."

Like a harassed schoolmaster unable to keep order, Blacas could not decide whether the diabolical Bonapartes were more alarming together or apart. He was horrified when Jérôme's repudiated first wife, the American, Elizabeth Patterson, arrived in Rome and was received by Letizia and Pauline: " They say Jérôme is coming here specially to make legal acknowledgment of his son . . . Madame Letizia seems especially desirous of this, and promises to provide for his future."

What Letizia especially desired was to carry out Napoleon's instructions that his family should settle in Rome and ally themselves with all the princely families. " That is to say," he had told General Bertrand in St. Helena, " all those that have produced popes, who command the world's conscience." Napoleon had thought that his name would remain popular in Italy : " The Italians will always consider the period when the Emperor tried to establish their independence as a lost opportunity. He roused the imagination of Italy . . . Prince Lucien, Bacciochi and Princess Elisa's children are naturally in their place in Rome ; Prince Joseph and the Queen of Naples should marry their daughters there . . . Madame should promise 300,000 francs to each of her grandchildren who settles in Rome . . . Lucien should make one of his sons a Cardinal." (Lucien's grandson did become one.) Blacas did not know of this advice, but, confronted by Elizabeth Patterson and her handsome son, he felt that an American Bonaparte, the New World coming to reinforce the Old, was more than he could bear. He might have been relieved could he have known that the last of the American Bonapartes was to die in 1945, in the person of a childless old gentleman named Jérôme Napoleon, who received fatal injuries when he stumbled over the leash of his wife's dog while walking in Central Park.

That autumn Letizia received a visit from Antommarchi, newly returned from St. Helena. He wrote of his interview : " Madame Mère's grief was still great and I was obliged to be very careful what I said, and to spare her feelings— in a word, to give her only an outline of what I had witnessed. On my second visit she was calmer and more resigned, and I gave her some details, which were, however, continually interrupted by her sobs. I stopped, whereupon the unhappy mother dried her tears and began to question me anew. It was a struggle between courage and grief, never was such heart-rending emotion seen. I saw her a third time, when she overwhelmed me with proofs of her goodwill and satisfaction and presented me with a diamond, which I shall never part with, since it is a gift of the Emperor's mother."

What did her the most good at this time was the arrival in Rome of Jérôme and Catherine. Lady Blessington gives a vivid picture of the three of them together :

Walking in the gardens of the Vigna Palatina yesterday, with our amiable friend the owner, Mr. C. Mills, we were surprised by the arrival of the Prince and Princesse de Montfort [as Jérôme and Catherine were now titled] and their children, with Madame Letitia Bonaparte, or *Madame Mère*, as she is generally called, attended by her chaplain, *dame de compagnie*, and others of their joint suite. Having heard that Madame Mère disliked meeting strangers, we retired to a distant part of the garden ; but the ex-King of Westphalia having recognised my carriage in the courtyard sent to request us to join them, and presented us to his mother, and wife. Madame Letitia Bonaparte is tall and slight, her figure gently bowed by age, but nevertheless dignified and graceful. Her face is, even still, remarkably handsome, bearing proof of the accuracy of Canova's admirable statue of her ; and a finer personification of a Roman matron could not be found than is presented by this Hecuba of the Imperial dynasty. She is pale, and the expression of her countenance is pensive, unless when occasionally lighted up by some observations, when her dark eye glances for a moment with animation, but quickly resumes its melancholy character again ; yet even when animated, her manner retains its natural dignity and composure, and she seems born to represent the mother of kings. The Prince de Montfort, and his excellent wife treat her with a watchful and respectful tenderness ; each supported her, and suited their pace to her feeble steps, listening with deep attention to her observations. She was dressed in a robe of rich dark-grey Levantine silk, and a bonnet of the same material, worn over a lace cap, with a black blonde veil. Her hair was divided *a-la-Madonna* [her own white hair], showing a high and pale forehead, marked by the furrows of care. A superb cashmere shawl that looked like a tribute from some barbaric sovereign fell gracefully over her shoulders, and completed one of the most interesting pictures I ever beheld. I must not omit recording that her feet are small and finely formed, and her hands admirable. Her voice is low and sweet, with a certain tremulousness in it that denotes a deep sensibility. She spoke of the Emperor Napoleon ; and her lip quivered and her eyes filled with tears.

"I shall soon join him in that better world where no tears are shed," said she, wiping away those that chased each other down her cheeks. "I thought I should have done so, long ago, but God sees what is best for me."

Sorrow, sanctified by resignation, has given to the countenance of this interesting woman an indescribable charm. The Prince and Princesse de Montfort led the conversation to other topics, in which *Madame Mère* joined, but by monosyllables ; yet her manner was gracious and gentle, and marked by much of that affectionate earnestness which characterises Italian women, and particularly those of advanced years and elevated rank. When we had made the tour of the garden, walking very slowly in order to avoid fatiguing her, she entered her carriage, into which she was assisted by Jérôme and my husband ; the ex-King and Queen of Westphalia kissed her hand, the latter performing the ceremony with as profound a respect as if a diadem encircled the brows of Letitia, and that she herself had not borne one. *Madame Mère* invited us to visit her, and at parting touched my forehead with her lips, and shook hands with Lord Blessington, saying kind and flattering things to us both. The gentlemen, including the Prince de Montfort, all remained with their hats off until her carriage had driven away, when that of her son and his suite followed.

There was something highly scenic in the whole scene of our interview. Here was the mother of a modern Cæsar, walking amidst the ruins of the palace of the ancient ones, lamenting a son whose fame had filled the four quarters of the globe and formed an epoch in the history of Europe ; her tottering steps supported by another son from whose brow the diadem had been torn, and who now, shorn of his splendour, reminded one of the poet's description of a dethroned sovereign . . . The other supporter of *Madame Mère* added much to the effect of the picture. The daughter of kings of the old legitimate stock and allied to half the reigning sovereigns of our day, she has nobly, femininely and wisely adhered to the fallen fortunes of her husband, resisted the brilliant offers of her family, and shares the present comparatively obscure destiny of him on whose throne her virtues shed a lustre. There is something touchingly beautiful in the respectful tenderness of this admirable Princess towards the aged mother of her husband,

and her unceasing and affectionate attention to him, and her children . . . Colonel Sebastiani told me that while her children were yet in infancy, Madame Letitia Bonaparte had been remarked for the dignity and self-possession of her manner and conduct. With a large family and a small income, she practised a rigid system of economy which never degenerated into meanness ; and this prudence seemed in her to be much more the result of a laudable pride, and principle, than of avarice . . . With Napoleon's quick perception of the effect produced by his near relations on those around him, and with the *fierté* which formed a characteristic of his nature, it was peculiarly fortunate that his mother's appearance was so calculated to assert with the rank to which she was elevated. Her tall and slender figure, her graceful demeanour, distinguished countenance and cold but polite manners, were well suited to the part she had to fill . . . The Duc de Reichstadt is said to occupy much of her thoughts, which, since Napoleon's death, revert continually to this interesting youth. There is so much self-control in the manners of Letitia that conclusions are drawn more from the expression of her countenance, significant shakes of the head, or deep sighs, than from her words. Though gracious and kind, she is neither demonstrative nor communicative, and there is a natural dignity about her that must ever check the incursions of curiosity.

ALTHOUGH LETIZIA NOW seemed to her great-grand-children immeasurably old, less a human being than a page of history mysteriously alive, she still had emotional trials ahead of her and the capacity to feel them with intensity. After Napoleon's death Pauline's health, never robust, began to deteriorate visibly and was not improved by the un-happiness of her last love-affair. She who had captivated so many remarkable men was herself captivated by a youth, who, though attracted by her beauty and flattered by her reputation, saw in her an older woman whose demands must be held in check. Neither this nor horrible physical sufferings conquered the gallantry that had always been the counterpart of Pauline's frivolity, and she who had throughout her life wept and laughed with extraordinary facility, showed a stoical calm when dying of cancer at forty-five. With her death nearly all of the remaining light in Letizia's life was extinguished. " They all die," she said, " and I remain here to mourn them. I am condemned to bury them after bringing them into the world."

Such hope as Letizia retained now centred upon her grand-children, to whom she was an enthralling but slightly alarming character, the heroine of the family and its beacon. Jérôme's children were to remember her as " an old divinity carrying such a weight of history that, in the midst of her coffee cups and the snuff-boxes that closed with a dry snap, one felt almost unreal." Jérôme's youngest son never forgot the " extraordinary atmos-phere of laurels and snuff " in her palace, nor the fact that even when the talk concerned nothing beyond local gossip, " one was aware of mighty shadows passing. A singular solemnity dominated an atmosphere that was both domestic and epic, one walked on tiptoe and spoke in a low voice. One was dumbfounded when one heard the idol's voice, sometimes saying things oddly at variance with the majesty of the setting. 'My children gave me a lot of trouble,' she said one day, 'but at least I spanked them soundly.' She never seemed to have been amazed by the prodigies of which she was the origin. Her son's rise had astonished her more than his fall. She accepted this fantastic story with the simplicity of a matron who remembers washing her children's clothes and is no longer moved by anything, not even by being idolised in her old age."

But even her grandchildren seemed bent on stealing a march on her. In 1827, disaster overtook Lucien's ninth child, Paul-Marie, a wild and violent character. After being expelled from the Jesuit college at Urbino, he had been sent to study at Bologna, where he fell passionately in love with a married woman, the Marchesa Herrara de Avaray, and fought two duels on her behalf. Then, at eighteen, he followed Lord Byron's example and sailed, aboard an English ship, to fight for Greek independence. Full of foreboding, Letizia wrote to Lucien that, however distressing it might prove, she would rather know the truth than continue in suspense. Soon afterwards news came that Paul-Marie had been found dead on the bridge of his ship. He had shot himself, whether by accident or design was never proved.

Two years later Paul-Marie's sister, the Marchesa Honorati, died, and that same year Letizia lost her faithful old Corsican servant, Saveria. "I feel it sharply," she wrote to Julie. "So long and tried an attachment is not to be found again." Mistress and servant had spent more than half a century together, and with Saveria went the only person except Fesch with whom Letizia could relive the days when the fabulous Bonapartes were neither princes nor exiles but turbulent children playing in the golden air of a Corsican garden.

A CALAMITOUS ACCIDENT befell Letizia four months before her eightieth birthday. While walking in Pauline's gardens with her chamberlain Colonna, an old family friend and her granddaughter, Princess Charlotte (the formerly irreverent Lolotte, now married to Prince Gabrielli and herself the mother of two daughters), Letizia came to a path too narrow to walk two abreast. Leaving Colonna's arm she went ahead, slipped on the stony ground, fell and broke her hip. (She told her doctors that she distinctly heard the bone crack.)

Lucien, Louis and Jérôme hastened to her bedside and summoned the best doctors available. She was too old for them to employ the apparatus usual in such cases, so they tried a new treatment invented by the famous Dupuytren and placed the injured leg in a bent position on cushions. The shock affected her system so violently that Fesch was granted permission to give her absolution on behalf of the Pope, a grace usually reserved for cardinals and sovereigns. Once again, however, her fierce will prevailed over her fragile body. Eight days after the disaster she was out of danger, though always in pain. A covered balcony, still to be seen on the Corso corner of the palace, was built to provide her with privacy in which to watch the life of the piazza below. This piazza was known then as the " *Ripresa dei Barberi*," on account of the Barbary horses that raced up the Corso during carnival and were caught up here by swathes of material draped all across the piazza to prevent the animals crashing to death against the opposite walls. Later, on her doctor's orders, she would be carried out for carriage rides. It was a matter of pride to her to keep the Imperial arms on her carriage well furbished, and when passers-by stared at her she said, " Twenty years ago, whenever I entered the Tuileries drums were beaten, soldiers presented arms and crowds flocked around my carriage. Now people peer at me from behind curtains and are afraid to display indiscreet curiosity. But this style is as good as the former! Politeness has replaced eagerness. Twenty years ago I was Your Highness ; to-day I am Madame Letizia." As Madame Letizia, she was glad to speak to any Frenchman among those who stopped to gaze.

While convalescing, Letizia received a visit from Caroline, whom she had not seen for fifteen years, and from Caroline's twenty-five-year-old daughter Louise, now married to the Comte Giulio Rasponi. Time had exhausted Letizia's resentment of Caroline's political perfidy. She rejoiced in the presence of her only surviving daughter and was glad to evoke with her the days when a young and handsome Murat had brought them news of Napoleon's early triumphs, days that though long past sometimes seemed nearer than the intervening ones. But time had not exhausted the Allied Governments' fears of the Bonapartes, and Caroline's presence in Rome was declared dangerous on the grounds that she was the widow of a soldier of fortune who had " dazzled Naples by his bravery and panache," and that her two sons were likely to " arouse public interest." No matter what their individual convictions, the Bonapartes were considered by thousands of Italians to incarnate the ideals and principles of the French Revolution as opposed to those of the reactionary Bourbons. In consequence, the gathering of Letizia's children at her bedside was considered an embryo conspiracy and Caroline was notified that force would be used against her unless she left Rome within a week. She protested with her usual dynamism, hoping for assistance from Metternich, who in the past had been her lover and had worn a bracelet woven of her hair. But the bracelet had lost its magic and Caroline was driven from Rome, never to see her mother again.

Soon after Letizia's accident, an even worse physical disaster befell her. She began going blind from a double cataract condition. In the long twilight that followed, before the final move into darkness, she heard from Jérôme of the July Revolution in Paris. An ultra-reactionary ministry headed by the unpopular Prince Jules de Polignac had driven even the mildest liberals to oppose Louis XVIII's successor, Charles X. On July 25th the King had passed four decrees, two of which violated the Charter so flagrantly as to amount to a *coup d'état*. The Paris workers began to mass two days later, and joined by the National Guard seized the arsenal, powder factory, city hall and Notre-Dame. By July 29th the capital was in the hands of the insurgents. Charles X fled to Rambouillet and abdicated in favour of his grandson, the Duc de Bordeaux. France did not want him either, and Louis-Philippe, son of the regicide Duc d'Orléans, became the new King of France.

As she listened to yet another story of mobile thrones and barricades, Letizia thought of Napoleon's son, a prisoner in Vienna. Had the Duke of Reichstadt been in France it was he who would most probably have succeeded Charles X. She was very weak now, and when Jérôme brought her the news that the French Chamber was restoring the Emperor's statue to the top of the column in the Place Vendôme, tears rolled down her cheeks as she pressed his hand. Yet the news revived her and that night she ate a little. For days afterwards she kept repeating in a low voice, " The Emperor's statue on the column! The Emperor's statue! " She had by her a little model of this statue, and touching it, she said, " If I had been in Paris, as in the past, God might have given me strength to go up inside the column and see for myself . . . my poor eyes, how I regret them." She did not know that in Vienna her imprisoned grandson was equally moved by this news. When the Baron de Larue was leaving Vienna for Paris he asked the duke if he had any messages to send. The young man, to whom his father's country was only a memory, replied : " I know no one in France to whom I can send my compliments, but please greet the Place Vendôme column for me." Nearly seventy years later these words were used with tremendous emotional effect by the play-

wright Edmond Rostand in his *L'Aiglon*, first performed by
Sarah Bernhardt :

L'ATTACHÉ : *Avez-vous pour Paris—car j'y serai le quatre—*
    Quelques commissions ?—L'honneur me serait doux . . .
L'AIGLON : *Je compte être rendu dans . . . l'Empire avant vous !*
L'ATTACHÉ : *Si, pourtant, avant vous j'étais dans le . . . Royaume?*
L'AIGLON : *Saluez de ma part la colonne Vendôme.*

Letizia slept little now, and on waking would ask to be
wheeled about her apartment so as to have the sensation of
movement. Most of her time was spent in the covered balcony
where, she said, " The sun still comes to see me like a friend,
although I cannot see it " : words that poignantly recall those of
Napoleon during the last months of his life, when he would
drag himself to the open window and say, " Good morning, sun,
good morning, sun, my friend."

The night that was closing in on her diminished neither her
pride nor her sense of the obligations pride imposes. At this
time some of her children wanted to attempt legal action against
the French Government for its failure to honour the sixth
clause in the Treaty of Fontainebleau, which promised an income to each member of the fallen Emperor's family. Outraged,
Letizia wrote to Julie :

" I have just received a letter from Ravioli [their man of
business] requesting my power of attorney to enable him to
demand the execution of the sixth clause of the Treaty of
Fontainebleau. He also wishes me to ask you to send him your
power of attorney for the same purpose. I have definitely
refused . . . such an act would be an outrage to the Emperor's
memory and most inimical to his son. Besides, it would be
completely base of us to beg for anything from a government
that has maintained the fourth clause of the law of January 12th,
1818, which banishes us in perpetuity. I have no doubt that you
will reject Monsieur Ravioli's proposition with disdain. I know
you too well not to be certain that you will never hesitate
between honour and money."

She wrote to Hortense in the same spirit, adding : " I have

warned Monsieur Ravioli that I shall disavow any move he might make in my name, and I have told him that even if all my children thought differently I would never beg from a Bourbon, were he ten times Duc d'Orléans. Honour must always have priority over money, and I will never outrage the Emperor's memory . . . Let us be careful of what is left to us and, if we cannot live royally, let us live like honourable private citizens, and not expose ourselves to humiliations or self-reproach. I wrote in this sense to Louis, Jérôme and Julie long before the question of the maintenance of the law of banishment was raised in France. If they had listened to me they would have spared themselves the shame of begging in vain." Determined to leave all she possessed to Napoleon's son, she was equally determined to leave him nothing she considered tainted.

Like her pride, her wits survived the disasters that had overcome her body. She still followed the course of world events and had scores of newspapers and books of history read to her, particularly those concerning her dead son, such as the twenty-eight volumes of *Victories and Conquests* published during the restoration ; the Comte de Ségur's *History of Napoleon and the Grand Army of* 1812 ; and Alexandre Dumas's play *Napoleon Bonaparte*, a favourite which drew tears from her. One of her readers, Madame de Sartrouville, had a habit of skipping passages that criticised Napoleon adversely. This vexed Letizia, and during a reading of General Lamoigne's Memoirs she asked, " Why do you stop ? Do you think I cannot bear the truth ? The author is right : Napoleon was not infallible. In putting Murat on the throne of Naples he committed an unpardonable error. He was not the Son of Mary but only, alas, of Letizia."

Among the grandchildren she knew most intimately, Letizia particularly favoured Louis's sons. The elder, Napoleon-Louis, was a scholarly, reflective young man whose interests included aeronautics. He often talked to his grandmother of his plans to invent a double-propeller for a dirigible balloon, and she would listen with a suspension of incredulity remarkable at her age. He remembered his uncle with intense admiration, and in answer to questions of his on this subject Letizia wrote : " The details I could give you about the Emperor are too puerile to be included in his story. He has indicated himself, in his memoirs, how history should be written. It is as a public figure that he must be considered. His exploits must be depicted in a manner worthy of him. His prodigious policies, his administration and his laws must be handed down to posterity. No task is harder or finer than that of the historian. The Emperor must appear to posterity in his colossal dimensions. His life is so rich that to enter into every detail one would have to write volumes, thus exhausting the reader and diminishing the hero."

But Letizia's advice to Napoleon-Louis was not all on the side of gravity, of which Louis had given his son too much. He married his cousin Charlotte, Joseph's second daughter—who cared so much for her family that when asked in marriage by the Marchesa Curtilepri's son she said, " *Quando si ha l'onore di chiamarsi Bonaparte non si cambia nome.*" (When one has the honour to be called Bonaparte one does not change one's name.) Thereafter he became very solemn, and Letizia wrote to him : " I learn with regret that you have lost the charming vivacity

that suited you so well. I am told you are sombre, show a
tendency to neglect yourself, and are as grave as an old man. I
understand that marriage has steadied you but, believe me, my
dear child, a young man who becomes old before his time is
quite as much in the wrong as an old man who conducts himself
like a youth. You have everything essential to happiness, take
advantage of this. I fear you are studying too hard. Your health
is too precious to too many people for you to have the right to
compromise it. Be as you were in Rome . . . and take care of
your appearance so as to resemble a young gallant rather than a
scholar . . . You have been too long without writing to me. I
warn you I am very curious as to how you are spending your
time, what are your occupations, your amusements, and your
troubles. Be sure that I am ready to share in all that concerns
you. How is your aerial research progressing ? "

There was no need to advise Napoleon-Louis's younger
brother, Louis-Napoleon, to try to resemble a young gallant
rather than a scholar. The future Napoleon III had spent most
of his childhood with his mother, the charming Hortense, and
he was as interested in pleasure as in politics, which he often
discussed privately with Letizia, as shown by this letter which
she wrote to him two months after the July Revolution :

Thank you for all you say about my birthday. Please heaven
I shall soon be better, for with all my courage and resignation I cannot but find it very wearing to be always seated
or lying down. As for the journey to Corsica, I do not
think that will be able to take place yet. We must see if the
French people, who have shown such energy and courage in
throwing off the yoke imposed by foreigners, will be duped
by a faction that has decided, with as much impudence as
imprudence, to settle a problem that should have been resolved only by the nation as a whole. By proclaiming the
Duc d'Orléans King without asking the nation's assent, the
Chamber of Deputies has violated all the principles of the
revolution and assumed a terrible responsibility.

Your letter is that of a young enthusiast. To judge

anything it is necessary to view it objectively, and while renderingj ustice to the vigour of the people of Paris, I am far from seeing a philosopher's revelation in these courageous combats. No one has ever doubted French intrepidity. Wait before judging. You see that I am preaching. I hope you will not take exception to this : my old head, tempered by experience and time, yearns to instil reason into your ardent young head, so beloved by me. However, it is better at your age to have too much fire than too little. So I hope that in spite of my sermons you will not doubt the pleasure with which I embrace you, nor my tender attachment.

Four months later the ardent young head was expelled from Rome as politically undesirable. Revolutionary outbursts were as prevalent as showers in spring that year. The drawbridge went up before St. Angelo, and pilgrims made way for cannon in the Colosseum. The Papal Government scented a Bonaparte conspiracy, and this time the Papal Government was right. Letizia's older grandchildren were as nervously excited as race horses at the starting-point. No sooner had the future Napoleon III been banished to Florence than the police swooped on Jérôme's palace and attempted to arrest his sixteen-year-old son, Jérôme-Napoleon, whose mother successfully appealed to the Russian Minister and the Württemberg chargé d'affaires. The boy seems to have been innocent of anything except admiration for his cousins, but the Papal Government understandably found it difficult to distinguish between so many tumultuous young Bonapartes, each bearing Napoleon as one of their resonant Christian names.

More serious was the result of a police raid on the home of Lucien's Intendant, Vito Fedele. This uncovered a written scheme to put the Duke of Reichstadt on the throne of a resuscitated kingdom of Italy. Responsible were Louis's two sons, the Comte Camerata (husband of Elisa's daughter Napoleone), the Duca Sante della Rovere, the Marchese Corelli, two brothers employed in the administration of Prince Borghese's estates, a couple of artillerymen from the Papal Army (one appropriately named Canonieri), a sculptor, a doctor, a coachman and the proprietor of a copying establishment. The insurgents were to assemble in front of St. Peter's, seize the arms at the depot, and march through the working-class districts distributing money to be provided—they hoped—by Letizia. (Letizia was suspected in Vatican circles of having offered a million francs to the conspirators—perhaps because she managed her investments so well that she was able to lend money to the Holy See for less interest than was charged by the famous banker Torlonia.) They would then attack the castle of St. Angelo, seize the Santo Spirito bank, capture the cardinals and governors of the city, occupy the prison and march on the Capitol to proclaim Louis-Napoleon regent until the arrival of Napoleon's son. Wilder plots have succeeded, but the Papal Government learnt of this one in time to defeat it.

At the end of January, 1831, Louis's sons left Florence for Ombria so as to be on hand when the revolutionary signal came from Parma and Modena. Lucien's sixteen-year-old son, Pierre, attempted to join his cousins, but was arrested and, with his parents' consent, interned for six months in a fortress at Leghorn. When Bologna rose against the Papal Government in February its new provisional government included the Bonapartes' former tutor, Colonel Armandi, and the Marchese Pepoli, husband of Caroline's daughter, Letizia Murat. Stendhal, who was at Trieste waiting to take up his post as French Consul at Civita Vecchia, reported that groups of bandits were active on both sides.

In her palace in Rome Letizia listened to accounts of her grandsons' unruly conduct " without seeming altogether displeased." Perhaps these fanned the embers of the fire that had burnt so brilliantly in her when she too was young and unable to resist the cry of " *Libertà o Morte !* " But she was too old now for such exaltation to last. Instead she would remember the fate of Napoleon's son and tell Hortense that whatever happened

Napoleon-Louis and Louis-Napoleon must not fall into the hands of the Austrians.

Equally fearful of this, Hortense procured an English passport in the name of Lady Hamilton from the English Minister in Tuscany, and hurried after her sons. At Forli she found only her younger son. His elder brother had just died of measles, of which there was an epidemic. So ended all Napoleon-Louis's hopes of writing history and conquering the air. Letizia wrote to his mother-in-law, Julie : " The blow we have received is all the more terrible because unexpected. Only time can heal such a cruel wound. I can easily imagine Charlotte's grief, and yours. I know by my own experience that it is very difficult to control grief caused by the loss of those we love, yet I beg you to do as I do and harden yourself against irremediable misfortune. I regret so much that we are separated in such sad circumstances. Together we would help each other bear a loss so agonising to all of us. Be brave, try to distract Charlotte from her grief. My heart bleeds, thinking of your situation. Ill and in sorrow, you have to force yourself to console your daughter."

Meanwhile, Hortense was smuggling Louis-Napoleon out of Italy. Still travelling as Lady Hamilton, she took him and a fellow conspirator, disguised as a valet, to Paris, where they were secretly received by Louis-Philippe and Queen Amélie, who gave them money for their journey to England. This journey aroused such suspicious comments that Letizia wrote to Hortense : " I admit I was distressed by your journey to France, and what I feared has happened : it is attributed to motives that have certainly never entered your head. The French Government's newspapers and agents say you went to Paris only to conspire. I am sure this is not so, but the effect is bad, and you must contradict these falsehoods. In the present circumstances we must expect to find our most innocent actions maliciously construed." To this she added a fortnight later : " Urge Louis-Napoleon from me to be more circumspect. Before taking any step, he ought to think of the consequences and remember that he is too young and inexperienced not to heed the advice of his parents and relatives. His pride must not be hurt by these observations, which are prompted by my tender attachment to him."

Letizia never saw Louis-Napoleon again, and he seldom took her advice to be circumspect. The year she died he entered France secretly and was deported to America, whence he returned illegally to see his dying mother. He was then expelled from Switzerland and, after taking part in an abortive rising in France, imprisoned in the fortress of Hâ. From there he escaped to England, but returned to France in 1848, first as President, later as Napoleon III.

A T CHRISTMAS, 1831, the Duke of Reichstadt succeeded
in sending his grandmother a portrait of himself for which
he had sat in civilian clothes so as to spare her the distress of
seeing him in Austrian uniform. His solicitude was not wasted,
for the almost blind old woman insisted on having every detail
of the portrait described to her as she hungrily ran her fingertips
over it. Her feeling for the grandson whom she could remember
as a handsome little French prince cheered by the Parisians as he
rode by in his miniature carriage drawn by two merino sheep
had been intensified by the report, brought from Vienna by her
granddaughter Napoleone, that despite all efforts to turn him
into an Austrian, Napoleon's son was passionately attached to
France and to the memory of his father.

A few months later her grandson's closest friend, Count
Anton Prokesch von Osten, a former Austrian ambassador,
arrived in Rome on a diplomatic mission, met Prince Gabrielli
and was asked by Letizia's granddaughter, Charlotte, now
Princess Gabrielli, if he would have any objection to calling on
Madame Letizia. Prokesch said that, on the contrary, he would
be delighted to do so, and a visit was immediately arranged for
the following day.

Accompanied to the Palazzo Bonaparte by Charlotte,
Prokesch found himself in a vast, sombre, silent room where
thick curtains let in so little light that the handsome furniture
had a mysterious underwater look. As his eyes got used to the
dimness he saw a sofa from which a " noble and venerable
matron," dressed entirely in black, was rising with Charlotte's
help. Half-blind and half-paralysed, she greeted Prokesch, then

278

leaned back and " in the softest voice in the world " invited him
to sit beside her. Her French was not perfect, but she managed
the language with assurance and discrimination. Stirred by the
historic nature of the moment, Prokesch spoke at length of the
Duke of Reichstadt, giving all the details likely to interest a
mother—except such a mother as Marie-Louise. Letizia
listened with increasing emotion, interrupted frequently with
questions, and exclaimed over her grandson's resemblance in
character to Napoleon.

She was pleased to learn that he was treated at court " with
all the respect due to him," but above all she wanted news of the
boy's health. Only three weeks before this interview she had
written to Hortense : " You tell me the Duke of Reichstadt's
health is not as bad as reported in the newspapers, and that he
has been seen on horseback in the streets of Vienna. It is a joy to
me to believe that and my heart seizes on this hope with avidity.
But since your letter I have learnt that he has had a relapse and I
am very much distressed by this sad news. Despite my un-
certainty as to the Duke's state (I oscillate between fear and
hope) I want to settle for the latter. He is young, and Nature
has so many resources . . . I want and need to believe that he
will be victorious in this struggle between life and death." In
this state of mind Letizia drew great comfort from all that was
said by Prokesch, who had no idea he was not speaking the
truth. He had received no direct news since he left Vienna, as
the Duke of Reichstadt was forbidden to write to Rome except
with special permission and preferred, just as his father had done
at St. Helena, not to write at all rather than submit his letters to
censorship or theft.

Contact with someone who had lately seen her grandson
revived Letizia's memories of the last occasion on which she
had seen him. She described their flight from the Tuileries, and
added bitterly that though she had often written to Marie-Louise,
her letters had never been answered. Everything Letizia had
felt, thought and wished for Napoleon's son as she meditated on
him in the darkness was summed up in the message she en-

trusted to Prokesch : " Above all, he must respect his father's wishes. His hour will come. He will take his place on his father's throne." Prokesch said that the tender prophetic way in which she spoke drew tears from him.

Then she painfully rose again and was led by Charlotte to her grandson's bust, beside that of his father. She indicated both to Prokesch, also those of her other children, saying a few words about each one. She again referred bitterly to Marie-Louise. Then she searched for a lock of Napoleon's hair that she wished Prokesch to take back to her grandson. Unable to find it at once, she promised to send it to him that evening, together with a miniature of herself.

Prokesch kissed her hand and prepared for dismissal, but she detained him as if unwilling to relinquish this living link with her grandson. He said later that as he knelt at her feet, " her whole person seemed to grow more imposing, and an air of majestic dignity enveloped her." Trembling, she laid her small hands on his head and said, " Since I cannot go to him, may his grandmother's blessing be on your head. I shall soon leave this world, but my prayers, my tears and my wishes will be with him until the last instant of my life. Take him what I have laid on your head and entrusted to your heart."

When Prokesch rose, Letizia embraced him and for a moment they stood together in silence. He and Charlotte helped her back to the sofa and he took his leave. That evening Letizia sent him a miniature of herself with a lock of Napoleon's hair enclosed in the back of it, a miniature of Napoleon as First Consul and one of Caroline. Next day she added to these a lacquer box of mother-of-pearl counters, each stamped with an N and the Imperial crown. The English Admiral Malcolm had brought these from China to St. Helena as a gift for Napoleon, who had used them when playing the Spanish game of *hombre*. She wanted to collect more of Napoleon's personal belongings for her grandson, but Prokesch left Rome before she had time to do so. Nor would more time have availed her. On July 22nd, 1832, the day after Prokesch's visit to Letizia, Napoleon's son died in

Vienna of tuberculosis. He was twenty-one, and as he realised he was dying he said, " Between my cradle and my tomb is a great zero."

When the news reached Letizia she cried out : " This last way of losing my son is perhaps more painful than the first. Am I destined to outlive all my children ? "

M OVED BY ETIQUETTE as she had never been by her heart, Marie-Louise wrote to her mother-in-law for the first time in seventeen years. Even during her son's last illness she had neglected him for her current lover, and all she could find to say to Letizia was that God had disposed of him. Letizia was so sickened by this hypocrisy that she asked Fesch to answer the letter for her. Meanwhile she herself wrote to Hortense : " I have received from Marie-Louise a letter of which you will find a copy enclosed. The Cardinal and I are in mourning. Lacking courage and strength, I can add nothing to these few lines." A month later she wrote again to Hortense : " Your letter of August 17th has just arrived. It finds me ill and overcome. I try to summon courage, but there are some misfortunes against which it is useless to harden oneself. This is one of them. It has reopened all the barely-healed wounds of my heart, and my grief is increased by the details I hear every day. I am desolate at seeing, in so short a space of time, children whom I had hoped would close my eyes flung into the tomb just as they were arousing our finest hopes."

Nevertheless, she refused to forget the living to whom the future of her family belonged. As soon as she had recovered a little strength she altered her will, in which she had left all she possessed to Napoleon's son. A copy of her new will, drawn up by the notary Battista Giuseppe Offredi on September 22nd, 1832, is kept in the Capitoline Archives in Rome (*Instrumenti e testamenti sez. XX. vol.* 140. 1835–36). As character-revealing a document as Napoleon's will, it begins :

Her Highness, by the grace of God sane of mind,

intellect, and spirit, sane too as regards speech, hearing, and bodily capacities save that of sight, and being bedridden and not wishing to die intestate, has resolved to make her will, over the signature of Signor Bernardo Crede.

Offredi read the complete will in the presence of two lawyers and eight witnesses. When the reading was over and the will signed, he closed it with white thread and eight seals of red Spanish wax, each stamped with the Imperial eagle.

Letizia began with a declaration of faith in the Catholic Church. Arrangements for her funeral were to be made by Fesch, and, considerately practical to the last, she specified that he was to be given 7,000 scudi for immediate expenses, and to donate whatever remained of this sum to charity. She listed the churches where she wished masses to be said for the repose of her soul, also the sums to be distributed to the poor in each of the parishes concerned.

The bulk of her fortune, officially estimated at 1,700,000 francs, unofficially at 3,000,000, was to be equally divided among Joseph, Lucien, Louis and Jérôme, after smaller sums had been put aside for Caroline and for Elisa's children. Her palace was left to Joseph as eldest son, but its value was to be taken into account as part of his share of the whole estate. Legacies were to be given to Colonna, Rosa Mellini, her lawyer Natali, her secretary Robaglia, her doctor Antonini and to all her servants, on condition they were still in her service at the time of her death. Her family portraits went to Fesch. She annulled all her children's debts to her, except for 300,000 francs borrowed by Caroline in 1815, which was to be added to the total to be divided among all her children. In a codicil she left her heart to Ajaccio.

Neither grief nor sickness had lessened her determination that all she had accumulated should be of use to her dependants, and her will included a complete inventory of all her household goods, ranging from bread-baskets and mustard-pots to massive silver-gilt dinner-services. Even her clothes and bed-linen, including the sheets between which she expected to die, were carefully portioned out. It is a will entirely devoid of waste or sentimentality, animated throughout by her instinct to fulfil her responsibilities to church, family and loyal dependants. She left nothing to cherished grandchildren (except to the three who were to receive their dead mother's portion), because she knew that her children would in turn faithfully hand on all they possessed to the next generation.

Having put her affairs in order, she was far from giving up all hold on life. Instead she set about trying to obtain possession of the arms and heirlooms Napoleon had bequeathed to his son, which were now rightfully hers. These included the swords he had worn at Aboukir and Austerlitz, the sword of John III of Poland, a watch that had belonged to Frederick the Great, four hundred books from his library, and a collection of uniforms, snuff-boxes, miniatures, comfit boxes and medals. Her cousin the Duc de Padoue served her as intermediary, and the last letter she ever dictated was to him about this final struggle for family rights made in a spirit no more and no less militant than had driven her as an obscure widow to try again and again to obtain for her children the money owed to Carlo for the mulberry groves that had seemed so promising to young Louis XVI and Marie-Antoinette. She was more successful in her last struggle, and, thanks to her, these treasures are still in the family.

AT EASTER, 1833, Elisa's twenty-year-old son, Frédéric-Napoleon, was thrown from his horse while riding in Rome, and killed. After being told of this Letizia remained silent for several hours, then said : " There is a fatality weighing on the third generation of Bonapartes, they all die violent deaths." Among the letters of sympathy she received was one from a French deputy, Monsieur Sapey, who suggested out of respect for her age and griefs that the Chamber of Deputies abrogate the law of exile in her case. She immediately answered him :

Those who realise the absurdity of the maintenance of the law of exile against my family and who nevertheless propose making an exception of me, have never understood either my principles or my character.

I was widowed at thirty-four and my eight children were my only consolation. Corsica was threatened with separation from France. The loss of home and possessions did not frighten me. I followed my children to the Continent. In 1814 I followed Napoleon to Elba, and in 1816, despite my age, I would have followed him to St. Helena had he not forbidden this, and I resigned myself to living in Rome, a prisoner of state. Either as an extension of the law exiling my family from France, or as the result of Allied protocol, persecution stopped many members of the family who wanted to join me from coming to Rome. I decided to do without company, and hoped for happiness only in a future life, since I was separated from those for whose sake I value this life, and who represent all my memories and joy. What equivalent could I find in France that would not be poisoned by the injustice of powerful men who cannot forgive the glory won by my family ?

Let me be left alone, in my honourable sufferings, to carry my integrity to my grave. I will never separate my lot from that of my children.

Julie, fourth child of Joseph's elder daughter, Zenaïde, and of Lucien's eldest son, Charles-Lucien, could just remember her great-grandmother at this period as " an old lady always dressed in black and lying on one of those uncomfortable divans for which Canova's sculptures and Gérard's pictures have found a niche in the history of art. Visitors were received by Colonna . . . dry, angular, in satin knee-breeches and buckled shoes. Madame would rise slightly to receive us, but as she was blind she had to touch us to recognise our faces. ' You are very beautiful,' she said one day to Maria [Lucien's thirteenth child], who indeed had regular features illuminated by huge dark eyes."

Always appreciative of beauty, Letizia intended the women of her family to enjoy her jewels, of which she had an inventory made two months after her eighty-fifth birthday. Among those to whom she particularly wished to give pleasure was Jérôme's wife, but Catherine died a month later in Lausanne of inflammation of the lungs. She was only fifty-three and, until now, had never caused her husband or his family a moment's grief. After Catherine's death Letizia would be given no fresh cause to mourn in darkness. She had not far to go now.

Among Letizia's last visitors was the first of her future biographers, Félix Larrey, a young doctor visiting Rome with his father, Baron Larrey, former surgeon-in-chief to the Grand Army and described by Napoleon, who left him 100,000 francs in his will, as the " most virtuous man he had ever known."

The Larreys were welcomed to the Palazzo Bonaparte by Fesch, whom young Larrey described as " of lively intelligence, with an affable air, a penetrating gaze and fluent speech." They were then led into a vast square room, its walls hung with silk. Beside a large window from which the tower of the Capitol could be seen stood Napoleon's white-curtained bed, on which lay Letizia, immobile but attentive to the least sound. Her features were still beautiful, but her eyes had turned opaque and grey from cataracts and the face was so thin that it resembled " a medallion of a Roman empress."

Carlo's portrait hung over the bed and the room was populated with busts and portraits of all Letizia's children, also the bust of the little King of Rome that Lady Holland had sent to St. Helena as a gift for Napoleon. Joséphine, Hortense and the future Napoleon III were included in this personal pantheon of public history.

Fesch motioned to Baron Larrey to sit down in the chair beside Napoleon's bed. Letizia leaned towards him and said, " I am very much touched by your kind visit, Baron Larrey, and I thank you with all my heart. I feel as if I were seeing you to-day as I saw you in the past, you whom the Emperor loved and esteemed. I know how he spoke of you during his exile, and I remember the words of his will at St. Helena." Then she gave him her thin trembling hand.

Much moved, the baron presented his son. As the young man bent to kiss her hand Letizia said, " Come near, my child, let me embrace you and touch your face so as to know what it is like, since I cannot see it." Young Larrey could scarcely speak for emotion, but Letizia put him at ease by gently questioning him about his mother, his sisters, his studies and plans for the future. Because of his Napoleonic background, she instinctively spoke to him as if he were one of her own grandchildren.

After a silence during which she appeared to be assembling her thoughts, she asked Baron Larrey about his situation in France, his birth-place in the Pyrenees and his travels and campaigns, especially those in which he had accompanied Napoleon. She lost nothing of his answers and young Larrey observed that she had the rare talent of knowing how to listen. Both father and son noticed that, as if in compensation for her blindness, her hearing was phenomenally acute. Presently Baron Larrey feared they might be exhausting her and made a move to leave, but her wish to keep them longer was obviously due to more than courtesy. When they inquired about her health she said that what she found hardest to bear was her immobility.

Two hours after their arrival she collapsed into a semi-somnolent state, reacting only to the sound of her children's names, any one of which made her raise her head to the light and open her sightless eyes. When they took their leave she gave them her blessing and said, " May you be happy. As you are going to Florence you will doubtless see my children. [Louis and Caroline were there.] Give them my news ; they know I do not forget them. Farewell, my good Larrey, thank you for coming to see me with your dear son. Your visit has done me good. Remember me when you are back in France."

Outside, Fesch gave them the gifts Letizia had chosen for them, a magnificent gold-lined onyx snuff-box with a cameo lid for Baron Larrey and for each of them a cameo of Napoleon's head.

ON JANUARY 27TH, 1836, Letizia caught a chill that induced a fever. The doctors summoned by Fesch seemed to be curing her, but she knew better than they and asked for the sacraments. It was carnival time and Rome echoed with gaiety and tumult, but, out of respect for Letizia, no fireworks were set off in the Piazza Venezia. Of all her children, only Lucien and Jérôme were present at the final parting. Joseph, recently returned to Europe, was refused permission to go to her, as was Caroline, and Louis was himself too ill to travel.

Thirty years later Keats's biographer, Lord Houghton, told Augustus Hare : " I had a very narrow miss of seeing Madame Mère, and I am very sorry I did not do it for it would only have cost a scudo. She was a very long time dying, it was a kind of lying in state, and for a scudo the porter used to let people in behind a screen which there was at the foot of the bed, and they looked at her through the joinings. I was only a boy then, and I thought there was plenty of time, and put it off ; but one day she died."

Letizia remained lucid and calm throughout her last illness. She had been so long in darkness that the past was more vivid to her than the present, and perhaps than the future which she envisaged as " where no tears are shed." Half her life had been passed in Continental courts and palaces, but her most cherished memories concerned the island she and Fesch and old Saveria had kept alive in their hearts. She could remember the days when the names of Letizia, Fesch and Saveria were inseparable from those of Mamma Saveria, Mamma Fesch, Zia Geltruda, Zio Lucciano, Zio Napoleone, the Ramolinos, Casanovas,

Arrighis and Giubegas. As she remembered, these figures grew mysteriously younger, were joined by a group of handsome children—King Joseph was once more Giuseppe, the Emperor once more Napoleone, surrounded by Lucciano, Maria-Anna, Luigi, Maria-Paola, Maria-Nunziata and Girolamo. Then the children grew smaller, vanished. " The cries of the dying, the groans of the oppressed " rose in the smoke of a battlefield and Letizia felt her horse move beneath her, a horse that was still there as the cries and odours of the battlefield made way for the sounds and scents of the *macchia* as she rode up to Corte to meet a youthful Paoli, his horse caparisoned with crimson velvet and gold lace. Then this too faded and she was once more a child herself, Letizia Ramolino in the summer of 1764, walking proudly and timidly up the steps of Ajaccio Cathedral to give her hand and heart to Carlo-Maria Buonaparte.

It was seven o'clock in the evening of February 2nd, 1836, when Letizia fell asleep for the last time. Fesch, who had remained beside her throughout, closed the sightless eyes that had seen so much. He was seventy-three and had never known life without his sister.

Letizia left four sons, a daughter, ten grandsons, eleven granddaughters, thirteen great-grandsons and fourteen great-granddaughters when she at last joined her favourite child, not only in death but in history and in legend. That same year, in the centre of Paris, Napoleon's Arc de Triomphe was at last completed.

LETIZIA'S DEATH WAS announced only briefly in the
Diario di Roma and the Papal Government ordered that her
funeral be a very simple one, as if fearful that even the wreaths
of exiled kings might have the power to stir dormant Bona-
partism. This enforced austerity had some unexpected results.
For example, the Palazzo Bonaparte was left so unguarded that
the French painter Gigoux, in Rome by chance at the time, was
able to walk in unchallenged.

There was no one on the staircase to announce him, and no
one in the ante-room of Letizia's apartment. All the doors were
open and the rooms appeared deserted. It was as if some mighty
tide had receded, leaving behind it an unnatural silence. In the
third vast room Gigoux found the dead Letizia lying in state on
a bed covered with silver-fringed black velvet, the canopy topped
by four silver eagles. He wrote home that he had never seen so
beautiful a face. Another Frenchman, Joseph Méry, who also
chanced to see her lying in state, wrote that from the room in
which she lay one could see the Campidoglio : " What a combination ! The grandeur of Rome competing with the grandeur
of the woman."

A requiem mass was to be said for her at Santa Maria-in-Via-
Lata, an eighth-century church built over the one where St.
Paul supposedly lodged. Carnival was still rampant when the
funeral procession set out and confetti fell on the coffin, while
here and there an anti-Bonapartist whistled or shouted at the
little cortège. The Bonapartes had been forbidden to display the
Imperial arms on the black draperies over the entrance, but an

Imperial eagle surmounted the initials L. R. B. and the inscription : MATER NAPOLEONIS.

After the modest ceremony, the coffin was transported to the little Etruscan town of Tarquinia beside Civita Vecchia, where the French Consul, Henry Beyle, now known to the world as Stendhal, was just beginning to write his *Mémoires sur Napoléon* : " I feel an almost religious sentiment on writing the opening phrase of the history of Napoleon. It concerns the greatest man to appear in the world since Cæsar." In this exquisite little town of medieval skyscrapers and painted Etruscan tombs, Letizia's body was placed in the church of the Sisters of the Passion. The word " passion " in the sense of suffering was a most appropriate one to associate with Letizia's long life.

Born in the reign of Louis XV, she died the year before Queen Victoria came to the throne of England, and throughout this long period of cataclysmic changes, her personal life was intimately connected with history's leading actors. As an adolescent she fought in a local struggle for independence ; as a young widow she brought her children safely through a national revolution ; as a middle-aged woman she saw her favourite son found an empire in which three of her other sons were kings and one daughter a queen ; as an infirm old woman she lived on intimate terms with tragedy, with which she had always been acquainted, yet thanks to her love for her children she was never condemned to the limbo reserved for those who outlive their hearts. Nor would she ever collaborate with disaster, and it is on account of her capacity to love and to resist that even in her ashes live her wonted fires.

Epilogue

1951

Fear no more the heat o' th' sun,
Nor the furious winter's rages ;
Thou thy worldly task hast done,
Home art gone, and ta'en thy wages.
Golden lads and girls all must,
As chimney-sweepers, come to dust.

SHAKESPEARE : *Cymbeline*

L'espoir est une mémoire qui désire.

BALZAC : *Un Prince de la Bohème*

LETIZIA WAS NOT TO remain long among the Etruscans in Tarquinia. She and her family had been great travellers when living, and dead, they continued to travel.

Four years after Letizia's death the King of France, Louis-Philippe, obtained permission from the English Government to bring Napoleon's body home from St. Helena and grant the wish the Emperor had expressed in his will to be buried on the banks of the Seine amid the French people he loved so well. On the twenty-fifth anniversary of Napoleon's arrival at St. Helena, Louis-Philippe's sailor son, the Prince de Joinville, reached Jamestown aboard the *Belle Poule*. When the coffin was opened Napoleon was found to be perfectly preserved and looking as if asleep. The English garrison escorted the coffin to the harbour, accompanied by cannon fire and the music of the "Dead March" from *Saul*, and the *Belle Poule* sailed for France during a magnificent sunset.

Kneeling crowds lined the banks of the Seine all the way from Rouen to Paris, and units of the National Guard presented arms as the catafalque sailed up the river. Four hundred veterans of the Grand Army gathered at Neuilly and Courbevoie, wearing their old uniforms and headed by Lieutenant-Colonel Loubers of the Elba battalion. It was bitterly cold the night before the catafalque reached Neuilly, but the veterans slept at the posts they had taken up, rolled in their shabby old coats, the last ghostly bivouac of the Grand Army. When the cortège formed at dawn they refused to make way for the municipal authorities, saying, "You forget that the Emperor always marched in the midst of the Guard." In this way they escorted their Emperor to

Paris. The city was in a state of delirium. A million people had gathered for the occasion; a statue of Napoleon had been placed on the Arc de Triomphe; balconies on the Champs-Élysées had been rented at 3,000 francs each; and the crowds repeatedly sang " *Vive mon grand Napoléon !* " and Monnier's song :

> *Ami certain de la valeur,*
> *Fidèle amant de la victoire,*
> *Il eut pour marraine la gloire,*
> *Et pour père le champ d'honneur* . . .

Victor Hugo was one of the 100,000 spectators who occupied the six tribunes erected in front of Les Invalides. He said that the sun emerged from behind the clouds just as the " mountain of gold " of the catafalque appeared amidst " a roar as solemn as thunder." The King, the royal family and the dignitaries of state were waiting at Les Invalides. When the cortège arrived it was preceded by a chamberlain who announced : " The Emperor ! " Then the Prince de Joinville stepped towards his father the King, and said, " Sire, I present the body of Napoleon." Louis-Philippe answered, " I receive it in the name of France." Napoleon was home.

A hundred years later the King of Rome's body was brought from the Habsburg vaults of Vienna to lie beside his father. At last Napoleon and the child for whom he had longed were re-united under the golden dome of Les Invalides.

Eleven years after Napoleon's body was returned to France, Letizia's grandson, Louis-Napoleon, recently elected Prince-President of France, ordered Letizia's body to be taken back to Corsica where she had bequeathed her heart. She was escorted from Tarquinia with all the pomp denied her when she had died. The body of Cardinal Fesch was also sent back to Corsica at that time.

When the Second World War broke out, Letizia's great-great-grandson, Louis, Prince Napoleon, the present head of the house, who had been raised in exile in Belgium, volunteered for the French Army, but was refused. Nor would the British Navy accept him. He joined the Foreign Legion and served in Africa, but was demobilised after the 1940 armistice and, since he was not allowed to live in France, went to Switzerland. Two years later he entered France secretly, intending to join the Free French Forces in Algeria. He was captured by a German patrol and interned, first at the fort of Hâ, then at the prison of Fresnes. Freed the following year (perhaps because the Germans still had fatuous hopes of utilising him, perhaps through the intervention of his cousin, the King of Italy), he got in touch with the Resistance and joined the clandestine Carol battalion which went into action beside the Allied troops during the Normandy landing. Among his fellow soldiers was his cousin, Joachim, Prince Murat, killed in this campaign. Prince Napoleon was badly wounded in August, but soon afterwards asked General de Gaulle, then head of the provisional government, for permission to remain in the French Army. With typical brevity and emotion, the general said, " Prince Napoleon has himself abrogated the law of exile." Equally typically, General de Gaulle refused to allow the last male Bonaparte to take the dangerous post for which he had volunteered. This time the Bonapartes were up against a man with a sense of history as keen, romantic and astringent as their own. The law of exile was legally abrogated in 1950 and Prince Napoleon's twin son and daughter were the first Bonapartes born on French soil for ninety-four years.

In 1951 Prince and Princess Napoleon visited Corsica, taking back the body of Napoleon's father, Carlo. Ajaccio was splendidly decorated with tricolour flags and red carpets, Imperial crowns and golden bees, and in this atmosphere of high celebration Carlo was at long last restored to Letizia and the Mediterranean island from which all this triumph and tragedy had sprung.

Bibliography

Biographies of Letizia Bonaparte

AUGUSTIN, THIERRY: *Madame Mère.* Paris, Albin Michel, 1939.
DECAUX, ALAIN: *Letizia Mère de l'Empereur.* Paris, Amiot-Dumont, 1951.
LARREY, FÉLIX-HIPPOLYTE, BARON: *Madame Mère (Napoleonis Mater).* Paris, E. Dentu, 1892.
PERETTI, LYDIE: *Dans l'Ombre de la Gloire, Letizia Bonaparte.* Paris, Plon, 1932.
VILLENEUVE, GERMAINE DE: *Madame Mère.* Paris, G. Flicker, 1935.
WILSON, R. MCNAIR: *Napoleon's Mother.* Philadelphia, J. B. Lippincott, 1933.

Other books consulted

ABRANTÈS (DUCHESSE D'): *Mémoires.* Paris, Garnier Frères, 1893. *Histoire des Salons de Paris.* Paris, Ladvocat, 1836-38.
ANGELI, DIEGO: *I Bonaparti a Roma.* Milan, Mondadori, 1938.
ANGERS, DAVID D': *Cahiers.* Paris, Plon, 1958.
ARBLAY, MADAME D': *Diary and Letters of Madame d'Arblay.* London, Frederick Warne & Co., 1842-6, 1904-5.
ARNAULT, A. V.: *Souvenirs d'un Sexagénaire.* Paris, Dufy, 1833.
AUBRY, OCTAVE: *Vie Privée de Napoléon.* Paris, Flammarion, 1939. *Le Roi de Rome.* Paris, Fayard, 1932.

BAINVILLE, JACQUES: *Napoléon.* Paris, Fayard, 1957.
BALZAC, HONORÉ DE: *La Comédie Humaine.* Paris, Bibliothèque de la Pléiade, 1951-9.

Bibliography

BARBIER, PIERRE et VERNILLAT, FRANCE: *Histoire de France par la Chanson.* Paris, Gallimard, 1958.

BERTRAND, HENRI GRATIEN DE: *Cahiers de Sainte-Hélène* (deciphered and annotated by Paul Fleuriot de Langle). Paris, Flammarion, 1951.

BEUGNOT, COMTE DE: *Mémoires.* Paris, Hachette, 1959.

BLESSINGTON, COUNTESS OF: *The Idler in Italy.* London, Henry Colburn, 1839.

BLOCH, MAURICE: *Les Mères des Grands Hommes.* Paris, Librairie Ch. Delagrave, 1885.

BOIGNE, COMTESSE DE: *Mémoires d'une Tante.* Paris, 1907.

BONAPARTE, JÉRÔME: *Mémoires et correspondance du Roi Jérôme et de la Reine Catherine.* Published by the Baron Du Casse. Paris, E. Dentu, 1861-6.

BONAPARTE, JOSEPH: *Mémoires et Correspondance Politique et Militaire du Roi Joseph,* annotated by Baron Du Casse. Paris, Perrotin, 1853-4.

BONAPARTE, LETIZIA: Correspondence, in the Misciattelli Collection, Primoli Museum, Rome.

BONAPARTE, LOUIS: *Observations de Louis Bonaparte, Comte de St.-Leu, sur l'histoire de Napoléon, par M. de Norvins.* Paris, Goetschy Fils, 1834.

BOSWELL, JAMES: *The Life of Samuel Johnson.* London, J. M. Dent and Sons, 1952.
The Journal of a Tour to Corsica; and Memoirs of Pascal Paoli, edited by S. C. Roberts. Cambridge University Press, 1929.

BOURRIENNE, LOUIS-ANTOINE FAUVELET DE: *Mémoires.* Paris, Ladvocat, 1829.

BYRON, GEORGE GORDON: *Letters and Journals of Lord Byron, with notices of his life by Thomas Moore.* London, John Murray, 1932.

CAMPBELL, SIR NEIL: *Napoleon at Fontainebleau and Elba.* London, John Murray, 1869.

CASTELOT, ANDRÉ: *L'Aiglon.* Paris, Le Livre contemporain, 1959.

CHARLES-ROUX, F.: *Rome, asile des Bonapartes.* Paris, Hachette, 1952.

CHATEAUBRIAND, FRANÇOIS RENÉ DE: *Mémoires d'Outre-Tombe,* annotated by Maurice Levaillant and Georges Moulinier. Paris, Bibliothèque de la Pléiade, 1951-2.

COCHELET, LOUISE (Mme. Parquin): *Mémoires sur la Reine Hortense et la*

Bibliography

Famille Impériale par Mlle. Cochelet, edited by Frédéric Lacroix. Paris, Ladvocat, 1836-8.

CONSTANT, BENJAMIN: *Mémoires sur les Cent Jours*. Paris, Pichon et Didier, 1829.

CHRISTOPHE, ROBERT: *Napoléon Empereur de l'île d'Elbe*. Paris, Fayard, 1959.

CHUQUET, ARTHUR: *La Jeunesse de Napoléon*. Paris, A. Colin, 1879-99.

DOUBLET, VICTOR: *Les Nouveaux Voyageurs en Suisse et en Italie*. Paris, P. C. Lehuby, 1845.

DUMAS, ALEXANDRE: *Mes Mémoires* (2 volumes). Paris, Gallimard, 1954-7.

DURAND, SOPHIE COHONSET: *Anecdotes sur la cour et l'intérieur de la famille de Napoléon Bonaparte*. Paris & London, Colburn, 1818.

DUTHURON, GUSTAVE: *La Révolution*. Paris, Fayard, 1954.

ECKERMANN, J. P.: *Conversations avec Goethe*. Paris, Editions Henri Jonquières, 1930.

FUGIER, ANDRÉ: *Napoléon et l'Italie*. Paris, J. B. Janin, 1947.

GARROS, LOUIS: *Quel roman que ma vie : itinéraire de Napoléon Bonaparte*. Paris, Editions de l'Encyclopédie Française, 1947.
Napoléon cet inconnu. Paris, Editions Beaudart, 1950.

GEER, WALTER: *Napoleon and his family : the Story of a Corsican Clan* (3 volumes). New York, Brentano's, 1927-9.

GOBINEAU, MARCEL: *Pauline Borghese, sœur fidèle*. Paris, Pierre Amiot, 1958.

GOURGAUD, GASPARD: *Journal de Sainte-Hélène*. Paris, Flammarion, 1944.

HARE, AUGUSTUS: *Walks in Rome*. London, George Allen, 1903.

HAZLITT, WILLIAM: *Life of Napoleon Buonaparte* (4 volumes). London, Office of the Illustrated London Library, 1852.

Bibliography

HORTENSE, QUEEN: *Mémoires* (3 volumes). Prepared by Prince Napoléon and annotated by Jean Hanoteau. Paris, Plon, 1927.

LA TOUR DE PIN, HENRIETTE-LUCIE DILLON DE: *Journal d'une femme de cinquante ans.* Paris, R. Chapelot, 1907-11.

LANCELLOTTI, ARTURO: *I Napoleonidi.* Rome, Staderini, 1936.

LANGERON, ROGER: *Decazes, Ministre du roi.* Paris, Hachette, 1960.

LANGLE, P. FLEURIOT DE: *Alexandrine Lucien Bonaparte, Princesse de Canino.* Paris, Plon, 1939.

LAS CASES, EMMANUEL DE: *Le Mémorial de Sainte-Hélène* (2 volumes with index, notes and commentary by Gérard Walter). Paris, Bibliothèque de la Pléiade, 1957.

LEE, H.: *The Life of the Emperor Napoleon.* London, 1834.

LEFEBVRE, G.: *Napoleon.* Volume XIV in "Peuples et Civilisations" series published by Presses Universitaires de France, 1953.

LENÔTRE, G.: *Napoléon. Croquis de l'Empire.* Paris, Grasset, 1932.
En suivant l'Empereur. Paris, Grasset, 1935.
Femmes. Paris, Grasset, 1933.

LIGNE, CHARLES JOSEPH, PRINCE DE: *Fragments de l'histoire de ma vie.* Paris, Plon, 1928.

LOCKHART, JOHN GIBSON: *Life of Bonaparte.* London, J. M. Dent & Sons, 1906.

LUCAS-DUBRETON, J.: *Le Culte de Napoléon.* Paris, Albin Michel, 1959.

MADELIN, LOUIS: *La Jeunesse de Bonaparte.* Paris, Hachette, 1937.
Le Consulat et l'Empire. Paris, Hachette, 1948.

MARCHAND, LOUIS-JOSEPH: *Mémoires.* Paris, Plon, 1952.

MASSON, FRÉDÉRIC: *Napoléon et sa famille* (13 volumes). Paris, Albin Michel, 1930.

MÉRIMÉE, PROSPER: *Romans et nouvelles,* annotated by Henri Martineau. Paris, Bibliothèque de la Pléiade, 1952.

MICHELET, JULES: *Histoire de la Révolution Française,* annotated by Gérard Walter. Paris, Bibliothèque de la Pléiade, 1939.
Histoire de XIXème Siècle. Paris, Michel Lévy Frères, 1875.

MOREL, PIERRE: *La Corse.* Paris, Arthaud, 1951.

MORGAN, LADY: *Italy.* Paris, A. & W. Galignani, 1821.

Bibliography

MORTON, H. V.: *A Traveller in Italy*. London, Methuen, 1957.
MUSSET, ALFRED DE: *Confessions d'un enfant du siècle*, annotated by Maurice Allem. Paris, Classiques Garnier, 1947.

NASICA, ABBÉ T.: *Mémoires sur l'enfance et la jeunesse de Napoléon*. Paris, 1852.
NORRIS, HERBERT and CURTIS, OSWALD: *Costume and Fashion in the XIXth Century*. London, J. M. Dent, 1933.

OLIVIER, ALBERT: *Le Dix-huit Brumaire*. Paris, Gallimard, 1959.
O'MEARA, BARRY: *Napoleon in Exile; or A Voice from St. Helena*. London, Jones & Co., 1827.

PEREY, LUCIEN: *Histoire d'une grande dame du XVIIIème siècle*. Paris, Calmann-Lévy, 1888.
PROKESCH, COMTE VON OSTEN: *Mes Relations avec le Duc de Reichstadt*. Paris, 1878.

RÉMUSAT, CLAIRE-ELISABETH-JEANNE DE: *Mémoires* (3 volumes). Paris, Calmann-Lévy, 1880.
ROBIQUET, JEAN: *La Vie quotidienne au temps de Napoléon*. Paris, Hachette, 1946.
ROGERS, SAMUEL: *The Italian Journal of Samuel Rogers*, edited by J. R. Hale. London, Faber & Faber, 1956.

SAUNDERS, LLOYD: *The Holland House Circle*. London, Methuen, 1908.
SCHERER, MARGARET: *The Marvels of Ancient Rome*. New York & London, published by the Phaidon Press for the Metropolitan Museum of Art, 1946.
SÉGUR, LOUIS-PHILIPPE, COMTE DE: *La Campagne de Russie*. Paris, Les Amis de l'Histoire, 1958.
SOREL, ALBERT: *L'Europe et la Révolution Française* (8 volumes). Paris, E. Plon, Nourrit & Cie, 1885-1904.

Bibliography

STENDHAL: *Vie de Napoléon.* Paris, Le Divan, 1930.
Mémoires sur Napoléon. Paris, Le Divan, 1930.
Journal (1801-1823). Text established by Henri Martineau. 5 volumes.
Paris, Le Divan, 1937.
Mélanges d'art. Paris, Le Divan, 1932.
Rome, Naples et Florence. Paris, Pauvert, 1935.
Promenades dans Rome. Sceaux, Pauvert, 1935.
Correspondance (10 volumes). Paris, Le Divan, 1933-4.
STORY, WILLIAM W.: *Roba di Roma.* London, Chapman & Hall, 1876.

TALLEYRAND-PÉRIGORD, CHARLES MAURICE DE: *Mémoires* (2
volumes), annotated by Paul-Louis Couchoud & Jean-Paul Couchoud.
Paris, Plon, 1957.
TARLÉ, EUGÈNE: *Bonaparte,* translated from the Russian by John
Cournos, London, Secker & Warburg, 1937.

VALYNSEELE, JOSEPH: *Le Sang des Bonapartes.* Printed privately, 1954.

VOX, MAXIMILIEN: *Napoléon.* Paris, Eds. du Seuil, 1939.
Correspondance de Napoléon (600 lettres de travail, 1806-1810), Paris,
Gallimard, 1943.

WILLIAMS, H. NOEL: *The Women Bonapartes.* London, Methuen, 1958.

Index

A

Abrantès, Duc d', *see* Junot
Abrantès, Duchesse d', *see* Permon, Laure
Antommarchi, 250, 261
Artois, Comte d', *see* Charles X

B

Bacciochi, Felice Pasquale, 105, 106, 107, 109, 123
Bacciochi, Frédéric-Napoléon (son of Elisa), 285
Bacciochi, Napoleone (daughter of Elisa), 253-4, 274
Balzac, Honoré de, 54, 104
Barras, 94, 95, 98
Beauharnais, Eugène de, 97, 164
Beauharnais, Hortense de, 98, 124, 125, 127, 135, 164, 222, 223, 227, 231, 245, 257-8, 273, 276, 282
Beauharnais, Joséphine de, marriage with Napoleon, 97-8, 100, 117, 163, 166, 201, 223; antagonism of the Bonaparte family to, 99, 101, 105, 124, 126, 156; her infidelity, 104, 108, 111; plans marriage of her daughter to Louis, 125; divorced, 164-5, 167, 173; her house, Malmaison, 111, 227; other references, 106, 121, 127, 129
Bernadotte, Marshal, 113, 177, 181
Bertrand, General, 196, 199, 211, 249, 250, 260
Biadelli, Maria, 27
Blacas d'Aups, Comte, 239, 260
Bonaparte, Caroline, marries Murat, 123; becomes Queen of Naples, 163; her treachery, 183, 195; her palace outside Naples, 218-219; her remorse, 219; seized by the Austrians, 220; visits her mother in Rome,